Caution to the Wind

ALSO BY TERRY PRONE

FICTION

The Scattering of Mrs Blake
Blood Brothers, Soul Sisters
Racing the Moon
Running before Daybreak
Swinging on a Star
Dancing with the Angel

May Need Renovation (as Pamela Rowan)
Honeymoon Hurricane (as Pamela Rowan)

NON-FICTION

Write and Get Paid for It
This Business of Writing (with Kieran Lyons)
Just a Few Words
Baa Baa Pink Sheep
The Fear Factor
Do Your Own Publicity
Mirror, Mirror
Talk the Talk
The Best Advice I Ever Got
Start Your Own Business (with Frances Stephenson)

Irish Murders 1
Irish Murders 2

Caution to the Wind

A Memoir

Terry Prone

Published by
Red Stripe Press
an imprint of
Orpen Press
Upper Floor, Unit B3
Hume Centre
Hume Avenue
Park West Industrial Estate
Dublin 12

email: info@orpenpress.com
www.orpenpress.com

Hardback ISBN 978-1-78605-196-7
Paperback ISBN 978-1-78605-207-0
ePub ISBN 978-1-78605-197-4

Printed in the EU

For today's Little Women –
Make no mistake, Jo's the one to follow

ACKNOWLEDGEMENTS

Jonathan Williams, literary agent, is an old, old friend who once shared an office in the Institute of Public Administration with Tom Savage and was surprised by my account of Tom's occasional physicality with others. He took *Caution to the Wind* under his wing and browbeat it into its present shape. The process shouldn't have been fun, but it was.

My son, Anton Savage, sister, Hilary Kenny, and friend from Abbey Theatre days, Fionnuala Kenny, read the manuscript and were helpful.

Jo O'Donoghue, my first editor, recommended I meet Michael Brennan of Red Stripe Press. Which in turn led to meeting Gerry Kelly, his partner, and Eileen O'Brien, managing editor.

Barry McCall took the best shots of my life, one of which is on the cover of Steve O'Neill's design.

Moira Prone, my mother, a born archivist, left beautifully filed cuttings, manuscripts and even the price-notes for the Shopping Basket Gay Byrne Hour item.

Aileen Gaskin, Aoife Phelan, Kate O'Brien of The Communications Clinic, were marvellous throughout the process and don't try hiring them away.

Elements of this appeared in another form in the *Irish Examiner* and *Irish Times*.

Contents

1

Happy Fourth Birthday

*I*t shook out crisp and sharp-creased but within seconds the hanky was a hot limp redness in Mr Trimble's hand. I knew it was my fault and tried to say sorry as I was handed to my mother. I tried to say I was sorry to my mother, too, because it was my fourth birthday and I had crashed the tricycle that was the best gift ever, but words couldn't find their way around the chaos of my mouth, where the handlebar had entered, driving baby teeth ahead of it into my tongue.

Getting to Temple Street Hospital I don't remember, but I remember the operating theatre, the nurses and the medical students, all laughing obediently at the surgeon while he held up a big needle with black thread and told me he was going to stitch up my tongue. I screamed the place down and he got impatient and told them to hold me still. Hands were forcing my mouth open and nothing but pain happened until they sat me up and the surgeon showed me the needle again and the shortened thread. He had a fat ball to his thumb. His thumb bent backwards as if it couldn't believe how smart it was. I hated him and it and the crawling subordinates, but they had power and I had none. Because of the stitching and missing teeth, I couldn't even tell the family how bad it had been. Bottled and boiled, I was, with a mouth on me like swollen sausages packed into too small a space.

That's the first memory. Before that, nothing. Except what was told to me. And what was told to me was that Hilary, my big sister, had tormented my parents for a sister from the time she was about four. She was just shy of eight when she was sent down to Loughrea in County Galway to stay with our cousins, the Clearys, because my mother had to be hospitalised for some weeks before the birth. Once she heard of my arrival, Hilary wrote a letter wild with enthusiasm to Mamma: 'I nearly jumped out of my skin when I heard I had a new baby sister and that I was going back on Friday. I would like you to call her Mary Pattrissa'.

I was brought home and screamed for six months solid. Not crying. Screaming. They tried everything but couldn't find the cause. The black hair all down my back did not dent Hilary's delight. Half a year later I had shed the fur, although some neighbours in Mount Prospect Grove in Clontarf would look into the pram and, smiling through gritted teeth, ask me archly if I was the little baby who had screamed loud enough to be heard on the other side of the green park. That oblong park, surrounded by 1950s' houses, was where we lived, in number 44.

As soon as I began to walk, I started to have accidents. A little horsing on the bed with Hilary caused a broken collar bone, then plaster and a sling for weeks. Long before I understood what they were saying, I learned to dread adults who smirkingly asked me, as I sported my latest bandage or Elastoplast, if I was 'accident-prone'. Every one of them seemed to think they were the first to have made this crack. The thing was, I was *completely* accident-prone, so photographs of me as a child show a plumply happy collection of bruises, scabs and occasional plaster casts.

Driving up the lamppost meant that, since my teeth were forced into my tongue and the surgeon with the horrible thumb repaired it without much subtlety, I ended up with a distorted tongue and a diminished capacity to speak. My mother searched around until she found Mrs Young, aka Miss McCloskey, an elocution teacher who operated out of Styles Road in Clontarf, where she devoted a conservatory to her classes. Miss McCloskey was glamorous, blonde, elegant and married to an Aer Lingus pilot. In her class, we sat on benches around the windows, facing her, and chorused twee poems at her. Sometimes we'd be called by name and would stand out in the middle to deliver the recitation. How much this contributed to me becoming understandable again, post-lamppost, I don't know. I do, however, remember, after maybe a year and a half of this, being brought into town one day to the Father Mathew Hall in Church Street, to something called the Feis. It was the first time I had been in a theatre.

Me and the other kids from the elocution class watched other children come out on stage and say poems to a woman seated at a table in the centre aisle. The adjudicator, my mother explained. Then the woman in the aisle stood up, climbed onto the stage and made comments in an accent I had never heard before. 'Where's she from?' I asked my mother, who asked me back 'How would I know?' This, while poking me to follow the rest of Miss McCloskey's class along the side and into a dark corridor where we were lined up in an order that wasn't explained and told to be quiet. The line of children snaked forward until one was out on the stage, reciting, and the next – me – was in the wings. The little boy on stage finished and as soon as he came off, I went on. I didn't know I was supposed to bow, so I lashed straight into the poem, which was called 'Bunny Rabbit', and began 'Bunny creeps out and caresses his nose …'

We weren't allowed to go back to our mothers in the auditorium, but were forced to stay in a green room (which was brown) until those who had been exceptionally good with the rabbit would be 'recalled' for another go, with the first, second and third prize-winners chosen based on their rendition of the second poem. I accepted I would not be among them, because one of the older girls had eaten the face off me for not bowing and suggested that I had singlehandedly brought the whole class into disrepute. Then my name was called and I was so unnerved that I again failed to bow to the adjudicator before embarking on 'The Postman':

Please, O Mr Postman,
Bring me a letter, do.
Tomorrow at the garden gate,
I will wait for you.
Bring one from a fairy
Who says she'll come to tea –
Then I'll put on my party dress
How lovely that will be.
But please, O Mr Postman,
If fairies you know none,
Write me a letter from yourself,
And bring it, just for fun.

One of the girls who was recalled mimed along with her poem, so we got the garden gate opening and shoulder-high gestures designed to establish fairy wings. The rest of us guiltily wondered if we should have done likewise. When the adjudicator went up on the stage, the mothers present, having spent the brief interval asserting to their daughters that they were a winner even if they didn't bring home a medal, suddenly went rigid with anticipation, thereby proving to their offspring that the 'everybody's a winner' stuff was the greatest load of …

The adjudicator warbled about various strengths and weaknesses deployed by the competitors and then did the reverse announcement of the winners, starting with the highly commended, i.e. consolation prizes. When I hadn't appeared by the penultimate prize, I was resigned and therefore astonished when she placed me first. I received a silver medal and knew from Miss McCloskey's face that this was of world-changing significance, although I was still going to get it in the neck for not bowing.

When we left the Father Mathew Hall, it was on to a bus and down the quays to the offices of the *Irish Press*, where my mother told the front desk I had just won first prize in the Feis, with the implied certainty that they would care deeply about this. Not minded to fight her certitude, they produced a photographer, and a shot of me with an enormous floppy bow in my hair appeared in the paper the next day. My maternal grandmother's letter arrived two days later:

22-4-58

My dear Terry,

Heartiest congratulations to you. You are wonderful to come up 'first' in such a big crowd. You really must have worked very hard and deserved your great win. I am sure MaMa and DaDa and your teacher as well as all of us are very proud of you not forgetting Hilary.

Your photo in the paper is beautiful with your lovely happy smile has captivated all of us. No wonder you won the prize. You are a brick.

GrandDa and I enclose a P.O. for 5/= as a little reward for work well done.

God bless you dear Terry.

That was typical of Nana. She wrote letters by the dozen every day, at least half of them, I suspect, to her most beloved daughter, my mother. Every one of her grandchildren received cards and notes at Christmas and on birthdays, and she always included a financial reward. My grandfather got credited, even though we all knew he had nothing to do with it and even less interest. Patrick Colfer was a tall, handsome, white-haired man who had driven a dray for Guinness and, during the Civil War, was frequently lifted off it by the cops because of his resemblance to Michael Collins. He was from Wexford and his happiest section of any year was the early summer when he went down to his family and fished on the Slaney. Granddad was authoritative and took no shit from anybody. His shit detector was a high one, so his children and grandchildren tended to circle him at something of a distance, with the exception of Hilary, whom he adored.

My grandparents lived in 47 St Thomas Road, off the South Circular Road, in a small terraced house not that far from Keeffe's the knackers, which meant that if the wind was not in the right direction, the ambient pong would almost bring you to your knees. The front door of '47' as we called it, opened into a narrow dark hall with bicycles stacked on one side. On your right was a plastic version of Millais' *The Gleaners* with the figures slightly raised and a slimy-sided container the size of an egg-cup full of holy water underneath it.

When we visited, it was straight through the door into the main room, with Tony, the gigantic black cocker spaniel, under the table on which sat the television, and Ronnie, the budgie, in the birdcage on top. Ronnie raced up and down his perch at enough speed to have earned him his name in homage to Ireland's Olympic gold medallist Ronnie Delaney. That's when he wasn't being let out, the windows having been carefully checked so he could not endanger himself by escaping. He would sit on top of picture frames, land on the mantelpiece and finally go for his favourite place; the top edge of my grandfather's newspaper. Granddad always let on to be irritated by this, but of course he wasn't, particularly if the bird was in a talkative mood. Ronnie had two modes of talk. One was mimicking my grandfather, 'Get up them steps' and 'Shut the bloody door' being two of his favourites, the second instruction addressed by him to grandchildren, the first to the bird himself. The other mimicry was of my grandmother's sweet little voice, murmuring 'Hello, Ronnie. Who's a lovely birdie?' Every now and again, Ronnie would run the full gamut and, no matter how often you'd heard his accurate imitation of the two of them, it would startle and make you laugh.

The window overlooking the tiny back garden had a mirror on it, sitting above a box with its own little curtain attached. That was where my grandfather's shaving gear lived.

The back garden itself was bleak. Up against a wall was the pantry, a cupboard with a mesh front in which were kept perishables like butter and milk. Since we had a big fridge at home, this was a constant source of worry to me, because I couldn't see how the milk could be kept properly cold, and warmish milk would give you the shudders.

Twin pear trees that never fruited stood on either side of the two big steps that led to a pointless paved walk down the middle of the rectangle to the fencing at the back. They belonged to Nana and she was convinced that, sooner or later, they would produce fruit. One year, Granddad, in what my mother's brothers thought was a funny joke, tied a few store-bought pears to the branches of one of the trees and, for a few days, my poor grandmother was convinced it had come good. She laughed at herself when all was revealed and I remember thinking the worse of my grandfather for it.

Nana had no guile and her grandchildren thought the world of her, not least because we got to watch her doing her diabetes injections and she'd let us inject the skin of an orange using the empty syringe. She was one of five sisters from a family in Westport who owned a butcher's shop – Bridgie, who lived in New Rochelle in upstate New York; Cis, who lived in Edinburgh; Kate, who lived down the west; and Nora, who was a religious sister in an enclosed order in New York. Our Nana's name was Mary Agnes, and she, along with Bridgie, represented for us the good side of the Geraghtys. Less popular was Kate, because she was a schoolteacher of ostensible sweetness whom my mother said had once jammed her foot into her boot before work and only that evening, when investigating why it felt tight, found a dead mouse in the toe of it. Cis was a flasher. None of us had the word at the time, but she was always finding reasons to expose her horrific underwear or breasts. We were supposed to love all grandaunts equally, but my mother quickly abandoned that principle in sensible reaction to the realities. From the age of about five, I knew that it was okay to dislike my grandmother's sisters but Decent Behaviour required you to keep a lid on it.

Aunty Nora, the enclosed nun, was let out once, when her nephew Marty was being ordained in Rome. On her way, she stayed with us and we got to watch her doing enclosed nun things. She wasn't allowed to use an iron to flatten and smooth the white shoulder-to-shoulder bib she wore in front of her black ankle-length robe. Instead, she washed it and then laid it out on a mirror, smoothing the wrinkles out of it by hand while it was still wet. It was remarkably effective but meant we couldn't use the mirror for the day.

The first time I realised that someone loved Hilary more than they loved me was in my grandparents' narrow back garden when I was about six. My grandfather was rooting about in the shed. I said something to him and he answered me without turning around. Then Hilary said something and he reversed out of the shed door, smiles all over the big stern face of him, and talked to her. The different reactions intrigued me and I watched her to see what had caused it. The difference between us seemed to be that I talked about me and expected him to find it interesting, whereas Hilary asked him questions about what *he* was doing. In the long slanted shadows of evening, I realised people liked to be found interesting. It just seemed like a good way of doing things, like running a hard-boiled egg under cold water to make it easier to peel. It also reduced the performance imperative; if you asked people questions about themselves, they did the talking and were happy without you having to kill yourself being entertaining. You should, I learned, watching Hilary, also try to remember what they said. I tried, although not much remains for quotation other than Granddad talking about 'blackbirds roaring in the back garden' and muttering 'Bitch' about the nurse who tweaked his toes through the blanket in the hospital the day before he died.

The second set of grandparents, my father's parents, dead long before I was born, left no more than a couple of legends. His mother smiled vaguely out of a faded photograph in our album. When Mamma would see it, she would do a half-shake of the head that was one notch short of a snort, and describe her, with withering contempt, as 'a woman who would – *and did* – take two buses to meet someone on the northside to learn a new knitting stitch'. That's the sum total of my knowledge of the woman.

Dad's father was a janitor at the local church and had been involved in some vague way in the War of Independence, storing guns in the basement of the church and transporting them in the big pram underneath whichever of Dad's brothers was the baby at the time. My mother regarded the old man as a dogmatic bullying know-all given to religiosity, whose only good point was that he read constantly. That said, her face always softened when she told us of Lorcan's baby. Lorcan was one of my father's brothers, and when his first wife died in childbirth, Lorcan could see no alternative to asking his parents to take care of the baby while he went out to work. Our family album had many pictures of the child as he grew from baby to toddler to young lad, but they stopped when he was about nine, because that was when Lorcan remarried and took the boy to live with him and his new wife, devastating his parents, who never got over the loss of the child who had been the centre of their later lives.

My father never talked of his family, although he didn't edit them out of the family album, which allowed Hilary and me to work out, with Mamma's help, which of his brothers was which. He had a sister too. My mother would acknowledge this with a slight shudder. We could make of that shudder what we wished. The family's ancestors, according to familial legend, had been Huguenots – the Van Proens – who had fled Catholic oppression to come to Ireland, which at that time had pockets of Huguenots, particularly around the Liberties, where they ran weaving factories. The Van Proens, with the perversity that seemed to characterise them, settled in Ireland, where they were free to stay Protestant, and turned Catholic instead. Only one Prone family lived in Dublin and one side of them (us) didn't talk to the other side. My mother indicated that my father had become principled over the others challenging their parents' will in order to overturn the amount of money left to a brother who had a learning disability, but we never found out if he had succeeded. Stories on my mother's side had a beginning, middle and end. Stories on my father's side had a beginning and a middle and you didn't ask for anything more.

My mother, when my ex-seminarian father happened along, was a glamour girl who could make anything for which a Butterick pattern existed. She had understated good taste, was tall and slender with great legs, and had a knack with accessories that enabled her to give the impression of having a limitless wardrobe. She was also a party girl who regarded dancing as essential as food and air. She could do anything from the Charleston to the hornpipe, and no weekend was complete without at least one visit to a dancehall. She had several boyfriends, including a lovely man named Addie Keogh who later named his daughter after her, and we always wondered what it was that attracted her so irrevocably to my father, seeing as how the only dancing he could do was the waltz, and even then my mother had to 'One, two three' under her breath to keep him right. He turned up at the Colfer family home one evening and produced an engagement ring. Mamma said yes, put on the engagement ring and went off to a dance with another fellow.

Her engagement put the skids under her elder sister Kitty, who suddenly married a pleasant schoolteacher named Seán Cleary – said wedding happening scant months before my mother's nuptials. Asked about this, my mother would shrug: that was Kitty for you. My mother, in early childhood, had been given an expensive china doll, and the very day she got it, Kitty had whipped it from her, swung it like a baseball bat and smashed its head off the wall. Kitty was devastatingly witty and so cutting that I steered clear of her whenever possible.

In our own home, we lived a binary life. Ice cream was acceptable, ice pops not. Cotton was right for underpants, whereas nylon was the cheap work of Satan. Saying 'Pleased to meet you' when introduced to a new person marked you as muck. Describing a napkin as a 'serviette' ditto.

Magpies were bad, robins were good. Comics were bad, books were good. Real coffee, burping on the cooker in a percolator, was good. Irel coffee was a cheapskate's version, therefore bad. Ornaments were bad, unadorned surfaces good. Televisions were bad, radios were good. Winifred Atwell was good, Russ Conway was bad. (Honkey-tonk

pianists were popular at the time.) Daffodils were good, chrysan-
themums were worse than bad because not only were they vulgar
in appearance and stench, but they harboured earwigs. Almost every
insect south of the ladybird was so evil that family legend recorded
my mother wrapping Hilary up, as an infant, putting her in the pram
and taking the bus to my grandmother's house, leaving a centipede in
sole possession of the Prone home in Templeogue. This was in 1942.
She caught the last bus back home that night, landing at the same
time as my father arrived on his bike, and sat outside while he went
on a search-and-destroy mission inside. The centipede, wisely, was a
no-show.

I knew snails were bad, but I didn't know how good worms were
until the day I decided to make several of them by subdividing an
original worm. My mother's horror was unbounded. Nothing I could
say – not even pointing to the moving sections to indicate how happy
they were – amounted to an acceptable reason or an apology. Someone
who would do something so evil might never, ever get back to accepta-
bility. My sister irrelevantly but irritatingly weighed in to point out
that just a few weeks earlier I had been convinced a big worm was
about to eat my tricycle.

But, then, animals were the bane of my childhood, particularly Bob
the dog, who daily assaulted me when I came home from school. The
bus conductor had to physically lower me to the pavement to get me
off his vehicle, because the minute my feet hit the pavement, Bob was
all over me, as tall as I was on his hind legs, barking, slobbering and
showing me his filthy teeth. Nobody at home had any understanding
about the horror of Bob. 'It's a bloody *Labrador*,' my father said. 'It's
only trying to be friendly.'

Even though I hated Bob with a passion so long-lasting that I
still regard black Labs as guilty until proven innocent, I nevertheless
campaigned constantly for a pet. Everybody else I knew had a pet, I
pointed out to my mother, breaking the implacable home rule that we
did not compare ourselves to other people. I was indiscriminate: dog,
cat or budgie would do me fine. My godmother, Mai Houlihan, heard

me beg so often for a pet that one birthday she gave me a full-sized birdcage with a pretend canary on the perch. If you wound it up, it sang a song. I hated that canary with a hissing low-level venom but obediently brought it out for her delectation every visit.

Asthma meant Hilary and I couldn't have furry pets. Bad asthma. Every winter we alternated, one of us in bed with bronchitis, the other working up to it. We got used to our fingernails turning blue through lack of oxygen. We also got used to idiot doctors who would tell us that we needed to concentrate on breathing *out*, not *in*. We had inhalers with big bulbs at the bottom and a delicate glass top that vaporised the medicine. Nobody made the connection with our father smoking like a chimney, in common with our mother. He smoked Player's untipped from morning until night. Mamma's cigarettes were tipped – fat lot of good that did – and she too smoked constantly. At one point, she and I shared a bedroom so she could watch over me trying to breathe through the asthma the two of them, unknowingly, gave Hilary and me.

She concentrated on removing asthma triggers. No feather pillows or quilts. Nothing with fur on it. Sheets pinned all the way around, so the blankets were enclosed and couldn't release their vile spores. No daisies or goldenrod in the garden – or in the neighbour's garden. No matter what she did, one of us would have a crisis sufficiently dangerous to justify asking the doctor to visit, sometimes in the middle of the night. Our doctor, grandfather to Brian O'Driscoll the rugby player, arrived whenever he was telephoned, his deep voice coming up the stairs preceding his arrival in the bedroom, the glance around for a surface on which to dump the big tan leather doctor's bag. He would prescribe ephedrine, which made your hands shake and played your fast heartbeat in your ears, and Sulpha, the white liquid antibiotic, which had a uniquely vile taste.

If Dr O'Driscoll couldn't fix you, and those occasions were rare, you went to hospital. I remember three weeks in Temple Street when I shared a room with a little boy who cried for his family in a continuum of terrified misery, those being the days when hospital staff told parents not to visit because it would only upset the little patient. I was not permitted to have the light on to read after eight o'clock, but was allowed to have the radio on. One night, I listened to a short story – a ghost story called 'The Barbican Room' – which had such a terrifyingly realistic and unexpected ending, I've spent half a century fruitlessly seeking it to re-read.

It was after that hospital spell that my parents bought me a goldfish bowl with two inhabitants whom my father, to my puzzlement, named Finn and Haddie. After about six months, I came down one morning to find Finn bent and motionless at the bottom of the bowl. My sister gently lifted him out and laid him on a facecloth while Haddie continued to circle, solo, mouthing at us. 'Flush it down the toilet,' my father recommended, which reduced me to screaming tears of revulsion until my sister held me firmly by the shoulder while she gave out yards to Dad and told him this goldfish was going to have a proper coffin and a proper burial and he should know better, a point with which my mother unexpectedly concurred. Still rocked by intermittent bone-shaking sobs, I watched while Hilary constructed a perfect coffin from white cardboard, inserted Finn in it and gently lowered the Sellotape-hinged lid over him. She handed it to me and led me out to the back garden, where she used my father's spade to dig an oblong hole near the swing and gestured me to insert the coffin. She then pulled soil over it and stood beside me, the spade upright so we were like three mourners, while she said a prayer that Finn would find a happy future home. His brother (or sister) followed him six months later, and that ended pets in our house.

The binary distinctions applied also to the neighbours. The Cliftons were on one side, and my mother approved of them, not least because, one day when she and Mrs Clifton were having a chat over the fence dividing our garden from theirs, they simultaneously noticed that Mrs Clinton's youngest, a gorgeous pre-toddler named Denis, who was sitting up in the pram, was humming *The Merry Widow Waltz* to himself. Mamma didn't *disapprove* of the Dowdalls on the other side, but she had reservations about the fact that Mr Dowdall, a builder who had a glass eye, was known to send workers for a particular plank having placed the glass eye underneath it. She felt that the least you could do, if you had a glass eye, was be discreet about it.

My mother had stories that either condemned neighbours for their failings, or amounted to moral lessons for Hilary and me. The story about Mrs O'Donoghue was that she had invited the neighbours in for tea and biscuits to view her new baby. Something about the stillness of the baby intrigued Ma, who slid her hand under the coverlet to find that the infant was secured to the bottom sheet and mattress by more than a dozen oversized safety pins. He had to be perfect for the viewing. No kicking off of coverings.

The warning stories included Leslie Slye, the beautiful girl who wore sandals with a strap across the back of the toes. When she was coming down the stairs one day, the front bit of the sole of one sandal bent backwards, tripping her and tossing her right through the glass front door. Everybody in the Grove could enumerate the resulting stitches. The moral lesson was that you should always wear sandals that had a front bit preventing the sole from turning nasty.

When the O'Connors' house went on fire one night, the moral lesson was not to play with matches, which, in combination with the Edward Lear limerick about the girl who did just that, made me slightly envious of the O'Connors (who I assumed had played with matches) and subject to nightly terrors that our own house was on fire. The O'Connors moved on from their fire. I never did. Every fire ever reported fascinated me. Parents 'beaten back by flames' when trying to rescue their children. Pugilistic poses of corpses. The imagined horror of drawing scorching heat into one's lungs with the prayer of fast-dying nerve ends …

My father had a much simpler attitude than my mother to neighbours. He didn't quite hate them all on sight, but the less he had to do with any of them, the better. Dad was a bit like the two fictional priests of whom Thomas Keneally wrote, 'because they loved nobody, they thought they loved God.' Dad loved the notion of community, so he joined local committees, worked his way to the top, fought with everybody, and left. He was visionary in his thinking, just not good at tolerating what my mother called 'do-gooders' for the long haul. So, although he was one of the people who established the credit union movement in Ireland and was close to John Hume, who at the time was president of the Irish League of Credit Unions, he eventually fell out with them too.

He never fell out with Jimmy Kelly, a fellow trade union activist, better known as James Plunkett, the writer of *Strumpet City*. When the author, before he became unimpeachable through literary fame, went to the Soviet Union to meet worker leaders there, the Catholic Church in Ireland roundly condemned him. Plunkett, in retrospect, might have acknowledged a certain 'Potemkin village' marketing of Stalin's USSR, but that wasn't what the Church was up in arms about. The very idea that an Irish Catholic would choose to visit godless Russia at all horrified the hierarchy, and they whipped up their followers, while James Plunkett was overseas, to condemn him. My father took pen in hand and wrote a passionate and well-argued letter in defence of his friend, which ended up on the front page of one of the weekly Catholic papers and caused him no end of trouble with other members of the faithful. My mother said that we should all be grateful that the Dublin Gas Company, where Dad worked, was a Protestant organisation where none of the top guys cared about the Catholic excoriation of Kelly or my father's guilt by association. Hilary and I thought him heroic. My mother had a way of tilting her head down and looking at you grimly when you articulated that kind of view. 'Yes,' she would murmur. 'Heroic.' Like when Mr Robertson, the chief executive of the Dublin Gas Company, offered Dadda a managerial position and he turned it down because he would have to leave the trade union. This principled stance cost money and prestige and my mother's lip tended to curl about such costly principles.

Most of the time my father's dislike of neighbours was persistent but relatively passive. On one occasion, however, he was in the scullery, sniffing the wonderful bowl-you-over scent of my mother's brown bread, which was cooling on a metal grid, when a mouse appeared and ran over the loaf. My father slammed the door into the main kitchen and turned on all the gas jets. As an employee of Dublin Gas, he knew all about the dangers of what came out of those jets but did not let that hold him back. The mouse reappeared, staggering, fell into the sink and gave up its short life, at which point my father opened the window and the back door and breathed deeply until the dizziness passed, then secreted the dead mouse in one of those six-unit cardboard egg boxes, headed out into the lane and left the egg box as an anonymous gift on the back wall of Mr Brennan's house. It was the only time his dislike of Mr Brennan showed up other than in the icy courtesy my father reserved for those he cordially loathed.

Inside the house, my father often knew the rules and broke them with determination and regularity. He knew all about electricity, but put silver paper in fuses, effectively disabling them, and did wiring of such creativity that for quite some time one wall in the scullery was live. If you put your hand on it, someone had to get you unstuck using a broom handle. Dad undertook work that, today, you'd get 'a man' to do. It wasn't that he had a particular affinity for plumbing and carpentry, it was that we couldn't afford to hire an external expert. My mother's bookkeeping was admirable, if sad, looked at through a lens of later financial ease. Every bus trip was costed, every purchase recorded, every refund acknowledged. She didn't enjoy any of it, repeatedly telling her daughters to work hard at school because freedom lay in having your own money.

Meanwhile, when anything went wrong, my father would fix it. Sometimes the fix would be effective and orthodox. Not often, though. He took a freestyle approach to electricity, carpentry and plumbing which sometimes left the fix visible or required it to have warnings attached. For the most part, things worked, although one Good Friday, the plumbing ceased to do what plumbing is supposed to do, and he announced that he was going down the manhole in the back garden and that if any of us used the toilet before he gave us permission, the consequences would be lamentable. With that, he disappeared out the back door, leaving my mother to explain the word 'lamentable'. Hilary cut to the chase by telling me that when you flushed the toilet the contents would land on Da's head. I asked how long he was going to be down there, and my mother said it didn't matter. We could still *use* the loo. It was just that we couldn't flush it, after use. When I visited the facilities about an hour later, I was so scared that I murmured 'Don't flush whatever you do' all the time. On this Good Friday, at some point, the conversation in the kitchen between my mother and me was arrested in mid-syllable by the unmistakable sound of the toilet flushing upstairs. When Hilary joined us, one look at our faces told her the trouble she was in. Within seconds, my father was standing there in extreme and sodden disarray. Mamma and I showed zero loyalty, pointing at Hilary and saying, 'It was her, it was her.'

My mother knew the rules for everything and enforced them ruthlessly. Sometimes even cruelly. 'Stand up straight,' she would instruct Hilary. 'Your neck is short enough as it is.' She could make anything from a raffia lampshade to a complete and beautiful version of Snow White's clothes for me. She could also cook or bake anything. She could turn out party food for sixty which not only tasted delicious but looked gorgeous. My father, on the other hand, cooked only two things, and I have never got over either of them.

The first of the twin horrors was porridge, which required a double boiler, infinite care and the sort of precision normally required when making a soufflé. The result was – well, porridge. Porridge is difficult to spoil or improve, in my view. It always comes out as spodge. My father's spodge, when you poured milk round the edges, rose and floated in the bowl like a rubbery UFO. I would attack it with the objective of swallowing it without tasting, and that meant getting through it in five discrete chunks. I tried to get away with four, but my mother tut-tutted at the size of what was on my spoon, so five ended up as the sentence I would serve, each and every morning, except in high summer, when I got paroled with cornflakes. I had learned to swallow, rather than eat, horrible things because among the 'treatments' at the time for asthma was a raw egg ingested first thing in the morning. It couldn't be flipped or the yolk broken, and to this day I gag at the memory of the firmly soft oleaginous, gelatinous mass going down, even though the course of treatment lasted only for a month. I swore that when I was grown up, I would never ever eat two things: porridge and cabbage. As an adult, I revised the rule about cabbage to 'occasionally and ideally raw or nearly so', but porridge stays on the banned list to this day. I would never engage in porridge-shaming, but I seriously mistrust people who announce that they start their day with porridge.

The other abomination cooked by my father was called brawn. Brawn began, horribly, with a sheep's head steeping in a bucket in the scullery. The trauma visited upon a small child by having to pass by this skeletal dead thing with its eyeholes staring out can never be erased. The heads seemed twice as big as any reasonable sheep would need. We never saw my father strip the meat off the skull, although he would have been charmed to share the task with us, so I honestly don't know what happened between the time when the bucket with the skull in it sat in the scullery and the moment when a pleasing little bowl of horror was reverently placed on the tea table.

The bowl had a lightly gilded network design all over it, interrupted on either side by a scene of a shepherd and shepherdess in improbably clean and fancy flounces. It now seems to me to have been gratuitously cruel to present something made from a dead sheep in a bowl decorated with gambolling lambs, but that's the way it was. Brawn was a kind of coarse pâté, tasting like I imagined chilled turds might taste. It had many drawbacks, undoubtedly the most pronounced of which was that it was not amenable to unchewed swallowing like the raw egg yolks and the porridge. How my father could take such pride in producing something that provoked retching still puzzles me. Back then, it was just one of the awful contradictions inflicted on children. My father pronounced it delicious, my mother contradicted him with her face but made us eat it anyway.

Another of those contradictions was the relationship between my mother and father. Close but fraught is how it might be characterised. Any time my mother was due home after my father would have gone to bed – if, say, she was visiting her mother – she would come home to find a love letter or comic poem written in pencil on the cream Formica kitchen table. A wipe of a dishcloth and it was gone, which now seems a shame. Weekends, he would set out to do something that would please her when she got home from spending Saturday afternoon with her mother. Like painting all the kitchen chairs and her vintage sewing machine an almost neon green. She didn't speak to him for nearly three months and never got over the sewing machine. Every time she used it thereafter, she would stand for a second or two with her eyes closed before sitting down at it to work.

We called them 'coolnesses,' the cold wars that were erratically constant between family members. Your mother might be cooling you. Or Hilary might be cooling Dad. So at mealtimes, you'd get frigid requests to 'Kindly ask your father for the salt.' I heard 'kindly' so often in a tone that would shatter glass that I had to relearn it later as a quite positive term.

A buoyant nature was not an asset when you were on the receiving end of a coolness. I would get an unmerciful dressing-down from my mother, the clear implications of which were that I had by my execrable actions brought the Prones, seed, breed and generation, into possibly terminal disrepute. I would acknowledge my infamy, grovel fruitlessly in the face of my mother's grievous disappointment, and slink upstairs, where a few minutes later I would have forgotten the whole thing and burst into song. Forgetting you were being 'cooled' exacerbated the original crime by proving you *didn't care* about how hurt my mother was.

Every Sunday, we had two visitors for a tea of sliced ham with lettuce and tomato. They were my godmother, Mai Houlihan, a civil servant from Cahirsiveen, and Gerry Marrinan, a Columban father from Antrim who'd been in the seminary with Dad before being ordained and serving in Korea. When the Pacific war broke out, Gerry found himself parked in Navan, writing the Pudsy Ryan column, a mildly funny offering ostensibly from a schoolboy, in *The Far East* magazine. He got to go to America, and met Bing Crosby on the set of a film in which Bing played a priest, generating a magazine cutting with Gerry, in full Roman-collared black priestly uniform, standing beside an identically dressed Bing. Gerry was impregnably calm and reasonable. When Hilary complained of having too much homework, he pointed out that nobody had ever died of homework.

Mai and Gerry were generous and I still have some of their gifts, including a matched set of Edgar Allan Poe's writings from Gerry, who also introduced me to G.K. Chesterton, having mentioned him in a debate, led by my father, on how nobody really knew how good life probably was in the USSR. (This was before we knew Stalin inflicted lethal starvation on millions of his people.) I was trying to understand what communism was, and Gerry quoted Chesterton to the effect that, under capitalism, only the chimneys of the rich get swept, whereas under communism, the chimneys of rich and poor alike were swept, but you weren't allowed to own your own soot. I opened my mouth to ask why anybody would *want* to own their own soot and got a look from Hilary that made me close it again, unenlightened.

2

SPECIAL DISPENSATIONS

*P*ale grey shadows, still and stiff, ghosted one into the other. Slow march to whipping speed, you tried to focus on even one of them before it joined the others in a stalwart slide. Trees by the side of roads lit only by the headlights of Gerry Marrinan's car, flipping into darkness as we drove home, me in the portion of the Volkswagen Beetle behind the back seats, padded about by coats, hands sliding from the satin smoothness of their lining to the rough sack carpeting of that uncushioned little segment of the car.

We'd be coming home from Dalgan, the rhythms linking and slipping, engine noise and passing shadows. At some point, as if in response to an unspoken instruction, someone would begin to hum a tune. Someone else would pick it up and the songs would line up in an unacknowledged playlist, the inevitability of the next melody foreordained by the last notes of the previous one.

Heart of my heart,
I love that melody,
Heart of my heart,
Brings back sweet memories.

When we were kids on the corner of the street,
We were rough and ready guys –
But oh, how we could harmonise.

Followed by:

Oh, give me land, lots of land, under starry skies above,
Don't fence me in.
Let me ride through the wide open spaces that I love,
Don't fence me in …

My mother would lead, with my sister's pure soprano taking the harmony line and my father trying to make like Paul Robeson. Gerry didn't sing much; he'd be concentrating, as he always was, on the road. He was a beautiful driver as defined by the times, the consensus being that a few scoops of good whiskey before he got behind the wheel never impaired him a bit; maybe even improved him. I learned all these phrases at four and five, never questioning why people referred to them as 'scoops', never wondering why they always talked of 'good' whiskey as if somewhere in the world folk willingly, even eagerly, drank bad whiskey.

Memories of the journeys are layered with legend, so I believe I remember what I probably do not actually recall, like the night when Gerry, watching wavering headlights coming towards us, said 'This guy's going to hit us,' in a quiet voice, sliding the gear into neutral and braking. The other car, driven by a man who had perhaps too many scoops of good whiskey in him, did hit us. Details were exchanged and a civil parting achieved. Gerry murmured that one of the advantages of the VW having its engine in the back was that he didn't have to worry about the collision having damaged it. 'Here we go again,' he said, and someone sang, as if it was the necessary next phrase, 'Happy as can be, all good friends and jolly good company.' That song might yield to 'On the Sidewalks of New York', and then Hilary would start on Harry Belafonte's 'Scarlet Ribbons'.

The songs sung on car journeys home might overlap with the songs sung at home, but not by much. At home, my father would play LPs of the D'Oyly Carte Gilbert and Sullivan operettas, my mother would turn up the radio when Burl Ives came on with mystifying lyrics like 'Jimmy crack corn and I don't care', or Hil would carefully lower the gramophone needle on Pat Boone records. Her bedroom was dominated by posters of the handsome, clean-cut singer with the lovely voice – the singer who faded away to nothing over the decades.

The main journey involving the VW and Gerry as driver was the autumn highlight of our year, when he would host an elaborate formal lunch for us in Dowdstown House, about a mile from the Columban Fathers seminary in Dalgan Park near Navan. Dowdstown House had been the dower house of an old estate, possessed of beautiful views over grounds rolling down towards the slow River Nanny. Everything about it was grand. Parquet flooring my mother tiptoed over, lest her high heels pock the old chevroned deep-shining wood. Low-level iron radiators half-warming each room. Great glass cases of formal Korean and Chinese court gowns and robes. Toilets with overhead tanks from which descended chains with wooden dowels at the end. A formal dining room. And the library, where we spent most of our visiting day. Oh, the library, with its floor to ceiling mahogany bookshelves filled with leather-bound volumes of history and theology. The library, with its wonderful circular add-on room at one corner, where quiet study or daydreaming could happen.

Between the windows and on the walls of the dining room hung Chinese artwork of breathtaking delicacy, annotated down the side with mysterious characters. Close to the door into the dining room stood a carved wooden trolley laden with decanted sherry, bottles of brandy, and enormous siphons of lemonade, white and red, and soda water. Watching those siphons spew forth their fizzed-up contents made me drink much more than I wanted to, just for the chance to have another go at the small pump handle. After lunch, we would sit around the roaring log fire in the centre of the room and talk until my father or Gerry or both snoozed and I was carried away to have a nap in the bishop's bed. I never learned who the bishop was or what he thought of a six- or seven-year-old napping in his bed, but I remember the elaborate cornices on the ceiling of his room and the four posts coming up from the corners of the bed. I imagined they were there to prevent him from falling out.

Our year was hung between such highlights. The birthday parties where everybody had paper crowns and got to eat cornflake crispies, made in our house with Cadbury's Dairy Milk chocolate. None of your old cooking chocolate, with its sour after-taste, for us. Birthday parties with the nervous moment before you blew out all the candles. Nobody ever specified the consequences for failing to blow out the four or five candles on one exhale, but we knew they might be serious. My most vivid birthday memory is of a child from a few houses down throwing up over her balloon, and Hilary, present as the guardian older sister, decisively tossing the puke-slimed object into the fire, where it exploded with widely distributed nastiness.

Some of the highlight days were pretty ordinary, rendered exceptional only by their placement in the calendar. St Patrick's Day was an oasis in the desert of Lent. On that day, you could eat sweets, biscuits or cakes – whatever you had been coerced into giving up for Lent – so during the weeks before our patron saint's day, we banked every random chocolate bar or toffee and on that day ate a promiscuous assortment of sweet garbage. Other than that, and wearing shamrock to Mass, in our house we ignored St Patrick's Day. My father regarded the evidence for the saint's existence as thin and my mother loathed any display of patriotism. I knew a parade happened in Dublin city, but couldn't figure out why anybody would want to watch lorries going past with people standing on them waving.

Easter was a chocolate outbreak. Those old Quaker families, the Rowntrees, the Frys and the Cadburys, contributed the high-end offerings, with local brands like Lemon's bringing up the rear. Lemon's mainly seemed to make hard or boiled sweets which required committed long-term sucking in order to deliver even a second-class sugar high, inflicting mouth ulcers as part of the deal.

Summer holidays meant a month in Laytown, County Meath. Mothers and children were installed in wooden chalets with corrugated roofs, built in a U around a green space in the middle. Outside each chalet stood a sturdy barrel to capture rainwater, which some of the women preferred to tap water when it came to washing their hair, because the tap water was adjudged to be very hard. 'Hard' in water terms meant that milk would divide up into tiny white islands on the top of a cup of tea, and that the tea itself was more delicious than any tea since.

The men in the families tended to go back to Dublin and then visit at weekends, although some of them stayed for the final two weeks in August. It was in Laytown I learned to swim, or at least doggy paddle, on my father's instructions. I never learned to co-ordinate legs and arms, though, so my crawl and backstroke look like the progress of a spavined ewe. In the evenings, when I was in bed, Hilary would go to the Gallaghers' chalet, at the top of one of the legs of the U. The Gallaghers were marvellous musicians, and each evening they would drag chairs, guitars, spoons and tin whistles onto the veranda that ran the length of their chalet and create music while the sun set, the session breaking up only when darkness was profound. Hilary was part of this, even when a thunderstorm roared and those on the veranda were barely sheltered from the rain.

My mother worried about anybody going outdoors during a thunderstorm, and had theories about them. Whether it was electrical storms or clothes, one never knew where a theory, sprung fully fledged from her, ended, and where scientific facts came in.

'Two thin ones are better than one thick one,' she maintained, talking about the warmth induced by wearing two sweaters. That didn't mean she ever put either of us in a thin sweater; instead, making us wear two thick sweaters. If a little of what you fancy does you good, her reasoning went, a lot of what you fancy does you a power of good. Because she herself retired to bed like a smacked dog at the smallest rumble of thunder, I always assumed that her electrical storm advice wasn't up to much. 'Don't shelter under a tree,' she would tell us. 'Don't put up an umbrella. Don't go near a window. Lie down in the middle of a field.'

The last was a bit impractical because fields were scarce in suburban Clontarf. Later, in school, learning about electrical storms, I came racing home, full of joyous surprise. 'Hey, you were right about not sheltering under a tree.' She looked insulted and said of course she was right; she wasn't stupid, you know. My mother always felt herself to be at the mercy of elemental forces obeying no known laws. Electricity was out to get you and if it failed through the normal household channels, it would come at you in the shape of a thunderstorm and if you used the phone when thunder was about, the lightning would come down the flex and fry your brain through your ear.

Laytown was the first occasion when I did something that made my mother cry. During August, the Laytown Races are run along the long beach for several days. Another visiting kid and I wanted to experience the races up close and decided that crossing the road from where the chalets were situated was perfectly safe, as was scrambling down the grassy cliff from the road to the beach. So we did it. Not long after, a race began. We could hear the horses in the distance, coming closer, thundering closer, closer until we could feel their hoofbeats through our bare feet on the hard sand and hoofbeats became heartbeats. It happened twice, that life-changing wonder, and might have happened thrice were it not that a search party found us two runaways and dragged us back to face our respective mothers, who confounded us by crying and hugging and reproaching us for what we knew not. I never saw the little boy again. I presume that as far as his mother was concerned, I was bad company, and as far as mine was concerned, the same applied to him.

Laytown was also where I brushed, unknowingly, against a figure now part of Ireland's theatrical history. During the holiday month, we had temporary tickets allowing us to borrow books from the Laytown library. The librarian was a completely circular old lady who rarely said anything. Then, one day, as my mother handed over the books we were returning, the little roundy lady looked at the big picture story book borrowed for me and opened it at a picture of Captain Hook standing athwart a crocodile's wide open mouth. She looked at it for a long moment and then turned it around to me. 'Who's he?' she asked in a voice so soft, only a child could have heard her at first go. I stepped up beside her (her big comfy chair and desk were on a plinth, raised off the library floor by about a foot), turned the book rightways around, and went three pages back to where the character was introduced. I told her all about him and how scary he was with his hook for a hand and his eyepatch, which, I confided, was a bit like the one I had had to wear when I had a stye on my eye. She said nothing. Just listened. Nodded. Indicated I should go on. Then mashed her mouth together in a way that wordlessly conveyed to me that she now understood a story the essence of which had eluded her up to that point. Hilary grabbed me off the plinth and marched me into the Children's Books section. The librarian smiled at my mother, who, for once, didn't know what to make of the situation. The librarian asked my name and wrote it down, careful to get the spelling right.

'That little girl will be an Abbey actress,' she told my mother and went on to deal with the small queue that had formed. On every subsequent visit, the librarian nodded to me as if we had come to an agreement of some sort. Meanwhile, my mother began asking around about the little round figure in the tiny library, and discovered she was Máire Nic Shiubhlaigh, one of the earliest members of the Abbey Theatre Company, who had abandoned acting after ideological disagreements with W.B. Yeats, all-powerful for several decades in Ireland's national theatre. Once I was old enough to go to the theatre, whenever we were in the Abbey, we would visit the Jack Yeats painting of her, slender, distant, wistful and beautiful in her youth. It was a wintertime pilgrimage undertaken every year when we dutifully, if resentfully, attended the Abbey's Irish language pantomime with, one year, Sinéad Cusack playing the princess and T.P. McKenna playing the prince. The Abbey's was one of three pantomimes we would see every year. The Olympia had Jack Cruise and the Gaiety had Maureen Potter.

My mother would decide when to buy the tickets and whether to go for matinees or night-time performances.

But then, Christmas was more or less owned by my mother. The signs would be there for a while. Cellophane packages of raisins, sultanas and almonds piled up side by side in kitchen cupboards until one weekend we would find the kitchen table taken over by the butter-coloured thick delft mixing bowl, and by neat squares of waxed paper, onto which went steepled piles of newly grated suet or breadcrumbs. Invariably, we skinned bits off our knuckles as we grated, occasioning gruesome cannibal jokes from my father, and we always asked why the puddings and cakes had to be done so far in advance.

'They have to mature,' Mamma would say, her hair wrapped up in a scarf knotted at the forehead, Rosie the Riveter-style, to help her perm withstand the steam generated by boiling the puddings. Some mothers made plum puddings in muslin bags, which produced circular offerings like black snowballs, but Mamma had a series of Pyrex bowls, over the top of which was stretched greaseproof paper retained in position by triple circles of twine, tightly knotted, although she said the boiling water would tighten the twine anyway, so the contents would be safe while the flavours, as she put it, 'melded' into each other. Even at the lowest gas burner setting, they simmered with enough vigour to move around the Pyrex bowls, making grumbling noises.

'Meld', we would murmur to ourselves. 'Meld.' If it was a word, it was peculiarly a pre-Christmas word, never used at any other time of the year. As we chewed the word, she would tell us again about the time that our grandmother had mislaid a pudding after its first boiling and had not found it until the following year. 'She gave it its second boiling then and everybody agreed it was simply the best pudding any of us ever tasted,' she would say, turning over and over the ingredients for her own pudding in the huge bowl with slow, sure, unhurried movements. She had big hands, my mother, big hands to span the octave on a piano, big hands to comfort a fallen child, big, skilful hands to make and mend. Nothing was beyond them, and their contribution to the economy of our household was significant, if unacknowledged. Curtains and lampshades, dresses and coats, cakes and roasts were turned out, and the word 'bought', as in 'a bought cake' was always pejorative.

Those hands came into their own at Christmas. It was Mamma who, one day in early winter, would ask what everybody was giving up for Advent, the question carrying the assumption that you were giving up something and it had better be a serious self-deprivation, a real and present postponement of gratification. The flavours of Christmas burst with particular vividness on tastebuds that had been having a thin time.

In the church, a few weeks before Christmas, one porch area would be curtained off with blackish-grey 'sugar paper', which would be pulled aside on Christmas Eve to reveal the Holy Family positioned around an empty centre area, looking with appropriately awed and affectionate expressions at a blank space where, on Christmas morning, the baby Jesus would be placed on a little straw crib, his hands raised to shoulder level as if acknowledging applause.

I thought it was kind of tough on Our Lady to be left kneeling for days before and after she had a baby, but then the baby, when it made its appearance, wasn't like any baby I knew. It was always thin, the Baby Jesus, with long slender six-month-old limbs and a fine-boned, knowing face. You never saw a baby Jesus that was roaring its head off, although sometimes you saw swaddled clothes, crisscross ribbons holding the cloth tight and the baby's arms and legs with it. You'd find yourself surreptitiously stretching out your own arms and legs in sympathy with the cramped infant.

Every household, of course, had its own crib, a much smaller version than the one in the church, but more colourful, since the church statues were of white marble, whereas the characters in home cribs wore colourful clothes, with the exception of the shepherds, who never got to wear anything other than beige and brown. The three kings arrived a few days after Christmas and were ritually moved a bit closer to the action each day thereafter. I insisted that the king carrying the gold (he happened to be black and have a jewelled turban rather than a crown) be in prime position, because I believed he had his wits about him, whereas the other two were just wasting Our Lady's time. She's there in a stable trying to cope with a new baby, an old husband leaning on a tall crozier thing as if he had no energy, a whole load of sheep and shepherds and a star overhead so bright that it would let her get no sleep, and three kings arrive with gifts. Gold she certainly could use. But frankincense and myrrh?

The lesson you were supposed to draw from it, I'm sure, was that you should be grateful for any gift at Christmas, no matter how rotten it was. If your aunt gave you half a dozen prickly woollen vests, you had to behave as if she had given you three puppies and a bike, throwing your arms around her and telling her how beautiful they were. I thought this was a cod, and was sure the slightly vague expression Our Lady had in every crib meant that she was giving serious consideration to pelting the two dopier kings with their presents.

In the last couple of days before Christmas, the house was filled with an excitement like bubbles in newly applied wallpaper. Our mother would pat down the excitement and it would just surface somewhere else, irritating our father, who was to be found in a vile temper, going through the Christmas lights one by one to find the dud that was on strike and had brought out all its comrades in sympathy. The lights were the first thing to go on the tree each year, so while he did his diagnosis and rescue, we lifted the lids off the big flat cardboard boxes that had come down from the attic, each filled with smaller boxes, each subdivided like a noughts-and-crosses game with light card keeping the baubles separated and safe from one another. The ornaments I liked best had been hand-made by my mother years before.

Gerry's present to Mamma every year was a subscription to the American *Good Housekeeping* magazine, which arrived in the post every month. Ma didn't believe that teenage minds like Hilary's could be trusted with all the information in that magazine (particularly a regular column entitled 'Can this marriage be saved?') so she kept

Good Housekeeping stashed between the mattress of her bed and the frame. Hil and I regarded this as something of an invitation or at the very least a test of our individual discretion. Each of us pulled it out and read what we liked in it. Neither of us told the other. Both of us kept our mother content that she was protecting us from Yankee corruption.

It was in *Good Housekeeping* I first encountered Bad Breath, which, it seemed, was one of a rake of social errors you could commit unbeknownst to yourself, which would result in your rightful exclusion from decent society. I became so fearful of Bad Breath that I got into the self-testing habit. Hilary would ask why the hell I kept breathing into my hands, but it was an order to cease and desist rather than a genuine question. In the early pages of every edition was an ad for a pointy bra made by Maidenform. The conceit was that the model wearing the pointy bra had a dream which put her in a reasonably public situation, wearing nothing but her Maidenform bra above the waist.

The December issue of *Good Housekeeping* was almost completely given over to Christmas decorations, cuisine, wrapping and gift ideas. One year, they printed coloured shapes you were supposed to cut out, pasting one on either side of a piece of similarly shaped thick cardboard. Some were round, others oblong, some lantern-shaped. Our mother neatly did this, threading strong silvered cord through the top. Out they came, every year, with their round-mouthed carol singers and bell-wielding town criers of Pickwickian embonpoint, standing in snow, or skating on smooth ponds, hands tucked in muffs, scarves flying out behind them. Only one failed skater figured — a child young enough to be portrayed with feet splayed, straight-legged, arms in the air like a figure X.

While we lined up the ornaments, putting strings on the ones that had shed their loops, Mamma sat at the kitchen table gently pulling the long thin explosive bit out of the Christmas crackers, in deference to my terror of the things. She did it as if she was de-stinging a bee. A contradiction in terms, those crackers were.

It was as if our mother had done a course in Christmas, and that only she knew the secret rules. In other houses they didn't know the rules, and we allowed ourselves to feel quietly superior. Not knowing the rules meant putting your Christmas tree in the front window ('vulgar display'). Or putting balloons on the tree ('crude and out of proportion'). Or spraying the tree with glitter ('easier than proper decoration, but not as effective'). Our mother knew that a tree should have hundreds of little decorations, each in its preordained place, lots of lametta, painstakingly hung, string by string, never thrown on in bundles, and a star at the top that looked into the room and didn't tilt to one side.

Our father was a bit player during the holiday season. His moment of glory came when we had all written our letters to Santa, and dad would tell us to throw them in the fire. Each Christmas we did, expecting to see them destroyed by the flames, and each Christmas, with some trick of draught management achieved by quickly opening or closing a door, my father ensured that they flew, unburned, straight up the chimney on their way to the North Pole.

It was our mother who defined, on Christmas morning, what was 'an absolutely ridiculous' but nevertheless acceptably early time to get out of bed and start unwrapping, as opposed to what was actually still the middle of the night. Because the stockings were hung up downstairs, we had no way of knowing when Santa had arrived. The stockings were special, too. Our mother figured that ordinary stockings were no damn good for Santa purposes, so she knitted up a few, using a great deal of ribbing in the leg, and making each stocking fit to contain the leg of a small giant. The ribbing meant that the stocking could expand at points to accept an oddly shaped item, and the result was that Christmas morning saw a deliberate 'postponement of gratification' as each of us turned our stocking around and around, noting any long shape that went from one side to another, as if a snake had swallowed a ruler sideways on, rather than longways, poking the softish box shape which seemed to have something round inside it, and – carefully – jolting the whole stocking up and down to hear the rattles.

No matter what we wanted, we got it. Santa first brought me a plastic clarinet I never learned to play, then the most beautiful lacquered zither (ditto) and later a pogo stick. I had fallen in love with the idea of a pogo stick because a character in the comic *Judy*, or *Bunty* perhaps, used hers to leap tall buildings in order to save people from some potential disaster, but once I had it, and I was the first of my friends to have a pogo stick, I found that all it did was rattle your fillings while never rising more than a foot off the ground.

Such limitations were never evident on Christmas morning. Indeed, limitations seemed there none, as we went through the stockings, reaching the toe, where a tangerine (rare at that time in Ireland) and a Crispin competed for space. The Crispin was a wafer biscuit coated in chocolate, and we knew we were not to even consider eating it before Mass. We had barely opened our gifts when we had to get dolled up to walk to the French Sisters of Charity convent on Mount Prospect Avenue, where my father served Mass every day and where, as a result, we were honoured guests for Mass on Christmas morning. My father concentrated on his Catholicism, rather than his socialism, when he was with the nuns, and when they rustled out to welcome us on Christmas morning, we were warmed by referred affection. The French Sisters of Charity wore vast headdresses of starched white cotton and full-length gowns. Sometimes, they would clip together the wings of the headdresses with tiny clothes pegs, but that was only to keep them from flapping while they did housework. On this one morning, every headdress was freed to whisper to the one beside it and the one in front of it, like a field of white flowers rustling in a breeze.

Once Mass was over, Dad's starring role was finished, and from then on Mamma was like a theatrical director, managing every other phase of the day. She decided all that moved. She allowed us to choose a toy each to bring to '47', where our grandparents lived, and got us scarfed and mittened, ready for take-off, long before the taxi arrived. The taxi was such an experience, with so many details to be examined, that I sometimes missed when the driver had asked me a question such as 'What was the best present you got this morning?' I was always thrown by that one. Every present that Santa or my parents gave me was equally wonderful. I was missing a one to ten scale by which to select the best, so often simply held up whatever item I had been permitted to bring with me.

When we were dropped at St Thomas Road, free, on that wonderful day, of the usual scent delivered by Keeffe's the knackers, the house would already be crowded. Uncle Donal, the youngest of my mother's many brothers, might already have arrived with his glamorous, always smiling, wife, Kay. Uncle Pat, the former RAF man, might be there with his tiny English wife, Peggy. Uncle Martin, who seldom spoke, and then only in a shy whisper, would be there with Maura Harris. For some reason I never got a handle on, Maura never became 'Aunty Maura' and always retained her maiden name. Maura Harris was the ultimate complement to Martin, who had, as a kid, been spotted by a Manchester United scout and brought to live in England as a future team member, returning home after ten days half-dead from a homesickness that seemed to stay with him. Maura was the life-lover he needed, dressed with a careless panache, one manicured hand always clutching a cigarette. Dermot, another uncle, would be there with Marie, his wife, who had been a nun, which gave her an obscure glamour. At that point, remember, nuns were nuns for life, and one of the bestsellers of the 1960s, called *I Leap Over the Wall*, written by a former nun, was passed from hand to hand as covertly as pornography, with its details of head-shaving and other sisterly rituals.

One Christmas morning, Dermot noticed me eyeing his newly poured glass of Guinness and asked me if I would like to taste it. Neither my mother nor father being within vetoing distance, I nodded and he held out the tall glass, which I knew was filled with a chocolate-flavoured drink topped off with whipped cream. The first mouthful failed horribly to live up to expectations. I sat there, cheeks distended, Dermot and the other uncles roaring with laughter at me. My mother walked in from the scullery and in an instant worked out what had happened. 'Swallow it,' she instructed. I did. Which made the experience even worse and left me with a life-long mistrust of

Dermot, who had no idea his drink had given me PTSD of a liquid sort.

Mamma's brothers, in appearance, career and behaviour, were diversity in action. Fergus, for example, was a gentle gambling addict who lived in London, returning briefly when he was flush with money and disappearing when the cash ran out. His siblings rescued him from one disaster after another, realising eventually that there was ultimately no saving him. His disease defined him and sucked the life out of him.

Brendan was the survivor of a pair of twins. The other twin, Seán, had been my mother's pet. As his favoured older sister, she took the roundy little toddler everywhere she could, buying him whatever she could afford in the way of treats. He had only to see her to put the two little arms up to be lifted, to be cuddled, to be swung, to be hugged. Then, when Seán and Brendan were about four, came scarlet fever. Brendan suffered it and shook it off. His twin didn't, sinking into fevered pneumonia. My mother sneaked into the room where he lay and he opened heavy-lidded eyes, registering who she was. 'Doh away', he told her, not old enough to pronounce the tired dismissal correctly. 'Doh away.' It stayed with her for ever, that saddest moment of her youth, that plea for inattention by a febrile tot, that loss of her ability to love him out of it, to kiss him better. 'Doh away,' she would repeat, wonderingly, to Hilary and me when we were children, then teenagers, then adults, the pain of it never going, the repetition never turning into a bid for sympathy.

Brendan was too young to remember his sibling and did not have a shadow over his childhood. He arrived into any situation giving stick to whomever was there, getting laughs from the moment of his arrival, the sweary Dub with the deep singing voice. He, like our grandmother, had had type 1 diabetes from his teens, and had to do all the measuring, injecting and diet control required by a fairly brittle version of the complaint.

Uncle Brendan would tend to arrive for true Christmas lunch with former or current residents of the Los Angeles Society's home, where he was the director. By the nineties, Los Angeles had two homes, one in Conyngham Road near Islandbridge and one in Blackrock, to address the needs of young boys sleeping rough in the capital city. The boys were on the streets because their parents were alcoholic, drug-addicted (although that was only beginning to be a problem in the sixties), mentally ill or dead. A bunch of private citizens got together the cash to buy first one house, then two, and the then Eastern Health Board paid for the staffing. Brendan had no third-level education and wasn't a social worker by trade. He was a believer. Not just a religious believer, although he did have a strong faith. No, Brendan's belief was in potential. Like John Hume, he saw education as the key to releasing that potential in the homeless lads who came into the Los Angeles home. The *Irish Times's* Pádraig O'Moráin, profiling him when the organisation met with some opposition while planning the opening of a third home in Dalkey, wrote of Brendan:

> His conversation is peppered with references to boys who got four and five honours in the Leaving Certificate. He talks with great pride of the boys who came to the society from broken homes – broken by sickness, death (one boy's parents committed suicide within months of each other), desertion or drink – and have gone on to get an education, work, 'meet a nice girl, settle down and be happy'.
>
> The boy whose mother used to put him into shops to shoplift, disappear when he was caught, and then beat him up in front of the Gardaí when they brought him home, came to the society at the age of 13 and had been out of school for two years at the time. Mr Colfer got him going to school and into an athletic club. After four years, he got a scholarship to an American university where he did a degree in business organisation and marketing. 'Now he earns $33,000 a year,' Mr Colfer says like any proud parent. He showed me a recent letter from the boy, who now calls him 'Dad'.

The Los Angeles boys, once they arrived on Christmas Day, took instructions from Nana, who knew each one of them like an extra son or grandson. My mother was second in command and served as Patton to Nana's benign Eisenhower. It was Mamma who delivered the ticking-off of a tantrum-thrower (always done in another room, so as not to taint the general atmosphere) or the cheering up of someone who had broken a vital part of a toy and the identification of a guest likely to be able to fix it. All were her tasks.

She wore an apron most of the day. A special Christmas apron, white, with lace around the rounded hem. My grandmother wore a much more comprehensive apron because she was the one most likely to be spattered with hot fat or other liquids in the kitchen. My mother would work beside her and around her, murmuring one of those maternal axioms to which every generation intellectually agrees and – practically speaking – ignores: 'Clean as you go.'

The year my grandmother threw the turkey on the kitchen floor was the best. By a mile. Not that she did it deliberately. She would have tracked that turkey from egg upwards, in order to make sure it was fit for family consumption, the way she did every year. By the time any of her grandchildren were five, they could imitate her turkey spiel, the way kids now sing television ads. It came from Mr Geoghegan, and Mr Geoghegan could be trusted. Not like a lot of farmers who just did turkeys at Christmastime to make money. We had the idea that Mr Geoghegan, whom none of us ever met, and whose first name we never learned, did turkeys at Christmas as an art form, for the appreciation of a select few aficionados.

The grandchildren also grew up with a completely false notion of turkeys. We thought they were always the size of an ostrich. This was because my grandmother had two daughters and six sons, most of them married and possessed of several children, almost all of whom pitched up for lunch on Christmas Day in her house, so the turkey had to feed about sixty people. It was a mystery that it could, subsequently, generate leftovers, but my grandfather always maintained with some bitterness that he was eating turkey in various guises until St Patrick's Day.

Even if Mr Geoghegan got the scale and feeding of the bird right, my grandmother still worried about its dryness. She did a sort of consumer satisfaction survey on each and every guest on each and every Christmas Day, checking if they thought it wasn't a bit dry. My sister gave me an awful kick under the table the year I said it didn't matter if it was dry, weren't we all going to be pouring gravy on it anyway? The bird was made to fit into the oven somehow in the middle of the night and left there to cook, except for Nana's constant visitations for basting and worrying in equal measure. Eventually, it was placed on an oval plate the size of the Isle of Man and brought to the table for us all to greet with wonder and joy.

This one year, however, it made it onto the warmed oval plate fine, and then our grandmother turned to face her audience. Too quickly did she turn. That turkey left the plate like a ball leaves Federer's racquet – all topspin and speed. Not bad on distance either. It hit the heavily decorated table doing about 30kph and headed longways through the glasses, salt cellars and lemonade siphons, gathering the tablecloth with it like a bridal train. When it ran out of table, it made an attempt to get to the sideboard but, dropping short, landed on the floor in front of Tony the spaniel, who always stayed, safe from being stood on, inside the four legs of the TV table in the corner. Tony nearly had a seizure. Not only had this huge brown hot thing arrived without warning, but it was blocking his escape. It was the first and only time I ever saw a spaniel cry, but Tony's grief was nothing compared to my grandmother's. She threw her apron up over her face, a gesture I later saw in productions of *Riders to the Sea* but at the time thought she had invented, and keened like a banshee.

The younger kids were unbothered by any of this because they hadn't much in the way of embedded memories of the way the turkey was usually served, and therefore assumed this was normal, give or take. Their fathers exchanged glances; filled with covert 'fair dues to her' admiration: it had been a hell of a throw. My mother rose and put her arms around her own apron-concealed mother. And my sister lost her usually formidable self-control. She laughed. She put her hands over her face to stifle it, but it spurted out between her fingers. Which made everybody else laugh, too, although Dermot's wife Marie grabbed a table napkin and put it over her mouth with Victorian gentility.

Two of my uncles then did the sensible thing. One of them lifted the turkey with towels over his shirted arms and put it on the table, then gathered up his end of the tablecloth while another brother did the same at the far end, with stragglers removing cutlery and crockery until they could carry the avian corpse back out to the scullery, all the time assuring my grandmother that it had touched nothing in its flight. I thought this was an awful lie, but my sister explained that they meant that the turkey hadn't touched the floor, much, with any part you'd eat, and could be presented as pristine and germ-free. Two of the Los Angeles boys set to clean the floor, patently delighted with a task that would put them low enough to fall around laughing without anybody taking it amiss.

My mother took my grandmother to the sitting room, where, normally, nobody ever went, partly because its chairs were covered in horsehair, which gave bare legs the sensation of being stabbed with a million small needles. Back in the kitchen, my sister organised everybody into a kind of battlefield triage. By the time my mother brought Nana back, her apron sodden with tears, everything was almost perfect, although the turkey looked as if it had been through a fight and the ham was so perfect in comparison it seemed to be looking down on the dishevelled bird. My grandfather, who had gone out into the garden and smoked his pipe during the repairs, was heard to mutter that the next time she was going to wreck something, maybe she'd start with the Brussels sprouts. This caused a fresh onset of tears, from which we were all distracted by an explosion in the scullery. The lemonade siphon, fortunately sitting in the sink, its fizziness exacerbated by unexpected travels and collisions, had lost its top and was fountaining its contents at the ceiling. It was at this point that Ronnie, the budgie, spoke for the first time. 'Give us a kiss', he instructed everybody. 'Give poor Ronnie a kiss.'

'Later,' my sister said crisply. 'We're a bit busy this minute.'

We spent the next hour reassuring my grandmother that all was well, although she kept spotting bits of turkey juice on the wallpaper and getting upset all over again. At least nobody was dumb enough to tell her that firing the turkey around made it a lot easier to serve, since its legs were already semi-detached. But the fact is that, of all the Christmas dinners she ever cooked, this was by far the most delicious.

After a lunch that lasted until late afternoon came snoozes, voluntary in the case of uncles, involuntary and no-choice in the case of the younger children. We would wake up in a tidied world where someone would turn out the room lights, so that at one end would be the crib with its star, at the other the sparky brightness of the Christmas tree and in the middle the glow of a dying fire. Everybody had a song. The younger ones might sing 'Silent Night' in Irish, because we'd learned it at school, but other songs had nothing to do with Christmas. Donal's offering was 'The Wild Colonial Boy'.

It was our mother who permitted Christmas Day to start, and it was our mother who put an end to it, gathering us into the taxi and, when we arrived home, allowing each of us to take with us one special toy, to sit on the floor beside the bed if it was awkwardly shaped or breakable, to be tucked in beside us if it was soft. She would allow bedroom doors to be left open to allow the distant glimmer of tree lights. 'Special dispensation,' my father would mutter. I would ask for special dispensations later in the week, but after St Stephen's Day, along with ploughing through leftovers, we knew we were moving away from the spangled wonder of Christmas, the highlight of the year, and back towards normality, where special pleading didn't work and special dispensations didn't happen.

3

THE KEYS TO THE KINGDOM

I hated primary school, although I loved Mrs Barrett in Junior Infants. She taught us to knit, and I thought this was so cool I gave my father a tutorial so he could share the thrill. I mixed art and knitting together, producing a knitted girl still extant in a polythene bag because my mother wouldn't let anyone throw it out. That, in itself, was unexpected, because she had no time for craftwork, even though she herself was superb at it: 'If a machine can do it, let the machine do it. It'll do it quicker and cheaper than a human.' I hated school because everything that made sense at home got mocked in school, right down to the intervals between the buttons on my cardigan. OK, my mother was a bit obsessive about draughts and so the cardigan I wore when I was six had twenty-six buttons down the front and took for ever to put on and take off. In our house, nothing got pulled over your head without being unbuttoned. Ever.

St John the Baptist Primary School for Girls in Clontarf had those speckled marble walls that curve at the bottom into the floor. You still see those bendy walls in buildings preserved for their Victorian value, like the wonderful Eye and Ear Hospital on Adelaide Road. There ended, however, any similarities between the Eye and Ear and our school, which had no Victorian architectural value, although it had its moments, particularly the period after lunch, when seagulls the size of bald eagles descended on the playground to pick up the crumbs that fell from our lunchboxes. Hitchcock's movie *The Birds*, when I saw it years later, seemed dull compared to our playground, viewed from classroom windows. Thousands of big white birds with primeval faces screamed at each other every day for an hour. That hour necessarily followed school lunchtime, which resulted in castoffs and discards all over the playground.

Those lunches, eaten around noon, were a form of differentiation between Our Family and The Rest. Our lunches were neatly enveloped in something called Cut-Rite, which some American relative sent to us at my mother's request. It was the equivalent of waxed paper, but a definite cut above, the way my mother saw it; the wrapping of a sliced pan put around a sandwich. I watched the lunches of other children and decided all of them did better out of the deal than I did. For starters, some of them had sandwiches made of extra tall bread called a batch loaf. I proposed to my mother that we might venture into batch loaf experimentation, and she said 'A *batch loaf?* I hardly think so,' in a tone that would convince you batch loaves were made from rat droppings. I gave up on them and concentrated on the jam. Some of the girls had jam sandwiches every day and I envied them like they'd been assumed into heaven. When I expressed this envy in a wistful winning way at home, my mother sat me down and gave me my first lecture on nutrition. Tomatoes are full of Vitamin C, which helps cuts to heal. Eggs are full of protein, which builds bones. I should be grateful for the good lunches I got every day which would make me grow big and strong.

I did not want to grow big and strong. I wanted to grow small and weak. Small and weak was the way to everybody's hearts. But my sister, overhearing this conversation, took me aside and told me the secret to surviving the home/school battle lines was silence. I should just shut up. Not tell the girls in school what my mother said. Not tell my mother what the girls in school said. Of course she was right, and of course, almost every day, either in school or at home, I would blurt out something that made me the hate figure of the day.

The other part of lunch was the flask holding hot tea. Every flask came bearing warnings. The interior, brilliantly shiny glass, was infinitely fragile and would break if you looked crooked at it. Nothing compares to the sinking horror of holding a broken flask, its outside suddenly burning hot because the liquid within was no longer prevented from reaching the metal cladding, rattling to the touch, filled with shards. If you broke a flask, your parents didn't buy a new one. They bought a new inside bit and fitted it painstakingly within the outer metal.

Primary school pulled together all the talents I didn't have. I was no good as a runner, so when teams lined up for chasing games at lunchtime, I was always last to be picked. If I got lucky, two teams of ten lined up, leaving me as the spare. I didn't feel wounded or diminished by exclusion because I hated all the things the teams were being welded together to do. In any kind of gathering, I quickly learned not to take the instruction 'Big girls to the back' personally. Every line-up, every group in a photograph, obeyed this law. The tall ones went to the back, the small ones went to the front. It was more than positional, though. It was pretty clear to me, as one of the ones in the back row, that the thing to be, in school, was ethereal. I mightn't know the word, but I sure as hell knew the reality: watery little girls, especially if they had long hair in ringlets, were beloved of teachers and parents alike, whereas sturdy stumps were not. They were the Clydesdales, whereas the little ones needed minding because they had sensitivities and sweetnesses the big lumps didn't. In reality, they could have the sweet sensitivity of rats with a sense of entitlement, but oul' wans on the way to Mass in their little black hats patted them on the head, visiting VIPs went down on their hunkers to them, and teachers saw them as delicate. Sick kids, I realised when I saw the first film version of *Jane Eyre*, where a juvenile Elizabeth Taylor died of consumption, had to be slender and beautiful. Being built like a pillar box made teachers believe that you were really malingering. Nobody welcomed you back, except sardonically, and when you had been ill you were left to catch up on stuff you didn't know you had missed. I still don't know all the words of Ireland's national anthem because I was out the week they did it.

The smells of school included perspiration, although that got worse in secondary school, when hormones sneaked in; and the toilet. Most of the pupils went to the toilet a few times a day. I learned to manage on one visit, because the toilets were like the later dirty protests in the Maze Prison, when Republican prisoners lived naked and smeared their excrement on the walls. Scoil Eoin Baiste's children did the same. Or some of them, anyway. Nobody ever talked about it or did anything about it, but it meant that whenever you went into a cubicle, you spent your time in there gagging.

School, otherwise, was designed for clean people, and I was dirty by nature. Not smelly disgusting dirty, but if ink could be spilled, I would spill it, and when we were filling our headline copybooks with capitals and lower case joined-up writing, as much ink got onto the pages through spillage as through writing. I came home each day, my beret sitting on its rim on my head because my head was too big for any standard beret, my woollen stockings at half-mast and the contents of my school bag, as my mother put it, 'streeling out in every direction'. And that was before I encountered Bob, the black Labrador whose greeting left me half-dressed, half-mad and so miserable I just wanted to be hugged for a long time by my mother, who always complimented me for being so brave when the objective evidence, even at five or six, I recognised, was that I was an abject and embarrassingly noisy coward. The only time my father witnessed my dance of death with Bob, he looked at me as if I was a half-wit and asked me why I didn't kick the dog if I didn't want to play with him, which is a bit like recommending that you tie knots in the tentacles of an octopus while it's eating you.

When I had survived Bob and arrived home to be mopped and consoled, I would sit at the kitchen table with my home lunch (as opposed to the school lunch) and my mother would go out into the scullery and start banging saucepans about as she cleaned up, except on Monday, which was wash day. On Monday, Mamma would put her hair in curlers and cover it with a soft cotton headscarf with fringing at the edge, which she knotted above her forehead. Then she would set to on the washing, clouds of steam billowing around her. Handkerchiefs and other items requiring to be sterilised went into a great Dutch oven on the gas cooker and were boiled for ages, before being taken out of it with a big wooden tongs, rinsed and hung up on the clothesline. When the hand-washed items joined the boil-washed articles on the line, the next step was to pick up a long pole bifurcated at the top, get the middle of the clothesline into the divided bit, shove the clothesline upwards so it took the shape of a loose fat W poked up in the middle by the pole, and secure the pole in an indentation in the ground. Then it was time for rinsing out receptacles.

Whatever my mother was doing in the scullery I regarded as cover for my out-loud story-telling. I had a serial going that involved two girls, Ruby Dean and Jennifer Marshal, each in a wheelchair – wheelchairs at that time being my definition of glamour. Half the characters in the books I was reading with my father were in wheelchairs, although many of them got miraculously released from them. Katy in *What Katy Did* was in a wheelchair, as was Heidi's pal in the eponymous children's book. Ruby and Jenny also attended a boarding school. I knew nothing through personal experience of boarding schools. Indeed, I had never met anyone who had attended a boarding school, but Enid Blyton, Jane Shaw and a rake of other writers set many of their stories in those schools, so I knew the details as if I had boarded from the time I was six months old, which is probably what my family would have liked. As a result, the stories I told out loud in the kitchen, while my mother clattered about in the scullery, were all set in English boarding schools where everybody played hockey and went ice-skating in the winter and called St Stephen's Day Boxing Day. They also wore plimsolls. I had no idea what a plimsoll was, but my characters donned them at strategic intervals in my narrative.

Every now and again, I would pause and call out to my mother 'Are you listening?' and she would impatiently tell me that she had more to be doing with her time, which would allow me to continue, convinced of the privacy of my storytelling. Of course, as she told me long years thereafter, she was listening to every word, entranced by my capacity to craft a narrative about imaginary people inhabiting a world that bore no resemblance to my own. The best part, she maintained, was the edge-of-the seat crisis on which each episode ended. It was, according to her, like the early black and white episodic movies, where each thrilling episode would end with the heroine tied to the rails of a railway track with a huge locomotive looming over the horizon or some equivalent unlikely challenge.

In the Grove, at that time, there were many families with children ranging from babies with observer status, sitting in the front garden in a pram, to secondary school kids who wore uniforms to school. Of the age group I played around with, Anna Coughlan was my *bête noire*. Anna was everything I wished I could be: tiny, pretty, ringleted. Plus her father, Joe Coughlan, led the Metropole band, which meant he didn't go to catch the bus until three o'clock in the afternoon, because his working day began at dinnertime. We kids would all stop what we were at in order to mark this untypical timing, and he would salute us with a rolled-up newspaper before striding on, the big straight-backed handsomeness of him. Once he went around the corner at the top, we would unfreeze and get launched again on whatever game we were playing. I was always afraid that Anne Sheehy, who lived in the corner house where they had a huge, beautiful garden full of berries and hiding places, would choose Anna over me as her best friend. Particularly when I was sick, I figured Anna would move into Anne's affections and I would never be allowed back in. Her living next door to Anne was another advantage she had over me.

Four of the families around the Grove were Protestant, which worried me because they were pleasant and I felt didn't deserve to go to hell, the way our religion said they were going. You couldn't get into heaven by the front door unless you were Catholic, and so even if they were let in, it was going to be in a second-rate, discount kind of a way. When I raised this with my mother, she did the air-wave gesture signifying that I was paddling in deeper waters than was appropriate for my age. 'I wouldn't worry about it,' she would say, which is like telling a panicky adult not to panic.

At some point, a girl in one those families got pregnant. She disappeared, ostensibly to mind a sick aunt in England, and when she came back, everybody behaved as if the reason fabricated to cover her absence was the truth. Everybody knew, but everybody let on they didn't know. She was colluded back into our community without comment or judgement.

The other crisis was when the O'Connors' house went on fire. I didn't wake to the sound of the fire engines arriving, so it was only the following day that I learned about the fire and that everybody had survived uninjured. The house had great flame-shaped smoke stains rising from the lower windows and from where the front door had been, up over the whitened render above.

Fire had never been anything other than a domestic friend up to that point, but the O'Connors' misfortune engendered in me a terror of nocturnal fire. I would be just about to go to sleep when I would see – for absolute definite I would see – the tell-tale signs of fire downstairs in the form of a slight difference in the darkness in my room. I would bang on the floor to alert everybody to their immediate danger, and someone would come up to me. My sister's knees clicked as she came up the stairs, and that clicking was the most frequent noise, no doubt because one of my parents told Hilary to 'Go and calm your sister down.' Hilary would arrive in a tearing temper, convinced I was making it up because any idiot could see there was no fire and would I just do what I was supposed to do and go to sleep and not be annoying everybody. People, she would tell me, silhouetted threateningly in the doorway, couldn't be running up and down stairs because I was imagining things. I would whimper and argue just in order to keep her there for a few minutes more, but Hilary saw through me and would depart, giving the door a bang that shook the whole house in a statement of her irritation. I loved that. If Hilary knew I was right, I reasoned, she would never bang the door at me like that, because God would smite her for it. It didn't strike me that God left Hilary amazingly unsmitten, despite her being a girl who would have won an Olympic medal if door-slamming counted as a sport. Hilary never saw a door she didn't want to slam, and her volatile personality presented endless justification for it. She did the reverse, too, opening a door with such sudden force as to weaken its moorings. She once did that to the upper half-door of the hot press, which came unstuck, bucketing down the stairs and into family legend.

Sometimes it was my mother who came to reassure me that the house was not on the point of general ignition, and that was okay, because she seemed to understand why I believed it was. My father rarely climbed the stairs, but when I heard the heavy sounds of his uneven gait, I dreaded it, because he would be quietly furious in a way that made Hilary's more noisy rage infinitely preferable.

My father smelt of cigarettes. Player's untipped with a sailor logo on a flat pack in his overcoat pocket on top of his unfurled clean hankie, shedding tobacco shreds on it. Everything belonging to him smelt of cigarettes other than his hankies when they were freshly ironed.

My mother smelt of cigarettes a bit, too, but mainly of good perfume. Never eau de parfum. She maintained that real perfume containing civet had staying power, whereas eau de parfum was just essentially sweet-smelling water that didn't last. My sister smelt of talcum powder, Imperial Leather talcum powder, and sometimes different scents, mainly after Christmas when she got presents of talc. My favourite was Cussons Apple Blossom.

Any time you needed answers, in our house, my mother was your source. The only time she blew it, in the advice-giving arena, was when I was too young — at four — to ask the question I asked at the tea table. 'Where do babies come from?' My father suddenly needed to refill the marmalade dish. My sister got an attack of something between snorts and sneezes. My mother glared at them, drew a deep breath and — untypically — started in the wrong place.

'Well, you know where kittens come from?' I nodded enthusiastically. 'It's the same with babies,' she began. 'From *cats?*' I shrilled.

Our home was bound about by certainties that, even if you didn't like one of them, still, in aggregate, provided an inarguable framework. One of those certainties was that, each evening, after work and after tea, while Hilary did her homework, my father would take me on his knee and read to me, his cigarette visiting the ashtray on the table in front of us, then retrieved for a long inhalation. This was the best part of the day for me, and I was always ready to promise anything in the hope of another chapter of whatever book was being read at the time. Indeed, reading time was so important that I learned to dread 'reconciliation', which happened every few months in the Dublin Gas Company where he worked. Reconciliation had something to do with bookkeeping and it meant that, coming up to the end of one particular week, my father would have to work late, and I was bereft of my favourite reader. Or, sometimes, bereft of *any* reader.

We had reached a particularly exciting part of *Black Beauty* one week when reconciliation happened, and I was so disconsolate, I sat at the end of the table with the book open in front of me in a sort of mourning ritual. Then I realised that I knew some of the words on the page. In fact, I knew most of them. I was so anxious to find out what happened next that I began to follow the lines, skipping when I came across a word with which I wasn't familiar. The next evening when my father was back to normal and ready to pick up, I pointed out the strange words to him and he explained them to me. Then he sat back and looked at the three pages that followed where he had left off, and asked me to pronounce particular words on those three pages. He asked me if Hilary had read those words to me. 'No', I told him, 'I didn't ask Hilary, I just kind of …'

'Kind of what?' he asked. I told him about finding out what happened next in the book by myself in some way I didn't understand and he beamed at me and told me I knew how to read. Then he asked me to read the next paragraph aloud, which I stumblingly did, and that got him to bring my mother and Hilary into the audience for yet another paragraph. Everybody was delighted, except me. I was slightly frightened that my father would stop reading to me, but he pointed out that each night we could sit down and I could read out loud to *him* until we reached the end of the book. That's what we did, and it was like being handed the keys to every kingdom in the world. Once I could read, I would never be lonely again. Once I could read, I would never be bored again. Once I could read, I could travel to infinity and beyond without leaving the kitchen or my bedroom. George Eliot said that only music could reach the depths of fear or grief in a human. Throughout my life, I've found that books do that too.

Books were full of children who had Adventures, but who also suffered and slaved up chimneys and were afflicted in ways that choked you with sympathy for them. Books were alive with animals, from bunny rabbits to tortoises, from hares to dromedaries, which I had never encountered in real life but loved through reading. I visited places I couldn't pronounce, finding myself in the position staked out by my maternal grandmother, a great reader with little formal education, who would spell words in the middle of a sentence. 'I just have a chest of drawers', she might say, 'but I might buy a b-u-r-e-a-u sometime.' Or, describing someone who bore up well under multifarious challenges, she would tell us that 'he was a s-t-o-i-c.'

Once I could read, the books all over our house became an asset, rather than merely a decoration. We had a sizeable dark wooden bookcase in the dining room with diamond-shaped glass windows, filled with my father's favourites, such as James Plunkett's short stories, Russell Braddon's accounts of the Second World War, and Neville Shute's bestselling novels. They were mixed in with my mother's hardbacks, including Beverley Nichols' essays about his cats, and novels like *A Tree Grows in Brooklyn*. Hilary's books included dozens of Dean Classics and Regent Classics, distinguished by logos of top-hatted silhouettes of men, constituting what parents regarded as basic reading: Dickens, the Brontës, Louisa May Alcott, Susan Coolidge, R.M. Ballantyne. I grew to hate Dickens with a great passion until I discovered that he had been paid by the word, which at least explained the verbosity. Ploughing through his work was greatly, if covertly, helped by sneaky loans of comic books from girls in school, which did 'strip' versions of such classics. So, for example, *A Tale of Two Cities* would be reduced to six pages of small pictures with bubbles coming out of the mouths of characters. Once you knew who was who and which of them was going to be heroically guillotined, it eased the journey through the actual hardback, although not by much.

But you discovered, once you could read, that, quite apart from being intrinsically rewarding, reading was regarded by adults as virtuous. A mother would shake her head in wonderment and proudly share with a neighbour that her child was 'always reading.' Reading being a virtue surprised me, but I realised that, for once, I was on the right side of the equation. If you played it right, you got rewarded for reading because you were seen as a better person. So if you announced that you'd finished *David Copperfield*, you might get taken to the film of the book. Or you might be handed a book by a writer named Jane Shaw, who was funny, by way of a vacation from more serious material. Dickens was never funny. When he moved into heavy carica-ture and weird accents, it was supposed to make you laugh, but didn't. Reading Dickens and Captain Marryat was the equivalent of eating your greens before you got to attack your pudding. It was insisted upon in the belief that you would come around to Dickens and Marryat, and generations of evidence disproving this thesis never discouraged the adults who advanced it. The only thing was to grind your way through the tedious books, knowing that something like *Little Women* awaited. Louisa May Alcott's book – together with its three sequels – was a wonderful discovery for me and half its female readers born since it was first published, with its central character, Jo, who was impatient of the constraints of her gender. Jo was not good. Jo was not one of those watery Dickensian heroines who willingly and smilingly died of TB or at the hands of a sadistic lover. Jo was rebellious and impatient. She made her sisters look like wimps (Meg) or bitches (Amy) and her mother look like a creepy, dutiful masochist overdue for a thumping.

Moving downwards from the books deserving of parental approval through the ones about which they were more iffy, the final point was Enid Blyton, whose series always had one 'tomboy' who freed generations of girls to try out excitements normally reserved for the lads, like tree-climbing, horse-riding and taking no shit from evil-doers. My mother maintained that Enid Blyton had a limited vocabulary, although she stopped pushing this after I entered and won an Enid Blyton essay competition open to entrants in Britain and Ireland, and received a handwritten letter of congratulation from the author.

The rules around books were set by our mother. *Reader's Digest* condensed novels were not permitted in the house. If someone gave one to either of us, it was put out behind the milk bottles in the porch the minute they left, on its way to where I don't know, because having it in the house even for a few hours endangered our literacy levels. Years later, someone gave me a guidebook for editors working for *Reader's Digest*, and it made perfect sense. Indeed, if applied to Dickens, it might have made him a tolerably good read. Another rule was that if you started a book, you had to finish it. No finding out, three pages in, that it was as interesting as a tutorial on mud. You had to show resolution and commitment by getting right to the end, unless the book was by Erle Stanley Gardner, the American lawyer turned thriller writer who created Perry Mason. Mamma regarded him as so bad, she broke the read-to-the-end rule in relation to his books. She wasn't into Dorothy L. Sayers or Rex Stout, but it was clear they qualified as Writers. My father adored Rex Stout. Stout's mother was such an addictive reader that she worked out the best way to keep her six or seven children from disturbing her was to sit in the middle of the main room in their house, a bowl of water and a facecloth beside her, a book on her lap. Any time any of the children hoved to, demanding her attention, she would briskly wash its face, which understandably caused them, over time, to leave her alone.

Every Christmas, Hilary would receive the *Girl* annual as part of her family present. She didn't get to read the weekly comic on which it was based, but a big red annual with a cloth spine hidden under the shiny wraparound would arrive every year, with its distinctive drawing of a young woman in profile wearing an Alice band, her hair flowing out behind her like the diminishing tail of a comet. The *Girl* annual was a marvellous mixture of strip-cartoon type series, including 'Belle of the Ballet', which inspired Hilary to want to become a ballerina. That ambition lasted for several years and much exercising, using the banister over the stairs on the landing as a barre. But the *Girl* annual also provided advice on how to figure skate and make macramé, balanced by more solid features. So, in the 1961 edition, an early chapter is devoted to a former child actor who went on to study zoology at university and to develop what the feature called 'a huge television audience'. A sketch of David Attenborough's youthful face (he was thirty-three at the time but looked younger) gazes admiringly at a somewhat mangy parrot at the top of the page.

The *Girl* annual taught me how to draw. I copied every movement of 'Belle of the Ballet', learned how to sketch the shine on satin by following the line drawings of queens, worked out perspective by gauging the size of characters in the distance as against those in the foreground. When my mother praised my drawings for being full of movement, it never struck me to give credit to the artists who filled each frame of a strip cartoon with characters leaping, cowering, falling or horse-riding at speed. They had to keep their readers with them, and characters, chin on hand, gazing reflectively into the middle distance weren't going to do that for them. Hence the constant movement I would cog.

If Hil and I begged, we had a 'reading tea', which meant that each of us could put our current book tilted up against a jug or jar on the table, and conversation was not required, except when some family member wanted the milk. The reverse of this was when I had done something so bad that it called for dire punishment, in which case I would be banned from reading books for a day, or if the sin was a mortaller, as many as three days. During those days, my soul shrivelled within me and I read everything in the public domain. Posters running across the bridge leading into Fairview. Instructions on the Vim tube. Ingredients and competition rules on the side of the cornflakes box. The depth of the desperation for print is difficult to describe to someone who has never suffered it, but it would take over my life for the duration of the punishment.

That was because, instead of being just one aspect of a rounded life, reading had become an obsession. I read everything. The instructions on tools. The warnings on aspirin. The newspaper.

In the early days, the newspaper of choice in our house was the *Irish Independent*, although that abruptly changed when, after only eighteen months, the thirty-six-year-old editor, Louis McRedmond, was fired. The Prone parents took exception to this, and from then on we were *Irish Times* readers. My mother would sometimes bring home from '47' copies of the *Irish Press*, Nana's favourite paper, indubitably because of its political leanings. My grandmother was a shameless IRA supporter who referred to them as 'our lads'. This sweet-natured and peaceable old lady never passed their fundraisers in front of the GPO without handing over a few coins. The *Irish Press* leaned towards republicanism and, more precisely, towards Fianna Fáil, which didn't go down well with my father, who was so left-wing he regarded the Labour Party as fellow travellers of the capitalism espoused by Fianna Fáil. He thought the Labour Party was honest but stupid, whereas Fianna Fáil was clever but crooked. We never tied down my mother's politics because she would sniff and announce that the franchise was secret for a good reason, although she did frequently mention that James Dillon was a wonderful orator.

One of the reasons for her bringing home the *Irish Press* was Captain Mac. Captain Mac ran Club na nÓg in the paper, which carried competitions like the first I entered on the instruction of my mother, the two prerequisites being that it be cliché-free and legible. My handwriting was and is so awful, it took me hours to meet that second criterion. Then off with us to Mount Prospect Avenue, where, nurgled up beside a gatepost, sat a postbox. So we stamped my entry for Captain Mac and I got to shove it in the mouth of the green box.

A few days later, my mother, in addition to the *Irish Times*, invested in the *Irish Press* to see if my entry had come up trumps on the Club na nÓg page. It had. She had the paper open on the kitchen table when I came home from school, so that over lunch I could read both my name and the promise that as a result of winning, I would, in due course, receive from Captain Mac a wristwatch, which was something nobody in my class owned at the time; and the piece of writing that had won me the timepiece. It was the first time I realised that your work looks a million times better in print. Something about hard copy elevates it above what it was when it left your hand or your machine.

Ten days later, a winner's certificate in Irish arrived, printed black and blue on cream card, with the icons of the four provinces at each corner. Dated 22 January 1960, it had a purple stamp reading 'Captain Mac' where a signature would normally be found. I was eleven, and this was the first time I had won a prize outside of the Feis.

When Hilary and I were children, perhaps because she could not then work outside the home, Mamma devoted a considerable amount of energy and brainpower to entering competitions and making us do likewise. Competitions today offer obvious choices, and winning is no credit to anybody. Back then, however, getting the prize demanded purchase of goods as a baseline, with demonstrations of skill thereafter. Next to homework, it was the priority in our house. My mother would buy the items that allowed for entry – in one case, enough teabags to fill six rubbish sacks that sat in the spare room for nearly two years while we drank our way slowly through them. She would put us sitting round the table and demand that we be clever or creative. Hilary was the clever one, spotting hidden clues. I was the creative one, coming up with the end of sentences that typically began 'I love my Vileda dishcloth because ...'

Our box room was always chock-a-block with purchases necessary for entry and with the prizes won. We rarely got to use those items. She would put small ads in the papers and sell them, earning what would have been patronisingly called 'pin money'. Our family was far from poor, but the grinding need to account for every penny, and the matching need to earn even tiny amounts of money in whatever way she could, developed in my mother a conviction she hammered home to me and Hilary at every opportunity: happiness lies in earning, owning and controlling your own money. We should never ever put ourselves in a financially dependent position. In the meantime, however, we were to avoid listening to mothers who said competition was a bad thing for children. Competition was good for children. It separated the wheat from the chaff. It also, she pointed out to us, gave us opportunities we might otherwise miss.

In my case, that meant learning what were known in the trade as 'dramatic solos' for delivery at the yearly Feis. One of the scenes was from a play called *Daddy Long Legs*, about a girl living in an orphanage who creates fun for the younger children, until she gets ticked off for drawing a chalk cartoon of one of the governors of the institution. Because she's seen only his shadow, she draws him like a daddy long legs, and the laughter of the children attracts the powers that be, who effectively court-martial her on a charge of making fun of a trustee. She says:

> I didn't mean to make fun of anybody. I don't think it's very funny now. I shall be very happy to go. Any place, anywhere would be better than this. I mean – I don't feel any gratitude because I have nothing to be grateful for. There is no charity about it. I have earned my living in the John Grier Home. I have worked from the time I was a tiny child. For three years straight I polished brass door knobs until you discovered that I was clever enough to do other things. And you haven't kept me all this extra time just for my own good. When I was eleven years old that lady wanted to adopt me. But you made her take another child instead, because I was useful. I might have had a home, too – like other children – and you stole it away from me. And you call me ungrateful because I'm glad to go? I don't care how hard it will be. Anywhere – out of the shadow of this place – you'd see. I've lived eighteen years in prison. I hate the John Grier Home!

It's a great speech for any young actor, threaded through as it is with pathos, anger, insight and defiance. That was the wonder of the Feis for me as a pre-teen. I watched Brenda Fricker playing Lady Macbeth, saw Joe Dowling deliver speeches. We got to see the best bits of dozens of plays by master playwrights, so we could quote Shakespeare, Shaw, Thornton Wilder, Synge and Lady Gregory. We watched St Joan condemn herself to the pyre, witnessed Nora tell her husband that she was leaving him and her children in their 'dolls' house', and were intrigued but slightly scared of the German play *Children in Uniform*, which introduced us to lesbianism without naming it. It was more educational than education, although, looking back, it also exposed us to prejudices that, at the time, seemed acceptable. Like Mr Sam McCready of Belfast, adjudicating at the Father Mathew Feis, who was reverently described in the newspapers as having come to Dublin 'in dread of the Dublin accent', fearing that he would not be able to understand the children. 'But this was elocution that rightly has earned Dublin the reputation for being the best English-speaking place in the world,' he said. Prejudice and patronage wrapped up together.

Because my mother had a natural instinct for public relations, as well as almost everything else, when I obediently entered and won competitions, she made sure the fact appeared in the newspaper:

Dublin girl is used to winning

Thirteen year old Terry Prone [this was in 1963], who has won a Gaeltacht scholarship in the Sunday Independent Essay competition, is a girl who seems to make a habit of winning. Last year she collected a Corporation scholarship worth £200, to be spread over five years, was first in her school in the Milk Board Essay competition and first in the Gas Company Cookery contest. This year, at the Father Mathew Feis, she walked off with no less than five prizes – three firsts, a second and a third. Terry says her latest success is really exciting and she is looking forward immensely to her trip to the Gaeltacht.

I had lied. The very thought of spending a month speaking Irish and living in a dormitory gave me the shivers, but I needn't have worried. My mother got me a health exemption and the *Sunday Independent* sent cash instead.

The Gas Company win was announced by a letter from The Directors, who requested 'the pleasure of the company of Treasa Pron at the Distribution of Prizes in the Company's Theatre, D'Olier Street, on Friday 25 May, 1962 at 3 p.m.' The fact that my father worked for them might have made them a bit familiar with the proper spelling of my name. I won the top prize with my scones. I suspect my mother helped on that one, more than she should have, because to this day I can't make scones worth a damn.

One year, the *Evening Press* ran an art competition to coincide with the Irish premiere of the Walt Disney film *In Search of the Castaways*, starring Hayley Mills. My first watercolour showed a scene from the story where the castaways, a family living in a tree on a desert island, experienced a lightning strike. Or their tree did. My mother looked at the painting as if it had maggots all over it, and index-finger poked me in front of her into the sitting room where a fire was burning in the hearth. She gestured at the fire. I looked at it and looked at her, terrified that whatever seemed so obvious to her was not obvious to me at all. She sarcastically inquired if any of the flames in the fire were coming out sideways. I shook my head. What was their direction, she demanded. Upward? I ventured. Precisely, she said, tossing the painting at me. When had I ever seen flames coming out sideways? I hadn't the courage to say that although I'd never seen sideways flames in reality, I'd never seen a tree struck by lightning, either, but I went back to the dining room and re-did the painting. It won first prize, which had three outcomes. First was that we got to see the film at a celebrity-studded showing, although, to my great disappointment, Hayley Mills was not among the celebs. Nor was Louise Mansfield, who had won a consolation prize. The Mansfield sisters, Thelma and Louise, were frequently the ones to beat in art competitions.

The second outcome was that the judge, painter Harry Kernoff, told my mother that he would take me on in his studio as soon as I left school because I had such talent. Kernoff was a genius who captured the working-class Dublin of his time with vivid humour. We have named one of the rooms in our Communications Clinic offices after him.

For Harry Kernoff to make an offer to effectively apprentice me in his studio was just extraordinarily generous. Although my parents would have been willing to let me do it, as opposed to going to university, I let it slide, because by my early teens I knew just how limited I was as an artist. What I could get away with in competitions was not enough to make me an adult artist and everything I drew or painted was so markedly short of what I saw in my mind as to be sickeningly disappointing. I had to keep working on art in secondary school for the simple reason that it was an easy and guaranteed Leaving Cert Honour, but the minute school was over, except for a few fashion sketches for the *Irish Press* women's pages, I abandoned art.

The first prize in the *Castaways* competition was a week in Butlin's holiday camp in Mosney, County Meath. I loved every minute of it. The entertainment was fantastic because the best comedians, singers and pantomime performers kept themselves solvent during the summer by working in the holiday camp theatre. The swimming pool had windows that allowed you to watch the legs of swimmers. Best of all was the skating rink, a smooth fenced-in cement area where you could hire skates. I spent hour after hour there, trying, with mixed success, to follow the instructions on how to do a figure-of-eight that had appeared in the previous year's *Girl* annual.

The rest of the family hated the week in Butlin's. Our chalet was the size of a garden shed, the beds so narrow it seemed an oversight that they didn't come with safety belts to stop you from falling off the edge. They were to prison design: a sturdy wooden shelf jutting out from the wall with a perilously thin 'mattress' on top of it. When my mother requested foam rubber pillows for her two asthmatic daughters, the staff reacted with such baffled incomprehension that she retreated and we slept with our heads on rolled-up overcoats. The food comprised spongy chips and puddings with a great deal of watery custard, and the regimentation drove my father nuts. Two sittings for each meal meant that you had to be at your table at a specific time and gone by a specific time. You might think that a man who came home from D'Olier Street every day to eat a speedy lunch would react well to Butlin's, but the difference was that his daily routine – getting home and back to the Gas Company – was self-inflicted.

Other than that exception, winning scholarships mattered. Our parents said at the time that they would send Hilary and me to secondary school, which wasn't free at the time, but that any scholarship money would greatly help the family finances. So a great sense of pride settled on me when I got a letter like this one from Dublin Corporation.

31 Lunasa, 1962
Bardas Atha Cliath
Secondary and Vocational Scholarships, 1962/63

A Chara,
I wish to inform you that the report received from the Department of Education on the results of the Examination held last Easter shows that you have qualified for the award of a Scholarship. The City Manager and Town Clerk accordingly has approved of the award to you of a First Year Scholarship valued £40 for the session 1962/63 …

Mise, le meas,
V.G. O'Brien, Assistant Principal Officer

Although I would have made it to secondary school without a scholarship, I might not have made it to speech and drama diploma classes at the Royal Irish Academy of Music in Westland Row without the entrance scholarship awarded to me by the Lady Superintendent in December 1961. Or found myself laboriously answering exam questions like:

> Describe the appropriate respiratory movements of the diaphragm, intercostal muscles, and the transverse abdominal muscles. What good effects do these movements serve in good speech delivery? (London College of Music Diploma Paper, Wednesday 15 December 1965)

It's only in retrospect that I realise how much our parents valued education for us. My father had a degree from Maynooth, about which he didn't talk, but then he didn't talk about anything to do with Maynooth. This was a time when the phrase 'spoiled priest' was still in the lexicon. We did pick up references from my mother to rules the seminarians had to follow, like never walking in twos. They had to always walk in threes as a way of preventing 'particular friendships' developing.

When it came to education, the formative experience for my mother was Louise Gavan Duffy's private pre-primary school. God alone knows how my grandmother learned about it or found the money to pay for it, but my mother adored every day she was there. 'Louise Gavan Duffy, without knowing it, showed me that there was a world I could enter by my own efforts and that it could be a joyful journey,' she wrote to me years later, when I was surprised to find, in a profile of writer Maeve Brennan, a reference to her attending the same school. Having discovered Brennan by accident, I was besotted with her.

'D'you remember a Maeve Brennan in Louise Gavan Duffy's school?' I asked her.

'The ambassador's daughter? Yes.'

'What was she like?'

'Obnoxious and crazy. Why?'

I told her about Brennan's years with the *New Yorker* and her tragic deterioration from eccentric isolation to demented dereliction, sleeping in Grand Central Station. My mother sat silently and then murmured that sometimes florid talent distracted those around you from getting you the help you needed.

Our mother might have started in a private nursery school but by the time she was in her teens, she had little educational choice. As the second eldest of a large and constantly growing family, she was required to make a financial contribution at home and so worked first in the Irish Sweepstakes and then in the Custom House – in an office where I was to work, decades later, as a ministerial adviser. Mamma talked lovingly of having worked in the Custom House, in a corner office with a window. The window rendered her visible to others, which resulted in the phone on her desk ringing one day. At the other end was an assistant secretary who, having observed her put on her hat, called to tell her to take it off because the working day had four more minutes in it. She wanted Hilary and me to bypass rules like the one that forced her out of the civil service on marriage.

She always seemed to know the law (civil and canon), the etiquette (Nancy Mitford was her most quoted source) and the financial implications (pocket money fine) attached to any misdemeanour and would apply whichever matched the crime once she had the facts. She took a standard police approach, issuing a formal warning before she interrogated you and brushing aside anything other than hard data. Once she had the data, there was no stopping her. She went immediately into either punishment or protection mode. For my confirmation, I had been put on the outside of the pew in the church. That was where they put people who were good at learning stuff off by heart who could be relied on to produce the right answer out of the catechism when asked by the bishop – or, in this case, the parish priest. The priest asked me if I would like a question on supernatural grace. 'Not particularly', I answered. He burst out laughing.

'In that case, I'd better pick something else,' he said and asked me a different question, which I answered perfectly. The next day I got sent home from school with a note to my mother. She unsealed it and read it in total silence. 'Put your coat back on,' she said. 'We're going down to that school this minute.'

When we arrived, the teacher involved met us, glowing in anticipation of apologies from my mother. My mother produced the note. 'It says here that when the priest asked her if she would like a question on supernatural grace, Terry said "I'm not particular." My daughter would never say anything so ungrammatical. I have no doubt that what she said was "Not particularly, Father."' The teacher looked confused.

'Let's be clear,' my mother went on. 'If a priest asks a pupil at an examination designed to ascertain that this pupil has reached the age of reason a question seeking to elicit a preference, it is absolutely correct for the pupil to express such a preference. We will hear no more of this nonsense.'

I would say that she turned on her heel and swept out of the school, except that I've never seen anyone successfully turn on their heel. She certainly swept out of the school, though. Nobody could sweep like my mother. I was constantly galloping after her when she did a magisterial sweep, because she had a good turn of speed as well as a touch of grandeur.

After I got lucky with Captain Mac in the *Irish Press*, she would read the junior page with ferocious attention before instructing me to write something on, say, not having a pet. The first draft, usually, would be savaged, but the response to the second or third would be warmer and eventually I would be told to produce handwritten copy. Before I moved into secondary school, the man behind the Captain Mac pseudonym wrote to me. I couldn't spell, he pointed out, and I couldn't punctuate, but I could write funny stuff and he needed funny stuff, so he would teach me how to do the other things. Tony Butler, senior journalist, then embarked on a series of free distance tutorials with a pre-teen in Clontarf whom he had never met.

'Do not *ever* use exclamation marks,' he wrote, in response to one of my submissions. 'Screamers are the mark of the rank amateur. They yell at the reader to notice how funny you are being. If your writing is amusing, the reader will notice without you yelling at them.'

Once, he put a PS at the end of one of his letters, asking if I could draw. Under Ma's tutelage, I crafted a letter of charming self-deprecation which nonetheless positioned me close to Leonardo da Vinci in experience, skill and genius. Well, he asked, why wasn't I illustrating the pieces I was writing for him? Investment was promptly made in black India ink and a pen and off went my articles and matching artwork neatly clipped to them. Tony Butler became a friend for life. Later, the two of us shared the same page in the *Evening Herald*, where I wrote a personal column and he pursued a number of crusades, one of which was to disabuse the world of its conviction that Seán O'Casey came from poverty. Tony never wasted an opportunity to point out in reviews of books about the playwright that he had, in fact, come from a Protestant family in the inner city which was not impoverished, but had affected a level of deprivation in order to make himself a more interesting specimen to Lady Gregory and W.B. Yeats.

I got lucky that a man sifting through hundreds, sometimes thousands, of handwritten entries from pre-teens, picked me out and decided to train me in journalism, free, gratis and for nothing.

4

PAINTING THE SNAKE

I knew secondary school was going to be a blast. Every second book I read proved it. Secondary schools had single desks, rather than the horrible shared ones with built-in inkwells characteristic of primary school. Secondary schools had uniforms with outdoor shoes and indoor shoes. Secondary schools had sporting teams. Secondary school had my older sister, who was a hard worker and loved by the nuns, who would therefore extend their affections to me.

For a while, I half-believed the Holy Faith Convent school would have midnight feasts and pillow fights, too, but that was because for a while I thought 'boarding' meant the same as 'secondary'. 'Boarding' later morphed into a maternal threat: if I didn't shape up, I would be going to boarding school the following year. That threat, over time, became the pea-canning factory threat, which held that if I didn't study harder, I would end up working in a pea-canning factory. I thought a pea-canning factory infinitely preferable to five hours of homework a night, but never dared to say that.

The uniform was a delight. Navy serge with skirt pleats stitched firmly down over the hips. A U-shaped bodice, crisp white shirt and striped tie. My father and Hilary spent ages standing behind me trying to teach me how to tie the tie, yelling 'It's perfectly *simple!*' at me. Whenever people tell you something is perfectly simple, it isn't.

When I started school that September, some of the promises were fulfilled. A line of wooden boxes in which to store our outdoor shoes during the day. Desks like the girls had in the English books I read, where the top lifted up for you to secrete your possessions. Assembly and an intercom and polished wooden floors.

But the 'big girls to the back' applied just as it had in primary school, and having a favoured older sister turned out to be a dead loss. Teachers, encountering the surname, would immediately express the threatening hope that I would be as good as Hilary at whatever their subject was, and I would stand there, earlobes swelling, face reddening, knowing I wouldn't. Also, there was the name thing. Because we came along before scans, and because our parents didn't want to refer to us, pre-birth, as 'it', they picked names that were unisex but also distinctive. Once a teacher had learned a name like Hilary Prone, it seemed to suffice for all members of the same family, so I learned to leap to attention whenever a nun said 'Hilary?'

Sister Euphrasia, the scariest nun, was at least eight feet tall and had that capacity (shared with my mother) of spotting your key weakness and sticking a metaphorical knitting needle in it. She was witty, in total control of the class and taught us French. About half her size was the sports nun, Marguerite, a tiny stub of concentrated venom who ordered immediate purchase by every first-year pupil of a hockey stick or a camogie stick. Looking at these implements, I decided I had a better chance of hitting a ball if I used the one with the fatter end to it, thereby in theory committing myself to six years of camogie.

The first day on the sports pitch was damp in that pervasive way where you know black mould is sprouting in the inside of your elbows. The grass was rooted in a slick slime that sucked at your boots and made you sink gently into it when you stood still, which I did a lot. Everything smelt of sweat and the outdoors.

Marguerite instructed a group of star players from a more senior year to demonstrate for us neophytes how speedy and exciting the game was. They slithered at one other at great speed and yelled a lot. Some of the newcomers on the sidelines with me seemed to find this exciting, so I thought it safer to put on an enthusiastic face, which I did up to the moment one of the fifth-year experts brought her hurl over her head in a swing involving the removal of two front teeth from the girl standing beside me. I moved quickly and efficiently, stripping off my raincoat and burying her face in it while I led her to the gate, where I knew my mother would be waiting in our white car with white leather interior. 'Teeth knocked out,' I said, and my mother responded as she always did in a medical crisis, with authority and compassion. She pulled the brick of 'man-sized' tissues out of the box she kept on the console and gently peeled my raincoat away from the girl's face. 'Don't press these against your face,' she told her. 'We don't want them to stick.' Then she drove her to the dental hospital, telephoned her mother from there, waited until the girl's father arrived, and came back to the car, where I was doing my homework.

'No camogie from now on,' she said when she got back in and that was the end of it. I regarded the camogie players in my class as dodgy. One minute they were normal. The next they were out beating hell out of one another. They, in turn, regarded me as a lazy, unpatriotic slob.

The more positive side of secondary school was that it did have a tuck shop, which was full of wonders, including a phenomenally, tooth-breakingly hard toffee bar lightly coated in what might, in shade, have been considered to be chocolate. The curious thing about this confection was that, like a spy, it kept changing its name. One year it might be a Tea Time Todi. The next year it would arrive in slightly different wrapping as a Flash Bar and, just as we got used to that, it would transform itself into a Honey Cap. I was faithful to that bar, whatever it was calling itself at the time. The tuck shop was run by Sister Bernard, who was beautiful and amiable. We all competed to be her assistant, for obvious and less obvious reasons.

Our lay teachers included Miss Ford, who because she taught Latin, as well as Irish, had inspired a little rhyme passed down from one generation to another: 'Fordibus sittibus at the deskoloribus.' I would carry her books to the teachers' room and she would talk on the way, pleased to have a volunteer listener, not knowing that I was being utterly selfish. Anything that got me away from my classmates was a good thing.

Art was Miss Mayne, who loved me because I won competitions. That she made Hilary's life a misery made me hate her. I believed my sister hated me, and I hated being my sister's sister, but enfilading fire at either of us united us in a fighting formation Wellington would have loved.

Music was Sister Fidelma. I opted, in that first year, fool that I was, to learn piano because my mother played so beautifully. My serial failure with musical instruments as Christmas presents demonstrated that I had neither talent nor persistence; and any motivation I had at the outset was eviscerated by Sister Fidelma cracking me across the fingers with a ruler when I made a mistake. I told on her and my mother sent a note to the headmistress, Sister Leontia, establishing that music and I were parting company, although I doubt she blamed Sister Fidelma. If she did, she forgot that I would have the same small spherical bundle of hatred for choir practice ('Big girls up the back'), and nobody got out of choir practice. So 'Fido' had plenty of opportunity to take me down a peg. This assumed that I was up a peg in the first place, which wasn't the case, but there's no arguing with the unspoken rules in school.

Maybe by accident, I was entered by Sister Fidelma in the Feis Ceoil and won a medal for a song that went 'I'll go my way a-singing, down the road to Arcady.' The great thing about this song was that, because by the third line it had bored listeners to coma level, social invitations to perform it dried up early. I loved singing around the house, but I knew I was never going to be anything as a singer other than the big coarse mezzo at the back of a choir.

I had a profound sense of not belonging, in school. I didn't belong in any of the gangs and I didn't belong in any of the groups that naturally form around particular subjects. I had fallen in love with history when

Hilary gave me Carty's *A Junior History of Ireland* to read when I was sick one winter, and had read enough history and absorbed enough through radio documentaries to be insufferable to any secondary school peer. The same with English. And the one absolute certainty about my outsider status was that I was never going to be a cool pop music groupie, even if I tried.

When The Beatles came to Dublin in 1963, the enthusiasm in the class took the form of tattoos on the back of the left hand; this location selected because it was the easiest for self-tattooing, which involved either blades or pen nibs and ink. When I told my mother about the amateur self-embellishment, she said my classmates would be lucky if they didn't give themselves blood poisoning, which is what sepsis was called at the time. Also, she said, how foolish they were going to feel in years to come when they had a career and had to keep concealing their left hand for fear people would see RINGO on it, tattoos being permanent. It didn't seem apropos to point out that the tattoos mostly said JOHN or PAUL, rather than RINGO. None of those tattooists was ever going to amount to anything, anyway, she concluded. Wrongly, as it turned out. One of them became a formidable and reasonably famous professor; she's on LinkedIn and all. No mention of the PAUL tattoo, though. I can't help but wonder if, today, she wears extra long cuffs on her shirts.

The Father Mathew Feis, on the other hand, loomed larger and larger in my life in the early years of secondary school. One of the regular contestants, Maria McGuire, was from the southside, pale, dark-haired and distant to a degree uncommon among would-be actors, most of whom want to be loved so badly they'll even relate to people they despise. Maria McGuire's distance seemed to be courteous, rather than contemptuous, but none of us knew for sure. On stage, she tended to perform with her head slightly tilted to one side, which added a note of irony to whatever part she was playing. Mostly she played queens. She turned up years later at the heart of terrorist intrigue, outing herself as having been the mistress of David O'Connell of the

Provisional IRA's Army Council, described by former Provo Kieran Conway in his memoir, *Southside Provisional* (Orpen Press, 2014), as, together with Ruairí Ó Brádaigh, 'responsible for whatever political strategy the Provisionals might have been credited with during the early 1970s.' O'Connell was good-looking, publicly silent and charismatic. Conway, who now runs a solicitor's practice in Dublin, met Maria McGuire in a pub with O'Connell, whom he portrays as patronising her, 'acknowledging with discreet winks to us that her real wish was to operate with an active service unit as we were doing, rather than engage in boring political work'.

Despite the patronage, O'Connell clearly found something personally attractive in this educated middle-class girl walking around Swinging Sixties Dublin in hot pants. According to Conway, 'Dave subsequently took her to Amsterdam as cover on an arms purchase operation where, unfortunately for him, in addition to losing the arms, he had a fling with her which became public knowledge. The fact that the mission failed, coupled with Maria's defection less than a year later and the revelation that they had been having an affair, did Dave long-term damage within the movement.' The 'defection' was revealed in confessional pieces by Maria in the *Sunday Times*, followed by a tell-all book that made not a whole lot of sense and an eventual career in the UK as a Tory local councillor.

At fourteen, I graduated to doing scenes from plays like *The Heiress*, adapted from the Henry James novel *Washington Square* about a rich, physically unattractive girl whose father bribes a young man to propose to her without her knowledge. The young man goes along with this, but later chickens out and jilts her. My diary for that year records the response of the adjudicator. 'Of course, when this lovely gel emerged from the back, I said to myself this cannot be Catherine, this gel is far too pretty. After all, Catherine is stated specifically to be a plain, almost ugly girl.' That was the first and only time I was ever found to be too pretty for a role.

That year, I produced this school essay:

My ambitions have suffered many changes down through the years, but I really know now what I will be. Ever since the very first day I appeared on the Fr Matthew [*sic*] Feis and won first prize I made up my mind to be an actress. My first love is for the theatre but I would not mind acting on radio, television or even films.

There is the feeling, in a theatre, of lots of people watching and listening, whereas on radio you speak into a very lifeless microphone and it seems you are speaking to nobody. I can say this with some authority as I have appeared on the wireless and all the time I felt that I could have gone home and nobody would have noticed the difference, although thousands must have been listening in!

I enter for the Feis annually and although I enter for mime, elocution and drama, the one I love best is the Drama competition. You sit in the wings, being very careful not to crush your costume, and catch glimpses of the competitor ahead of you, and find fault with her or him if possible. The curtain drops creakily and muffled applause is heard.

Then your drama teacher gives you last minute advice, to which (if you have any sense) you do not listen as she will muddle you into forgetting your lines if she can.

Then the curtain rises and you make your entry. This is great fun if you are acting a play by an author like Oscar Wilde, where you can sweep onto the stage in a great flowered hat and a huge crinoline, saying, in your deepest tones, 'What, pray, is this, Mr Worthington?'

As you turn majestically towards the stage-front, you are dazzled by those footlights which have lost their covers. These lights are also very hot, and if you stand too close to them your crinoline will soon notify you that it is scorching!

If you glance to the front, you will see a great, black void laden with cigarette and pipe smoke. At the back of the hall a great red sign says 'Exit' and in the dark, smoky place it looks as if it were hanging in mid-air. At the time you are not conscious of these things, but as your eyes get used to the brightness around you and the darkness in front of you, you see, in a sort of dream, row upon row of pale grey balls. These are the audience and you have to make them feel sad or happy as you want them to feel, as a sculptor carves marble into a figure to suit his ideas.

Lots of people say that if the audience applauds the instant you finish they think you are very good, but I think this is wrong. If there is a short interval between the end of your part and their applause, it shows that they are finding it hard to take themselves from the make-believe world you have created and put themselves back into real life.

Acting will give me a chance to fulfil my other ambition as I will be able to travel which is one of my dearest wishes, and to meet illustrious people. But if I am as famous as I hope I will be, I will be one of those celebrities. I think I have the right sort of temperament for it, as I have no nerves and my friends say I am a show off. So I think I would fit in that career pretty well.

Maybe one day my friends will say proudly to their children, 'I went to school with the great Terry Prone!'

My winning prizes (and being on TV) made some teachers overlook how bad I was in their subject. Up to a point. But only up to a point. Then they would take against me and I was goosed. I even got pulled from the back row to be put in a desk up front where the teachers could see me all the time, although I couldn't see how this improved their lives any. One of the coolest girls had a knack, when called to account, of leaning in a bored way on her desk as if overcome by the ennui of the school day. I tried to copy her, but had a tendency to fall over my school bag when instructed to stand up. The girl next to me, Treasa Drea, bought herself a long ruler and used it to send back belongings of mine that slid from my desk to hers. Since general slovenliness ensured I was never going to equal any of the cool girls, the only thing I could do, once I got upright, was to be pompous in my responses, using upmarket words. This was a good way to get hated even more by the other girls, while confirming to the teachers that they had been right about me all the time.

Once, when I was impertinent to some teacher, I was sent to the headmistress, and Sister Leontia decreed that I was not to attend that teacher's class for two weeks. During the time when I should have been in her class, I was to paint the statue of Our Lady in the main hall, which apparently needed a bit of refurbishment. I was supplied with the right kind of paint and had the best time serving this sentence. Our Lady didn't give much scope, because she was essentially a dress (white) and a long veil (blue). But the snake offered endless possibilities. Our Lady was standing on a snake, which still doesn't make sense to me, because nowhere in the Gospels does she meet a snake and she wasn't contemporaneous with Adam and Eve, who did. Or at least Eve did, to her cost. However, this statue had Our Lady's bare feet planted on the snake in two places and he had his tongue out as if he wasn't liking it. I gave that snake a magnificent Burberry plaid overcoat and a ruby red bifurcated tongue. And then, as a final gift to Satan, who seemed to have got the bad end of this arrangement, I gave him spectacularly crossed eyes.

Sister Leontia came to inspect the statue, pleased that I had given it a new lease of life. Quite properly, since she was a nun, she didn't look closely at Satan, so I went back to class and all was well for several weeks. I never mentioned the crossed eyes to anyone and had forgotten them when the intercom barked one morning and Sister Leontia's voice gruffed out of it: 'Terry Prone to my office immediately.' Even the classmates who didn't like me looked sympathetic as I slid out of the desk, fell over the school bag, did an "An bhfuil cead agam ..." at the teacher and went off to the headmistress's office. Without saying a word, she led me to the main hallway and nodded at the statue. I looked at the statue, starting at Our Lady's knee level and moving upwards, and looked back at her. It didn't work. A torrent of reproach washed over me and I was hit by the flotsam within it: In all her years ... The sacrilege! ... How could a girl with a sister like Hilary

Prone even *think* … Did I have no sense of responsibility to younger minds?

I stood, head bowed, waiting for the punishment, which was severe enough. I was to repaint Satan. Not only was I to repaint him with his eyes pointing the same way, but I was to repaint him with a proper snakeskin. I was to paint the other six statues in the school and I was to do it on my own time, and if my mother wanted an explanation for me being late home …

I painted those statues and had them inspected by Sister Leontia almost with a magnifying glass as I went. That was her mistake. When I had reached statue six, I sneaked back and gave our Lady's toes in the third version a good nail polishing in blue and scattered freckles across her nose. For all I know, the freckles and blue nail varnish are still there.

Being put out of any teacher's class was good for both sides. The teachers got a break from me and me from them. Plus, I got to avoid my classmates. Which sounds as if I didn't care, which is not true. I've never needed to be liked, but, God, it's horrible when you are disliked, and the majority of my teachers straight up disliked me. If they had decided I was stupid and lazy, all would have been well, but they decided I was *clever* and lazy, neither of which was true. I sat in apologetics class in religious knowledge and could understand all the individual words, but get no meaning out of the full sentences. I concentrated so fiercely in algebra, I thought my brain would squeeze out of my ears, but the subject still made no sense to me. Hilary devoted herself to helping me and frequently came close to braining me as a result, yelling, index finger hammering the page, convinced that I was pretending to be stupid. I was the genuine article, but I couldn't prove this to her.

I was bright enough to scorn girls who learned off geometric theorems, because those theorems fell into my brain like pieces of a jigsaw. I could immediately see the beautiful logic of them, and when a girl who had learned off the theorem got into trouble because, by leaving out one line by accident, she made the whole thing crazy,

I wondered at how somebody could be that stupid. Meanwhile, faced with my non-performance in algebra and arithmetic, my father and sister wondered how *I* could be that stupid. Not that it was just maths. Latin meant the word 'declension', which even now pleats me with terror. Irish was dominated by a depressing old bag named Peig and if she wasn't already good and dead, I'd have done her in. Irish also contradicted all the rules my mother and Tony Butler laid down for English, starting with 'No clichés'. In Irish, you actually got marks for learning off phrases that never merited repetition which later turned them *into* clichés. On the other hand, Irish involved an awful lot of learning off, and I was good at that. Give me an opening line like *Cad a dhéanfaimid feasta gan adhmad?* and you could rely on me for several verses.

Halfway through secondary school, nonetheless, I knew I was in trouble, and so did my mother. Ma understood I was working hard. She could see it. But she could also see I was like Dobbin, the horse in *Animal Farm*, working harder and harder to stay in much the same place. I needed six honours, one of them in Latin, in order to get into university and I had to get into university to avoid the pea-canning factory. Ma, at this time, was, fortunately, distracted on two fronts. A big fan of motoring correspondents, she religiously read Cecil Vard, who in his column during the sixties strongly approved of a French car called the Simca. Some upturn in the family finances allowed investment in a white Simca, favoured by my mother largely because Vard indicated that it was built like a tank and, if involved in a collision, was likely to outweigh the opposition. I have no idea what the number plate of my current car is, but I can reel off the number of that Simca: MZA 794.

The second distraction was market research. Attracted by a small ad, my mother applied for a researcher post with the Market Research Bureau of Ireland, and after brief training, was sent out on the road to knock on the front doors of family homes to ask the residents questions about their consumer preferences. They welcomed her as warmly as my father welcomed Jehovah's Witnesses, although he just wanted to crush them in theological debate, whereas the market research targets were astonished and delighted to be asked their opinions on anything. Mamma was furnished with questionnaires that were like scripts — they told her where she had to pause and where she had to probe, although she quickly found probing was rarely required. People told her the most intimate details of their lives, unbothered by her making notes, and at the end when she queried if they had anything else to offer, they always had. One man told her, apropos shampoo questions, that he had not washed his hair in forty years. His wife muttered that he hadn't washed his feet for that time, either, but my mother's form couldn't accommodate that. She did tell us that his hair looked remarkably clean and healthy.

She also conditionally dispensed anonymised packs of freeze-dried soup and baby food. To get the freebies, the family would have to agree to her coming back a fortnight later to explore their reactions to them. Sometimes the tests were done with the rigid distancing of a clinical trial. Not only would the recipients not know the real brand of the free custard powder, but my mother wouldn't know either.

On one occasion, as she was leaving a Corporation house with a tiny hallway, she noticed a yellowed drawing of a pair of boots pinned to the wall. The boots were bockety and the drawing was beautiful. Who had done that? she asked. John, when he was about eight, the mother said. 'I hope he went on to do art,' my mother said. 'He did' came the reply and the surname suddenly clicked with Ma. John Behan …

My mother not being on my case as much as in the past didn't stop the Leaving Cert looking like Mount Everest. I was sure of only three honours: art, history and, according to my teacher, Elizabeth Ahern, English too. Elizabeth Ahern was willowy, disorganised, quiet and baffled by the bitchery and smartarsery of a bunch of bright Holy Faith teenagers.

I suspect that most of the girls in my class, if they remember Elizabeth Ahern at all, would not retrospectively rate her as a good teacher. Those who responded best to bossy, dogmatic teachers regarded her sessions as free passes to idle. They talked, flew paper aeroplanes, went out to the toilets to have a smoke or read magazines. When required to deliver essays, half the class didn't bother, knowing that Miss Ahern didn't have much in the way of a punitive instinct.

One week, when she asked for an essay on snow, I produced something between a short story and a free-form poem. I did it with a sense of bored impertinence; let's see if this gets me sent to Sister Leontia's office. On Monday, Miss Ahern arrived looking like she'd recently taken some seriously life-enhancing drug. She glowed, she smiled, her gown billowed behind her. Normally it hung from her slender frame in a sad sack of dispirited chalk-dusted fabric, falling off one shoulder. I was ordered to the top of the class, and, for the first time in her presence, felt real dread. Whatever she was on had empowered her to a degree that scared the hell out of all of us. She handed me my copybook and told me to read aloud. When my reading wasn't clear enough, she told me to speak up. I occasionally lost my place in my appalling handwriting, I was so surprised. The faces watching me were wary. They didn't like the fact that the piece of writing contained uncommon words. They knew it wasn't a proper essay, so some of them gleefully anticipated that once I ground to a halt at the final full stop, I would be on my way to punishment of some sort. I finished. The room was still. That, in itself, was astonishing for Miss Ahern, whose classes tended to lock in firmly between anarchy and riot. She surveyed them with infinite calm.

'That is superb writing', she announced. 'It makes us see snow in a new way. You will be a writer,' she told me, gesturing me back to my seat with her long, pale hands. I stumbled over the strap of someone's schoolbag and swore as my elbow connected with a desk. Several girls made whispered comments in that hissing sibilance audible only to the perpetrator and the victim, never the teacher. But I heard nothing but that click that sounds when someone has put the key in the door of your adulthood, freeing you to be whatever you always dreamed of being. From that point on, everything was simple. I would be a writer. I had already decided to be an actor, but the two would go hand in hand. When I was asked to do a column for a newspaper at sixteen,

I wasn't surprised. When I was twenty and a publisher asked me to write a book, it fitted the pattern. When, years later, I won a Francis McManus short story award, that too seemed inevitable.

Inevitable didn't mean easy. No writing was easy for me. Particularly after a car crash in my thirties damaged the bit of my brain where words dance, it was hard. But the imperative had been set by a quiet introvert who drifted into my life like a frond off a dandelion puffball. I have no idea where Elizabeth Ahern is now. I've no idea if she considered herself a great teacher. I just know that I'm still grateful, still astonished by her generosity and her certainty. I thank her every day in my head and am sorry I don't know where to find her to thank her in person.

On the other hand, the Latin nun – Sister Marguerite, also the sports mistress – threw me out of her class a year before the Leaving Cert, ostensibly because I put a cheeky face on me, but really because she, like Hilary, thought I was pretending to be stupid. She announced to the class as I departed that she would give up teaching if I got an honour in Latin in the Leaving. Studying previous exam papers revealed that, one year, students were asked to translate into English a chunk of Latin written by, say, Horace. The following year, the chunk would be by another writer. The abomination called 'unseen trans' involved only four writers. The one who, the sequence suggested, would come up in my year was St Augustine. I checked the issue with my father. If I learned the *Confessions of Saint Augustine* in English off by heart from start to finish, then, on exam day, I would certainly spot a couple of Latin words that would clue me into context, and then I could produce my perfect translation, chewed-cud fashion. Even if I was only fair-to-middling in the other answers, this would push me into honours territory, would it not? My father, a Latin scholar, was perplexed by my inability to learn the language, but agreed that this peculiar approach might work. It just seemed – to him – to be more hard work than going at the task in the normal way.

My mother then worked out that the same might apply to French, and brought home from the library an English language version of the set text, a novel called *Le Drôle* – the Breton equivalent of Peig. Or so I had thought until I started on the English translation and found the sex bits that didn't appear in the school version and about which I didn't tell my mother.

The geography exam papers didn't have sex in them, but they did establish that if I was superb on the rest of the world, I could skip Asia. I skipped Asia.

This strategic approach to the Leaving Cert was time-consuming and matched what was going on in school not at all. About a year out from the final exam, I suggested to my mother that I go to school maybe one day a week. I showed her the roster. She agreed. When she met Sister Marguerite in Vernon Avenue and the nun told her I was absent from school more often than I was present, my mother looked down from a great height at her (not hard because the nun was so small) and raised an eyebrow. Marguerite knew better than to tangle with that eyebrow.

Come the exams and all played out according to plan. Six honours. One of them in Latin, where Saint Augustine did come up. Did Sister Marguerite give up teaching? No. Did anybody other than me notice? No.

Entry to college was assured, because I had scraped through pass maths. Trying to get a mathematical grip has left me with a conviction that counting is the essence of order. I do ten tasks a day. Five tisks make up a task, tisks being smaller components which don't merit being treated as the full deal. So whereas a Zoom meeting would count as a full task, an ordinary phone call is only a tisk. If a medic is poking about looking for a vein, you have to count to twenty before moaning. Sweets are eaten in fives. Books are read eight at a time, one hundred pages at a time. The dishwasher gets unloaded in twenties, with five items of cutlery adding up to one piece of crockery.

That's bad enough, but a worse problem is the nightmares, where I have just found out that I have failed the Leaving and am standing amid the shards of my hopes, waiting for my mother's condemnation.

5

ASK AN INTELLIGENT QUESTION

*R*adio was like breathing. In our house, it was a constant. From six a.m., weekdays and weekends, the BBC's news service could be faintly heard from downstairs as my father did his morning rituals. During the morning, my mother had *Music While You Work* on in the background, introduced by Eric Coates' eponymous signature tune, although she switched to Radio Éireann coming up to lunchtime, knowing that my father would arrive at twelve fifty-five on the dot to eat while listening to the lunchtime news, followed by *Topical Talk*. Sixty years later, if someone living in Clontarf said they'd like to go home from the city centre by bus for a three-course lunch, the reaction would be 'Good luck with that.' But Dad managed it every day, greatly helped by my mother's capacity to land a plate of hot food in front of him on the button. He maintained that one of the CIÉ drivers was going to give him an ulcer, and called him Psyche because he drove like a psychopath, in mad bursts of acceleration and sudden braking, none of it occasioned, as far as passengers could tell, by traffic or the roads. Psyche drove to the beat of his own drum, and it played a random rhythm.

Lunchtime radio consisted of sponsored programmes; fifteen-minute shows as sharply different from one another as were the brands that paid for them. The Irish Hospitals' Sweepstakes programme was presented by Bart Bastable, who brought a magisterial grandeur to flogging sweep tickets for an organisation whose success was predicated on breaking American law and having the populace wink at this transgression in the belief that it was fierce clever altogether – and in a good cause. Frankie Byrne presented an agony aunt show for Jacob's Biscuits, sounding so rock-solid certain about her advice that faithful listeners were later amazed to hear of a life where certainties were thin on the ground. Glen Abbey's show had the best signature tune ever invented: 'Lulu's Room'. The Walton's programme, presented by Leo Maguire, was perhaps the best-known and longest-running of them, ending with the curiously conditional instruction, 'If you feel like singing, do sing an Irish song.'

The very variety of the offerings trained generations of listeners to listen in fifteen-minute slots. *The Kennedys of Castleross* was an agricultural soap opera, broadcast from 1955 on a Tuesday and Thursday, starring the Abbey's Marie Kean as a long-suffering commonsensical widow, Vincent Dowling as her grown-up crisis-creating son, and a handful of other fine actors presenting the dilemmas of living in rural Ireland in quarter-hour chunks – for eighteen years. My mother parsed the dialogue on the fly, becoming enraged when characters articulated the statement, referring to an earlier reveal, 'Like I said.' Nobody ever used that phrase in real life, my mother said, and it was a mark of bad scriptwriting. This quintessentially rural Irish offering was actually written, in the beginning, by a Jewish New Yorker named Mark Grantham. According to the *Irish Times*'s Frank McNally, Grantham came to this country to study under the GI Bill after the war. Between them, he and another writer, Bill Nugent, wrote 800 episodes. Later, almost every impecunious writer in Ireland had a go, including playwright Lee Dunne and David Hanly, one of the early presenters of RTÉ radio's *Morning Ireland*.

It was employment as a *Kennedys of Castleross* scriptwriter that allowed playwright Hugh Leonard to get out of the Land Commission, a section of the civil service he regarded as somewhat short of intellectual stimulation. The other civil servants who worked there at the same time as Leonard loathed him and couldn't believe their luck that Radio Éireann was prepared to take him away. There was much sneering about how intellectually stimulated John Keyes Byrne (as they knew him before his pen name settled irrevocably on him) must be by crafting lines allowing Mrs Kennedy to invite a troubled character to sit down and have a cup of tea, which is what Mrs Kennedy did in most of the episodes, there being a clear need to resolve what might laughingly be called a crisis before the weekend, lest listeners fret. Actor Joe Kennedy tells the story of Leonard becoming convinced that the actors weren't studying the dialogue he'd created for them, this conviction based on the inadequacy – as he saw it – of their recorded performances. Leonard decided to lay a trap for the actors, inserting in the dialogue one week the following exchange:

Mrs Kennedy: Ah, Peadar, how are you?
Peadar: Grand, Mary.
Mrs Kennedy: I wish I could say the same for Christy.
Peadar: Why?
Mrs Kennedy: I'm worried about him, Peadar. His testicles haven't descended yet.

Marie Kean, in rehearsal, gave the line all that might have been asked of her; the other actors, taken by surprise, folded in laughter; and Hugh Leonard's point was proven.

The *IMCO Show*, which promoted a dry-cleaning operation, visited community events and workplaces, all of them filled with the kind of lippy oul' wan who has now lost independent life and been subsumed into Mrs Brown. These lippy oul' wans were at the stage in life where they had few expectations, a multitude of observations, and an eagerness to disclose the large number of children any of them had, which was always met with a huge round of applause, as if those present were relieved we weren't going to run out of people any time soon.

Today, radio vox pops tend to start with 'And how did you feel?' It might be, 'How did you feel when a six-foot wave inundated your kitchen?' or 'How did you feel when your lover stabbed you in the gizzard with the pinking shears?' Through the resultant sobs the interviewee paddles, puddles, even wades around in their feelings on behalf of the listeners. Fifty years ago, radio wasn't that much into feelings. At the top end of the social scale, people didn't have feelings because they were too busy being rich and also because being born with a silver spoon in your mouth tends to give you a stiff upper lip. At the middle of the social scale, people who had feelings were private about them because the concept of common decency still applied. At the lower end of the social scale, people who had them saw no point in expressing them because nobody at the other two levels was paying any attention.

After the news at lunchtime came *Topical Talk*, presented by men like George Burrows, who had a voice like small cannonballs rolling downstairs and who tended to talk about nature. Another presenter of this slot was Maxwell Sweeney, who was proper posh and whose real name was Eddie McSweeney. After a clutch of sponsored programmers, presented by wonderful broadcasters like Gay Byrne, Larry Gogan and Denis Brennan, the news and that day's *Topical Talk*, Radio Éireann literally and metaphorically ran out of steam. It closed down after lunch, abandoning its audience until it cranked back up at five o'clock. In our house, that meant moving the dial in early afternoon as Mamma shifted to the BBC's *Woman's Hour*, followed by someone reading a chapter of a book. She maintained that I was toilet-trained between the first and final episodes of Agatha Christie's *The Murder of Roger Ackroyd* and that I followed the plot better than the average adult. The reiteration of this family legend ensured that I never read *Roger Ackroyd* as an adult, because of the associations.

Later in the afternoon came *Mrs Dale's Diary*, which had in common with *The Kennedys of Casstleross* a central maternal figure who dispensed the bleeding obvious dressed up as wisdom in every episode and served as the moral guide for an entire neighbourhood.

In the evening, we tended to revisit Radio Éireann when they had quizzes and comedy shows like *The Foley Family*, which give Hilary and me the chance to imitate Dublin accents as interpreted by the Radio Éireann Players. However, around seven, if I remember rightly, the BBC Home Service's *Radio Newsreel* was the preferred option, followed by an hour-long documentary, which always seemed to be about the Second World War and included announcements made during that war by Alvar Liddell. Alvar Liddell was as familiar a voice to me growing up as the voices of my own family. As were the voices of Churchill, Montgomery and servicemen like Guy Gibson.

We knew which programmes were on which stations on which days, but that didn't mean we could do without the *Radio Times*, a tabloid-sized publication which combined page after page of lists, in tiny print, of programmes and their transmission times, with interviews with famous radio personalities and writers. In our house, you could safely lose almost any other publication, but if you lost the *Radio Times*, you were in dead trouble.

Our radio was roughly the size of me when I began listening. It was a Bush, and in case anybody missed the significance of the logo, it had a little green bush in a pot on the front. It was varnished, and the varnish, over time, cracked into a million tiny fissures. Later, it was moved upstairs and replaced, downstairs, by a Telefunken, which seemed to be the last word in modernity. My first love, though, was the Bush. With the room lighting turned down, it was the most comforting accompaniment to illness, and since, as long as I could remember, I spent winters floored by bronchitis and asthma, I learned to regard it as an enchanting friend, its back throwing long lozenges of light up against the wallpaper from the bulb deep inside. The number of stations on it seemed limitless, many of them based in locations of which you never otherwise heard, like Hilversum. I would lie with my right arm under the pillow, right hand clutching the rubber bulb of the glass asthma inhaler, transported to other places, other times, the drift to sleep interrupted only by the Hoover-wheeze of my own lungs. I was encountering concepts that never figured in Ireland, like vivisection. I was learning, through my mother's night-time choices, a nostalgia for a time, a music and a war I never knew.

One of the weekly enchantments was Alistair Cooke's *Letter from America*, which ran for 58 years – one of the longest-running radio series ever. Alistair Cooke, an Englishman who moved to the USA and took American citizenship, reported once a week on some aspect of his adopted country in a fifteen-minute audio essay which was fascinating because where it started never gave any indication of where it would end up. He presented with a casual precision and rarely allowed his own opinions to creep in, although he came dangerously close to it when reporting on the bus strike in Montgomery, Alabama, sympathising with the bus company and failing to spot that Rosa Parks was decidedly on the right side of history. Cooke presented her instead as an obstinate, trouble-making woman.

Whether it was Alistair Cooke or Frank Muir and Denis Norden, the oddity of the radio personalities of the time was how they united a family – us – who were never united about anything else. We listened as a group, for the most part, although Hilary tried to claim that her homework was greatly assisted by listening in her bedroom to Radio Luxembourg, the only pure pop station available.

The weekends were particularly great. That was when the BBC had their comedy shows. *Around the Horne* and shows like that were our weekly fix. We could sustain twenty-minute conversations as characters played by Kenneth Williams. 'Oh, don't be like that,' we would tell each other, not knowing that what we were repeating was Williams's high camp.

Kenneth Williams was also a regular on a programme called *Just a Minute*. It migrated to TV, although I never saw it on screen. On radio, it was broadcast in the middle of the day, presented by a man named Nicholas Parsons, who seemed happy enough to be the punchbag of the participants, who treated him – perhaps jocularly – as if he were a social-climbing twit with whom they could hardly bear to share the same air. Williams did the most delightfully melodramatic flounces, but other panellists, including Derek Nimmo, Clement Freud and

Sheila Hancock, also gave Parsons a hard time whenever he judged them to have failed in the programme's requirement to talk for sixty seconds 'without hesitation, repetition or deviation'. The weekly abuse did not stop Parsons from living to be ninety-six, missing only four of more than nine hundred recordings of the programme and working until a couple of weeks before his death.

Today, social media gives the same illusion of intimate relationship as radio did for us back then. Two men, known mainly by their surnames – Muir and Norden – we felt we knew better than we knew our neighbours and cousins, and we liked them a lot better, too. They happened upon each other when scriptwriting for others, and teamed up, not just as writers, but as panellists and personalities, delivering a humour that was never waspish, always amiable and invariably based on wordplay of some kind. On one of their programmes, they would be given a phrase in common usage and asked to propose a story to explain how it might have originated. On one occasion the phrase was the quotation from the melodrama *East Lynne*, 'Dead, dead – and never called me mother!' One of them rambled through an anecdote culminating in a teenage boy exiting a telephone box, complaining that it was 'Dead, dead – and never called me mother ...'

So much did radio programmes associate themselves with time and place that whenever I hear the theme tune from the musical *Carousel*, it reminds me, not of the movie, but of post-lunch listening on a Sunday afternoon. While my father dozed on the couch in the sitting room, looking exactly like the cartoon of Dagwood, Hilary and I would listen to the weekend movie show. Later, on Sundays, came *Sing Something Simple* (or, as my father inevitably called it, *Sing Something Sinful*), which aspired to and reached a level of melodic banality equalled only by weekdays' *Semprini Serenade*.

Radio as something you appeared on, rather than listened to, started for me with Radio Éireann's *Children at the Microphone*, presented by an Abbey actor from Mullingar named Pat Laide. It was where endless numbers of musicians and actors got their first run, in their teens or younger. Because radio was so important at the time, two of the people who went on to fame noted that, even then, it made instant local celebrities of them, they being Foster and Allen. 'There was a big hoor of a microphone hanging down in the dead centre of the room,' they remember. 'Pat would call us up to the microphone one at a time, and you would say your name, and where you were from. He might ask you a question or two, then you were on. You would play your selection, then retreat to the periphery again while the next hopeful came up to the microphone.'

When I was about thirteen, I was one of those hopefuls. Pat Laide had a beautiful voice and that actor's capacity to turn themselves briefly into a glowing spotlight that made everyone around them seem special. Meeting him on *Children at the Microphone* in July 1962 was my first experience of the transience of media relationships. Believing, by the end of the programme, that he and I were so *ad idem*, he might put in to adopt me, I was shocked to find that the minute the red light went off, so did he. In every sense. The producer, however, a man named Padraic O'Neill, who was better known as the greyhound racing commentator Paddy O'Brien, went to considerable trouble to convince me that I had a good voice for radio and that he would involve me in other programmes if I wanted. Of course I wanted, and, obeying my mother, sent him a polite thank you note after the appearance to ensure that he didn't instantly forget me. It took me a while to learn that the producer, not the presenter, is the important one to stay on the right side of. They paid me fifteen bob for being on the show.

The next opportunity radio offered – or seemed to offer – was *Question Time*, presented by Joe Linnane, one of the names and voices that defined Radio Éireann at the time. The weekly quiz programme, it was announced, would, for one season, be based around families, who could apply to take part. Four members of two selected families would then go to RTÉ in Dublin's Henry Street to compete. I decided that since my mother and father between them knew everything and Hilary and I knew a lot from radio programmes and reading, we would be unbeatable on this show, and I duly applied. Instant rejection. The producer told my mother in a telephone call that they would be delighted to have the Prones of Clontarf as contenders, but they would manage to do so without the youngest Prone. They were sure I was wonderfully well-informed, but someone that young? No. The heartless rest of the family, quite intrigued by the possibilities of appearing on radio, opted to invite a brilliant first cousin named Shane Cleary to replace me. It was obvious that Shane, who was not just a good scholar but a painter who also played the double bass, would do well in the quiz, but it was still irritating to find my family so willing to drop me over the nearest cliff-edge. I reasserted myself in a new role: trainer. I bought dozens of quiz books from Eason's and drilled the four of them on 'Who said …?' and 'What do you call …?' and 'What year was …?'. By the time they went into studio, they were match fit. They knew the date of the Defenestration of Prague. They knew what was the fastest land animal. They knew who had said you couldn't be too rich or too thin. They knew who had conducted the longest hunger strike ever. They knew the only disease that's been with us since pre-history.

They aced that first programme and were brought back the following week. And the week after. In August, they encountered the Farrells of Finglas, in September the Allens of Bray, in October the Minihans of New Ross. On 2 November 1962, the competition was the Franklins of Strawhill, Carlow; a week later it was the Dorans of Dolphin's Barn. In fact, their reign lasted for eleven weeks, with the Prones of Clontarf being mentioned in the newspapers. Those eleven weeks did include a few howlers. Once, my father was asked to provide the last word in the phrase 'Rack and …?' Without hesitation, he answered 'pinion', which met with instant dismissal by Joe Linnane, who moved swiftly on, only to come back to it a few minutes later, saying that his producer had decided that rack and pinion was a legitimate substitute for rack and ruin. He did it again in another programme, where he was offered 'As right as …?' and instead of producing 'rain,' he offered 'a trivet,' again causing the involvement of Higher Authorities, who came down on his side. Shane, asked to enumerate Shakespeare's Ages of Man, firmly opted for three, which made me, in the control room, so mad I couldn't speak. I was doing *As You Like It* in school and happened to know Jaques' speech off by heart. My sister was equally firm when asked the difference between an antiseptic and a disinfectant. 'An antiseptic kills wounds', she told the quiz master, 'and a disinfectant prevents wounds.'

Every week, we were in the newspaper:

7.30 *Question Time*: The Mallons of Coolock meet the Prones of Clontarf.

I can't remember which of the competing families caused the Prones of Clontarf to stumble and be defeated, but for years afterwards, my father would hold little semi-formal playbacks of the tapes of their better outings, and when, a little later, I appeared on a TV quiz for schools, I was introduced as coming from a family who made something of a speciality of winning quizzes.

That might have been my only television appearance, ever, were it not for Sister Annunciata. 'Nuncio', based on my Speech and Drama Awards, hurled me into debating. I could think on the fly and – courtesy largely of quiz books rather than in-depth reading – I could come up with a killer quote without warning. I could deliver my arguments with passion, arrogance and humour. I was, in short, worth watching and listening to. I knew how to play to an audience. I just didn't know how to think. Ideas came to me like an overturned box of buttons with no relation to each other or to the underlying fabric, for the pretty good reason that there never *was* an underlying fabric. I once saw a silvery waistcoat crafted entirely out of the ring-tops from beer cans and immediately thought: yep, that's my thinking process made manifest. Wearing it would create a stir, but there was no comfort or longevity in it and, ultimately, you had to ask why the hell anyone would be bothered making it.

I tried hard to fit my box of spilled buttons into the structures for speeches Sister Annunciata handed out, and the structures other teachers handed out to guide you when writing an essay, but the result was always poorly argued and trivial. I could analyse anybody else's speech and see where they were going wrong, but when I applied the same analytical thinking to my own speeches, the judgement was always the same. I was missing a crucial bit of the brain that handles this kind of process and no matter how hard I worked at it, I was not going to develop it. Nor did it help when my sister, wildly enthusiastic about her discovery of IQ tests, sat me down and put me through one of them and made no secret of the fact that I came out in the 'cretin' category.

In debating, I knew I couldn't do what I was supposed to do, and I knew, at the same time, that whatever I was doing was sliding me past the central problem. It wasn't imposter syndrome – I wasn't fearful of being found out, since I had already found myself out. Hard work could conceal natural deficits, and if I had to take six detours and put Christmas lights up at every crossroads to distract from my inability to take the intellectual high road, then detours and Christmas lights it was going to be. It was, it must be admitted, tough on the other three of the teams of four the Holy Faith Convent Clontarf sent out to compete in debating contests, because they never had a clue what was going to come out of my mouth and neither did I. Sister Annunciata cut through the whole issue by making sure I was always the last speaker of the team, which allowed me to berate and mock the other side, repeat the key points of my own side and get enough laughs to distract from the fact that the entire structure made the Leaning Tower of Pisa look like a miracle of solid balance.

Nuncio was a tall nun with an immense sense of her own assets, which included snow-white, beautifully shaped hands. Those hands, when she was not examining them with unconcealed admiration, she draped elegantly or used to stroke the weird roofing arrangement the Holy Faith nuns used to support their veils, which blocked their peripheral vision while making them unimaginably daunting. The squared-off white roof underneath the black veil was impressive enough, but they also wore a leather belt an adult's handspan wide that had a long loose end reaching to below the knee. This was used for corporal punishment, which was then legal, and so some of the more frequent punishers – including Sister Annunciata – had belts the ends of which curled upwards as a result of frequent use, sending the signal to potential offenders to watch out because the nun so armed was ever-ready to turn palms fuchsia pink, swollen and painful.

It was another teacher who caused my mother to take unilateral action long before campaigns to end corporal punishment got underway. Some nun belted Hilary. The next day my mother arrived at the school, demanded to see Sister Leontia, who in shape closely resembled the ageing Queen Victoria and indicated that if anybody in the school laid a hand, ruler or belt on either of her daughters in future, she would take them to court for common assault. My mother's account of verbal collisions with others tended to major on what she said, rather than on how the other side responded, so all we learned was that, at the conclusion of the meeting, Sister Leontia had agreed to restrain her officer class. This she did, although some of them maintained their position in the self-esteem battle by sneering aloud when faced with a situation that would normally have provoked a belt of the belt that of course Hilary Prone (or, later, Terry Prone) was so delicate that she couldn't be punished in the same way as others. In the face of Hilary proving to be a scholarly over-achiever, this died down a bit. The nuns and lay teachers adored her, and saw in her the promise she fulfilled by joining the Department of Education directly from school and serving as secretary to Dr Paddy Hillery, the minister who went on to be president of Ireland. Hilary became the first computer programmer in the Irish civil service and was known as the COBOL Queen.

Annunciata sailed into the classroom one day and announced that she had two tickets for *Teen Talk*. My parents didn't approve of television, so I had never heard of the programme. The indrawn breaths around the class indicated, however, that these tickets were invaluable. Nuncio then announced that she was sending a girl from sixth year and me to the programme.

'Sister, sister, you can't send Terry. She's only thirteen and you have to be sixteen.'

Annunciata favoured the naysayer with a menacing smile.

'Terry will wear the high heels she doesn't think I know she has, and she will *look* sixteen.'

Now, just as I know what I ate at important moments in my life when I should have been paying attention to what was happening rather than what was on the plate in front of me, so I can remember most of the pairs of high heels I have owned, starting with a pair of black patents with kitten heels, branded 'The Young Idea'. The second pair were powder blue suede with four-inch heels. These were the ones Nuncio had in mind. And yes, I owned them when I was thirteen. Up at the other end of me, I was still in broderie anglaise Peter Pan collars and outfits that precisely matched my age. From the ankles down, I was a showgirl.

As Nuncio doled out homework, I fished around among my classmates to find out about the programme. It was presented, I was told, by the most gorgeous man named Bunny Carr. *What?* Nobody knew why he was called Bunny, but he was. He was so handsome. and he had this wife in a wheelchair. The wife in the wheelchair seemed to make him in some way heroic and virtuous. The programme itself was a version of the classic *Question Time* format, with a panel of three adults from business, show business or politics, and an audience of teenagers to ask questions of the panel and contribute to the ensuing discussion. The programme had already given outings to undergraduates like Vincent Browne and Christina Murphy, who would go on to become household names. It was hugely popular, and the presenter was so adored that his fan mail took up three black plastic rubbish sacks a week in RTÉ. On Sundays, Dubliners would drive out to Sutton in the hope of seeing him, creating a slow motorised procession past the Carr house on La Vista Avenue.

'Ask a question,' Sister Annunciata instructed me. 'Ask an *intelligent* question.'

On the night, the sixth-year girl and I arrived separately and tacitly agreed we should continue that way. So I was effectively on my own in the big oblong lobby of RTÉ, which was much more imposing and elegant than it is now, albeit with the same sweeping staircase rising from floor level. On my own, but surrounded by groups of older teen-agers, the girls dressed to the nines and some of the guys wearing the uniform of dissent – scruffy everything. A tall handsome trench-coated man with a clipboard began to wander between the groups asking them what questions they'd like to ask, bantering with them, and making notes. Eavesdropping on my elders, I decided they weren't my betters, but rather an earnest cluster of worthies with questions like, 'If you were to bury a time capsule in our capital city representing Ireland in the nineteen sixties, what would you put in it?'

When the tall smiling bloke came to me, I said, 'I'd like to ask the panel why parents stop their babies from sucking their thumbs. It doesn't give you cancer, it doesn't make you fat and it's free.' He looked at me as if I was from a different species. 'Say that again?' I did. He wrote it down and walked away. A few minutes later we all formed a procession and were led into a vast studio, crowding behind a curtain that went up to a high light-gridded ceiling and formed a false inner wall. Coming around the corner of the curtain into the brilliantly lit studio was like stepping into a wonderland of sparkle, light and glamour. The panellists at their table. The presenter seated slightly away from the panel, a make-up artist powdering him. A man with a walkie-talkie on his belt picking individuals from the crowd of teenagers, instructing them where to sit, which frequently meant they were separated from their friends. Inevitably, I was put in the back row on the extreme right-hand side, which gave me a great close-up view of the set. It seemed to be constructed of chicken wire cut into the shape of leaves, with floor-level lights projecting the shadow of the leaves onto a coral-hued fabric stretched on a frame.

The presenter got up and walked the studio floor, telling every member of the audience, essentially, that they were on their own. If they waited for him to invite them to share their great thoughts with the Irish public, the Irish public were never going to hear those great thoughts because how could he know that – he pointed to one beautiful blonde girl in the second row and she offered her name: Richelle Courtney – how could he know that Richelle Courtney had a great thought lurking, ready for sharing? He then asked her what she was studying and she said medicine, at which the three grown-ups nodded approvingly. The presenter made smart comments to them over his shoulder and described them in jocularly negative terms to the teenagers. One of them was Cecil Barror, who presented a Bird's Custard-sponsored radio programme.

All the time the guy with the walkie-talkie on his belt was calling out times – 'Five minutes to air' – while cameramen spun around their great machines, their assistants pulled the fat flexes out of the way, and other guys used long poles to tilt the bright, hot lights one way or the other. Bunny Carr, the presenter, at one point indicated that the walkie-talkie guy was the floor manager, and a person to be reckoned with. The floor manager did an elaborate bow and announced it was two minutes to air. Bunny Carr promised to severely punish any of us who tried to wave at our mothers or who looked up if the microphone boom – 'Show them, Derek' – swung over our heads. Derek showed us, the floor manager said we had one minute to go, then started to count down from thirty, cued the boppity signature tune and off we went. Bunny Carr introduced the panel and then turned to the audience, sitting in tiered rows to his right.

'Our first question comes from … Terry Prone,' he announced and, sure enough, the camera boom swung right over my head. I asked my question. He put it to the panel. One of them just laughed it off as if it was too silly to engage with. One of them told me it was good that I was thinking of issues like smoking because smoking was so bad for young people. The third said you wouldn't want a generation of children with prominent teeth. The presenter threw it over to the audience, and the students present fell over themselves to insult the questioner and dismiss the question. We surely, they agreed, had more important topics to be discussing than thumb-sucking babies.

I had asked the question purely out of mischief and to be different, but once the war started, I started to believe in that question with a passion, and as soon as one of the audience finished excoriating me, I jumped in without invitation, told him he was patronising me, added that the panel had done likewise, and demanded evidence-based answers to the points I had raised, rather than reflex dismissal. This created even more annoyance, and the discussion got so hot and heavy that the presenter intervened and asked for the next question, which was more reasonable and led to a civilised discussion until the presenter suddenly asked me what *my* view was. I hadn't been paying attention because I was trying to work out exactly how the set/light arrangement worked, so I played for time by saying that I disagreed with everybody who had spoken thus far, which provoked an unwilling laugh and drew Cecil Barror on me. By the time he'd finished, I had worked up an opinion and delivered it as if I had always owned it. For the next few minutes, heat, light and adrenalin-fuelled opinions erupted from me on all topics. Then suddenly the programme was over. That was half an hour? It had felt like twelve minutes.

The lights went off and the place became dark, cold, ordinary. Some audience members grabbed the presenter, who embraced them enthusiastically while others took photographs. Some went up to the panel and engaged them in further chat. The rest of us, guided by the floor manager, headed out of the studio and across the lobby. I tried to ignore the degrees of separation imposed on me, clearly indicating that I had demonstrated something close to bubonic plague in the studio. Mid-sternum was growing the fat grey fear of what Sister Annunciata was going to say the following morning. Then my elbow was grabbed and a neat man with glasses pulled me gently away from the procession lining up to go through the circling doors. He shook hands with me and introduced himself as Denis O'Grady, the *Teen Talk* producer.

'Terry, we've never had a teenager on the panel,' he told me. 'But I was wondering if you'd like to be on the panel next week?'

'But all I did was cause fights!'

'Yes,' he beamed, and suddenly, all was clear. TV needed the good-looking, the articulate, the holders of worthy views. But what it needed even more was the contrarian, the individual prepared to go against consensus and fight their corner, in the process provoking everybody else present to fight *their* corner. I told Mr O'Grady I would be thrilled to be on the panel, gave him my phone number, and went home in a daze.

The next day was strange because nobody in my house had seen the programme, whereas everybody in the Holy Faith Convent had. Nuns stopped me in corridors. Teachers nodded at me as they set themselves up at their desk on the podium. Everyone in my class, including the ones who didn't like me, wanted a rundown from the moment I arrived to the moment I left. I did a mental dither about telling anybody about meeting Denis O'Grady and being invited on to the panel, and eventually kept schtum because I was afraid I'd have an accident or get sick and be prevented from appearing the following Friday.

On the Tuesday, my mother took me into town to buy me something to wear. I had dreams of frills, of gauzy sleeves with silver threads running through them. This was because I had no taste. I still have no taste. I can identify beautiful tailoring and perfect lines. But for myself, no pussy bow is too many and that's before we get started on the hair.

As we walked down Grafton Street, people turned to look at us in that way that makes you wonder if you've a tomato soup spill on your chest or your skirt tucked into your tights at the back. I checked. Nothing was obviously wrong. Then the lookers became accosters. Three. Ten. Thirty of them. Was I the girl off *Teen Talk?* When I nodded, they pulled out bits of paper and pens for me to sign my autograph. I wanted to tell them that I wasn't nearly important enough to get space in their autograph books, but my mother's quelling nod indicated that I should shut up and write. It was the writing bit that worried me, my handwriting then and now being a disgrace to the pen and me.

'Your signature will do,' Mamma muttered.

I also learned, from the blunt nudge my mother delivered, that you didn't hang about once you'd delivered your scrawl. I followed her at a trot into Switzer's, which was where Brown Thomas now stands, and was dragged up the big shallow steps to the womenswear section where I veered towards taffeta and ruffles. It wasn't much of a veer, because my mother was veering towards tailored blouses the way Sherman veered through Georgia. Within minutes, I had been fitted with the approving assistance of a woman my mother's age who congratulated her on having such a confident daughter.

'You're very kind,' my mother said, putting a full stop like a Garda roadblock at the end of the sentence: No more of this. Every now and again, then and later, she would accompany this never-changing response to flattery from strangers with a quarter eye-roll, soliciting their collaboration in not giving me notions. I was disappointed when we headed back down the magnificent broad staircase, because I had been hoping to get a skirt as well. Mamma said tersely that a skirt didn't matter: the panellists on *Teen Talk* were never seen below the waist.

On the Friday, I was the only teenager on the panel and had a ball, not least because my mother had sat Hilary and me down to work out the likely questions. Hilary was willing to help, but because she has a logical bent, kept pointing out that nobody would know what the questions were until the audience arrived and told Bunny before the programme started. (We were all, mentally at least, on first-name terms with the presenter.) 'Nonsense,' my mother said, who had a contempt for the masses which would have qualified her for any handy dictatorship. 'Those teenagers couldn't think up an original question to save their lives – that's why the thumb-sucking query worked.' So it shouldn't be beyond us to work out what they would ask on Friday. We got together a list and then I got peppered, in random order, with those questions and did, I thought, remarkably well at getting back answers to each of them. My sister seemed to agree. My mother, on the other hand, looked grimly into the middle distance before telling me that what I had said could have been said by anybody. It was *obvious*. There was nothing *new* about it. Did I seriously think Mr

O'Grady had invited me back to simper and say things any fool could say? She was going to give me an hour to think of better answers, she announced, before sweeping off about her normal tasks. Hilary scrunched the lower part of her face in a 'Don't blame me' grimace. I sat stunned by the realisation that I had to find ways to offer something that didn't fall under the headings of 'predictable' or 'routine'. Worst of all, I was going to have to leave the safe sanctuary created by consensus, and stand outside throwing stones.

It was the first time I understood my father's reverence for the church process called 'the devil's advocate', where, when a cleric is defending his thesis, one of the older clergymen present is instructed to come up with the devastating points the devil would make, were he present at the time. My father believed he should be the devil's advocate at all times. He would argue (retrospectively and remotely) with the priest who gave the sermon at Sunday Mass. He would argue with the presenters of radio's *Topical Talk*. He would argue with any book any of us was reading. What infuriated Hilary was that, half a century before Donald Trump, he would characterise as probably false what, to my sister, was clearly objective truth. Like the morning when Radio Éireann's first news bulletin announced that the Russians had put a satellite into space. It even had a name: Sputnik. Hilary, who was fascinated by outer space, was thrilled to hear the news, hushing us with a flailing porridge spoon until she had all the details. It was, apparently, going to be possible to see Sputnik lashing around the sky that night if it wasn't cloudy. My sister was ecstatic.

'You don't believe that, really, do you?' my father asked, pouring tea for my mother and himself.

'What do you mean? Of course I believe it. How could you not believe it?'

My father smirked and shrugged: 'Well, if you want to be that gullible, go right ahead.' Hilary began to breathe like a manatee and demanded his evidence for doubt, which even I, at seven, could have told her was not a good idea.

'Pure propaganda,' Dad said, taking the muslin off the milk jug. 'Pure propaganda to frighten the Americans.'

'How would a satellite frighten anyone?'

'Claiming that a Soviet satellite has been put in orbit will frighten Eisenhower that the Russians are winning the space race.'

Hilary, getting personally hotter while her porridge got colder, was unsure whether to go after the word 'claiming' or point out that Eisenhower wasn't going to be re-elected, so the only thing he needed to be frightened about was his next heart attack. My father never believed for a minute that Sputnik did not exist, but on this and on every other issue he forced Hil and me to look sceptically at everything we saw, read or heard and to come up with alternative explanations. This proved to be more than useful when prepping for *Teen Talk*, so by the time I arrived in Montrose an hour and a half before airtime, I had a head full of useful pictures, examples and stories applicable to almost any issue that might arise during the programme.

Sitting in front of a mirror framed in light bulbs while a make-up artist went at my face was the best part. She had sponges for applying make-up, and flat open containers of make-up that went from hard chalk to soft mush when water was applied. Max Factor Pan Cake, said the lid. This was foundation, and it eliminated all freckles and, as a result, made me look more grown up. Then she produced a silvery gadget that curled the upper eyelashes backwards, before going to work to put on eyeliner, followed by mascara. As the artist applied the soft stuff with a rolling motion, eyelashes that had been self-effacing became thickly assertive. The make-up artist, sweeping the cape off me, asked if I was happy. I couldn't tell her how happy I was. You can't say 'I look beautiful,' but I did.

I had learned from the first show that TV time goes four times as quickly as real time, and you can't ever afford to postpone anything, because the moving finger of TV writes, and having writ, moves on. So this time I barged in and blurted. I could feel the disapproval from the adults on either side of me, just as I could feel the delight on the part of the presenter. Bunny Carr had a knack of slightly insulting you as a way of approving of you.

'So let's go to our wilting violet on the panel,' he might say. Or 'We must now get the opinion of a future Abbey actress,' and everybody would know it was me he was talking about. Of course it was also a signal to me to get ready, and a signal to the camera. One of the cameras would circle and settle, a hand tightening the focus, and a red light would appear on it, indicating that this shot had been selected by Denis O'Grady in the control room for broadcast to the nation.

Like a child, I was learning rules I couldn't have articulated, even as I internalised them; the powerful reinforcer of learning that a camera would hover, waiting for the panellist most likely to say something. When the action moved away from me at one point, I had a sudden memory of bitter comments from actors about Cyril Cusack, a notorious scene-stealer, who was known to pull out a snowy white handkerchief in the middle of someone else's speech to draw the eye of the audience to himself. I didn't have a handkerchief, but in that moment, I realised I didn't need one. Nor did I need to speak. When someone else was on screen saying something boring, all I had to do was essay the tiniest head shake or raise an eyebrow, and two things would happen. The red light would appear on the camera observing me, and the presenter, noting that, would within seconds say something like 'So, Terry, I think we can guess you're in disagreement with Gerald on that one?'

The programme ended and Mamma took me home, pleased enough with the performance to describe it as 'functional'. Mamma had a thing about functionality. Anything that wasn't functional was a decoration, and she despised decorations. Our house was barren of china shepherdesses, brass bells and seashell-studded artefacts and she pretended not to see them in other houses.

At that time, you couldn't record a TV programme while it was being transmitted, so if you didn't have a television, you had to visit other people's homes to see it. Hilary went to her friend's house to see this second outing but my father was content to hear about it from his wife, who saw it in the green room. What none of us anticipated was that, because I had said something mildly anti-clerical, parish priests around the country would take acute umbrage, and preach about my sinful arrogance two days later. Which in turn led to commentary in newspapers. I became Controversial Teen Terry Prone. Denis O'Grady invited me back again, this time putting other teenagers – two lads of nineteen – on either side of me. The following evening, 15 November 1964, Gabriel Fallon, a director of the Abbey Theatre and TV critic of the *Evening Press*, registered the changes to the programme. 'I have been keeping a close eye on that intriguing programme *Teen Talk*, so ably presented by Bunny Carr,' he wrote. 'The new young panellists have acquitted themselves so well that I would be all for retaining them. Incidentally, Miss Terry Prone bears a remarkable resemblance to the young Sara Allgood. Whether or not this augurs well for her proposed career in the theatre remains to be seen.' (Sara, or Sally, Allgood had played mothers in movies, including *How Green Was My Valley.)*

I just loved going out to Montrose, visiting the canteen, meeting famous people – and being close to Bunny Carr, who was always funny. He would often have a microphone threaded down through his shirt and trousers and would claim that every time Charlie Roberts, the floor manager, trod on the cable he came *this close* to removing Bunny's slacks in the process.

Each time I appeared as a panellist, they paid me £5. The third time, Mamma was working and said she'd be about half an hour late, so I should wait in the lobby. When Denis O'Grady heard this, he wasn't having any of it. No, I would join his table in the canteen. Joan Collins, the programme's production assistant, brought me up and we were joined by Denis and Bunny at a table already occupied by three men. My diary for the day tells the story.

One man was an ordinary looking guy with a nice grin, who favoured me with it (the grin) and a dramatically dark man with a pale face and big flashing dark eyes. He looked vaguely Spanish.

'Oh, you're the girl from *Teen Talk*, aren't you?' I said yes and then burst out with 'Well, I don't really know your name, but I know your voice so well! Who are you?' At this point, Denis came over, followed by Gay Byrne's brother Al, and [the dark man] said to the general table: 'Isn't it wonderful that someone still occasionally listens to the radio?' Then he added to me, 'My name's Aiden Grennell' (of the RE rep.)

Joan Collins took me downstairs to meet my mother, and as we three walked down the corridor, we encountered Joe Lynch, who greeted me as the *Teen Talk* girl and started to talk to my mother, who was bowled over. He told her that while she might know him mainly as a singer, acting was his first love and his career direction, although he despised method acting. [With Joe Lynch, everything, conversationally, led to everything else. Bunny defined him as the sort of talker you adored for the first half-hour and whose second half-hour caused you to want to kill him.] As we stood in the corridor, we were joined by Denis Brennan and his actor wife Daphne Carroll. They leaned up against the walls of the corridor, talking, and I asked if they'd recommend a school of acting, and Joe said: 'Denis, you and I went to the S.H.K., didn't we?' I asked what this meant, and was told The School of Hard Knocks. Then a grey beard appeared at another door and behind it Cyril Cusack. Well, we stood there for about half an hour, Cyril's arm around Mamma's waist, talking. I didn't notice at the time, but all the time some poor idiot was trapped in the toilet, against which were leaning Mamma and Cyril. Eventually, after much rattling of the door, a red-faced man dashed out past us. As we parted, Joe Lynch complimented my mother on how I was dressed. 'Can't beat th'oul' tailored blouse,' he affirmed.

6

Dislocated Elbows and Real Tears

Miss Treasa Prom
Scoil Aisteoireachta
Your audition for above will be on Thursday next 9th Feb, at
5.30pm at the theatre.

That's what the card read. It didn't get my name right. The signature was illegible. And 9 February that year (1965) was a Wednesday. None of these speed bumps deterred me. Nor did the news that the audition would be overseen by Ernest Blythe, who had been managing director of the Abbey Theatre for more than twenty-three years.

Blythe, a northern Protestant, had been inveigled into the Irish Republican Brotherhood by Seán O'Casey. He couldn't take part in the 1916 rebellion because he was imprisoned for his republicanism at the time, but as soon as he got out, he learned the Irish language like a native speaker and became a government minister. Then he became a founder of Cumann na nGaedheal, writing speeches for leader Eoin O'Duffy. All of which made him anathema to my father. My mother, on the other hand, hated him because, as Minister for

Finance in 1926, he had cut the old-age pension by a shilling a week. She regarded him as rigid, authoritarian and politically stupid. By the time I auditioned for him, he was largely forgotten as a guerrilla fighter, a fascist and a government minister, but politicians would always associate his name with the one thing no politician should ever do: attack elderly voters. When, at home, we discussed the forthcoming audition, my parents' hatred of Blythe got a new lease of life from the rediscovery of his role in the Abbey. As Minister for Finance, he had made the Abbey the first state-subsidised theatre in the Western world. Blythe became a director of the theatre in 1935 at W.B. Yeats's invitation and from 1941 to 1967 he was its managing director. For nigh on two decades, in other words, the Abbey was run by an all-powerful bigoted bully.

The Abbey Theatre, at the time, was very different from the Gate. The Gate was all class and period English drama, plus Pirandello, Eugene O'Neill, Strindberg and Denis Johnston. The Abbey was all underclass and Irish peasantry, where no actor could get in unless they could act 'as Gaeilge'. The Irish language was one of Blythe's obsessions and he pushed it with the fervour of a late convert.

In 1965, the novelist Walter Macken became the first artistic director of the Abbey Theatre, but if anybody hoped this would back Blythe into more of a financial management role, they were much mistaken. He was across every decision in the theatre, right down to the selection of teenagers for the embryonic Abbey Theatre School of Acting. His dead hand when it came to the selection of plays meant that artistic leadership became the role of tiny theatres like the Pike, where Carolyn Swift and Alan Simpson took risks, got arrested (for staging Tennessee Williams's *The Rose Tattoo*) and created an excitement sorely missing from the Abbey's respectable, bland and boring productions. Seán O'Casey withdrew permission for the national theatre to stage his plays, and so, as Ireland was emerging into an era of theatrical possibility, the Abbey appealed to its audiences by staging John McCann and Lady Gregory potboilers. As potboilers went, both were top of the stove, but the paucity of new playwrights during the Blythe years drew savage criticism of the managing director. His response was implacable. 'Most people in Ireland', he wrote, 'are the habitués of farmhouse kitchens, city tenements or middle-class sitting-rooms and their loves and hates, disappointments and triumphs, griefs and joys, are just as interesting and amusing, or as touching, as those of, shall we say alliteratively, denizens of ducal drawing-rooms, or boozers in denizened brothels.'

Blythe had no qualms about invading the lives of his actors to save the theatre money. One of the best performers of the time, Máire Ní Dhómhnaill, was married to another actor named Geoffrey Golden. The Goldens had a fair number of babies, and although Máire worked in the theatre up to the last possible moment and returned to the stage at the first possible moment post partum (maternity leave being a concept far in the future), her fecundity irritated Blythe, who instructed her to replace the Golden double bed with two singles in two separate rooms, indicating that the theatre would financially contribute to this approach to contraception. Blythe had priorities other than coddling actors, and knew that actors are members of the ultimately disposable profession. As Maire O'Neill, a member of the Abbey Theatre company for several decades, once said: 'There's always someone younger and prettier coming up behind you.'

On the day of my audition for the School of Acting, there was a procession of young people outside the theatre, although none of them, as far as I could tell, was as young as I was. We were herded into seats and each received one of those tear-off cloakroom tickets with a number on it. This meant that if your number was in the teens or twenties, you got to watch several other Abbey aspirants before you were called. Nobody overreaches like the untalented, and so Juliet followed St Joan followed Portia, with Maurya from *Riders to the Sea* in there, too. The lads did Hamlet, Lear, and a couple of Shavian characters. One, with a strong Dublin accent, performed the scene where Mark Antony bleats loyalty over the dead body of Caesar. The young actor involved decided he needed some focus for his laments, so he turned a barstool on its side, confronting those in the auditorium with the sight of lumps of elderly chewing gum all down 'Caesar's' skinny legs.

When it came to my turn, my cloakroom ticket was taken from me and I was nodded to go up the rickety little steps. The stage was filthy and patched, but to stand looking out into the darkened auditorium of the Queen's Theatre in Pearse Street was to get some sense of the great old music hall it had been. The Queen's had been the home of the Abbey for several years following a disastrous fire at the old Abbey.

I was told to go ahead in my own time and I bowed, waited for a beat, got launched. I was lashing ahead with the shopping list scene from *The Playboy of the Western World*, trying, as does every novice, to invest the purchase of 'six yards of yellow stuff to make a gown' with subtle significance, when a voice called 'níos áirde' from the stalls. It was the managing director. I had been brought up on nothing but the best Grafton Street Gaelic, and this man spoke pure Northern dialect. Never the twain shall meet. I hadn't a clue what he was on about, but assumed what he offered was an adverse comment on the whole performance. As a result, I got quieter and quieter and more desperate as he got noisier and noisier and more irritated. By the end of the extract, the performance in the stalls was a good deal more rewarding than the one on stage because he was apoplectic with rage.

The tall man nearer the footlights – I learned later he was Walter Macken – rose and suggested I do my second piece. I was so frazzled that I couldn't remember what it was, which may have been fortunate, because if I had remembered and performed it as planned, I would have lined myself up in direct competition with at least five others who had chosen to do Shaw's St Joan, one of whom, Maria McGuire, future terrorist fellow traveller, had done an incomparable version. The tall man, seated again, looked up at me and nodded. Not quite 'get on with it', but close. In a moment of wild recklessness, I began the recitation I usually performed at family parties: Stanley Holloway's 'The Lion and Albert', which required a strong Lancashire accent. The recitation is about a family surnamed Ramsbottom, who went to Blackpool for the day and visited the zoo, where a lion ate young Albert. It had an early reference to Albert owning 'a stick with an 'orse's 'ead 'andle, the finest that Woolworth's could sell', Woolworth's being synonymous with cheap tat. When I said the line, tiny smothered laughs broke out among the other aspirant actors, and that small encouragement emboldened me to walk about the stage and deliver some of the lines to the unoccupied gods. Then I was back in the line-up of hopefuls.

When the last audition was over, we were asked to sit and wait. The man in the front and the man at the back disappeared. After an eternity, a woman came onto the stage and, using a torch to read from a jotter, announced she was going to call out the numbers of those who could now go home. If your number was called, you were done for. All those condemned sat politely until the list had been read, then formed a funereal coffle up the aisle and out into the sunshine. The woman on the stage then told the rest of us to stay put and disappeared into the wings.

Like survivors of gunfire, we sat with great gaps between us, facing forward, about twenty of us, fearful of hope lest it bring us to a worse form of execution than that endured by the departed kids. Facing forward, lest our expressions give us away. One of the survivors was Frank Grimes, the young man who had turned a barstool into Caesar. Eventually, the tall man came back, told us we had all succeeded and that we were now members of the Abbey Theatre School of Acting. As the others left, Joe Dowling, whom I knew and liked from the Feis, and I were kept back. Macken then talked to us quietly about the Abbey and how, when it went into its new home, it would see a new era of contribution to Ireland's history, Ireland's sense of community, Ireland's culture. He then told us we would pay no fees. Mr Blythe had given us both scholarships. We nodded, speechlessly.

When I got into our car, parked outside, I led off with acceptance and scholarship, which delighted my mother so much I never had to confess to having done 'The Lion and Albert' instead of something more powerfully dramatic. I did feel guilty when she gave me a silver medallion of St Joan, on a chain, to commemorate my acceptance by the school, but not guilty enough to confess. Ma moved swiftly on, anyway, to notifying the school about my prospective absences, conscious that the nuns were not likely to baulk at one of their own touching the hem of Sally Allgood. They didn't know I had lied about my age to get into the School of Acting, claiming to be sixteen when I was only fifteen and a half.

Frank Dermody, a producer in the Abbey, was the director of the School of Acting, a role for which he had neither qualifications nor competence. Dermody was a little pink bald guy who looked like a furious baby. He was permanently wound up as tight as a spring, with a lisp on S that made navigation through most sentences like white-water rafting. Everybody ended up soaked. He was also a binge drinker, which circuitously led to his extraordinary way of talking. When he went out to get drunk, he would quite sensibly decide to preserve his false teeth from the consequences of a possible fall. He'd take them out of his mouth, wrap them in a hanky, and secrete them in his coat pocket. Which was fine, except that he was also a pipe smoker, and when he got seriously drunk, he would shove his still-lit pipe into his pocket, where it would slowly set fire to the hanky, causing the melting of the false teeth into a shapeless lump of pink and white plastic. The first couple of times this happened, he replaced them, but around the third time he lost interest in his dentures and went gummy instead, which gave him an epic lisp and forced him to overemphasise everything in order to be understood at all. For us acting students, a training session with him was like trying to learn the pronunciation of Swahili from a deranged gorilla.

Not understanding him was the least of our worries, because there wasn't much of a curriculum. Guest lecturers would come equipped with a theme, references and exercises but, for the most part, Dermody was possessed by one thing: falling correctly. The number of roles in plays requiring an actor to fall out of their standing position and hit the floor in a fluid and uninjured way is relatively small. Dermody was nevertheless persuaded that if we could do that trick on demand, world fame would follow as day follows night. Whenever he was short of an idea for a class, we ended up falling down, never doing it to his satisfaction, thus forcing him to shout and lisp at us and then climb up on something to 'demonthrate how it thould be exthecuted.' He swore blind that if you fell relaxedly, you would not, could not, hurt yourself, and we generally accepted our bruises as the outcome of our own inadequacy. Most of the time, we were in a rehearsal room, which simplified the falling exercise, but on one occasion the lesson took place on the Abbey stage. Now the Queen's was legendary among the theatres of the time for having the third steepest rake in Ireland or Britain. The stage slanted from the back wall to the footlights as acutely as a ski slope. It was loved by directors and audiences but loathed by actors who, standing sideways, had the sensation that one foot was on a step. Dermody may have forgotten the storied rake of the stage, because when he landed after the perfect fall, he began to roll over and over, this greatly helped by his shape, which was spherical. He gained speed as he went, unable to stop himself, and was spilled into the orchestra pit, where he landed in the percussion section. We were way too terrified to laugh, but to this day I remember with some pleasure the five minutes of noise attendant upon him disengaging from the timpani.

Mainly, during what were called classes, the director of the Abbey Theatre School of Acting spewed and spat stories at us through his gums. One that frequently came up was how he had pointed out a pulsating vein in her neck to Siobhán McKenna. Neither the cause nor consequence of this were shared with us. Most of Dermody's narratives were designed to prove that we were in the hands of probably the best actor in Ireland and certainly the best talent-spotter. None of our parents could ever remember seeing him in any play, although my mother, going back through the play programmes she kept, found out that he was the one who had produced *The Plough and the Stars* the year before, when O'Casey had decided to lift his ban on the Abbey performing his works. Dermody's production had been spectacular, if traditional, with Eileen Crowe turning in a heart-breaking performance as Bessie Burgess. O'Casey himself didn't see the play, but his wife did; and based on what she told him, the playwright lavished praise on Angela Newman's interpretation of Rosie Redmond. Newman was beautiful in the role, particularly in the moment when the Young Covey, an undereducated gobshite stuffed with half-remembered Marxist phraseology, turns on Rosie and tells her to shut up, that she's 'only a prostitute'. Up to then, women playing Rosie had screamed the next lines back at the Young Covey: 'You're no man! You're no man!' Newman whispered those words and in that whisper was concentrated an infinity of misery and helpless resentment.

The odd thing about Dermody is that, even though he had such recent evidence of directorial competence from which to draw lessons, whether of blocking, lighting, design or performance for his students, he never mentioned *The Plough and the Stars*. Instead, his stories went much further back. Typically, these yarns had him standing alongside either Micheál Mac Liammóir or Hilton Edwards as they assessed a performance of a particular play, the accounts hinging on one or the other having a forehead-smacking moment when they acknowledged that the whole show would have died – *died right there* – were it not for the charismatic Dermody. '"Geniuth," Hilton thaid. "Geniuth".'

We doubted that, but after the first week, we knew we'd never have anyone as individual and as satisfying to imitate. In no time at all, Hilary and I were saying 'Oh, for *Chrithaketh!*' to each other, her version of a man she had never met based on my daily lisped rants. Things were going fine until the evening I asked a simple question at the tea table.

'What's your crotch?' I asked.

Hilary coped badly with this, her laughter colliding with a mouthful of tea. You might believe that a fifteen-and-a-half-year-old who claimed ignorance of what her crotch was could have been pretending, but that's the truth of it. I had never heard the word. Crotches were not part of our family conversation back then. Or since, now that I come to think of it. They just didn't surface casually in the familial discourse. So, other than my sister choking and apologising, the query proved to be a silencer. My mother, who had a genius for spotting implications, didn't answer the question but demanded to know why I was asking it.

Then I saw I was losing my audience. My father took his napkin from his lap, put it on his plate and silently walked out of the kitchen. This was seismic. This had never happened before. We sat, frozen, the three of us, until my mother put her own napkin on the table and followed him. I tried to establish, with Hilary's help, what had gone wrong, but neither of us could work it out.

Then my mother returned, put my father's meal on a tray and took it into the sitting room, before coming back and making a fresh pot of tea. Even the tea-making seemed a portent of something inchoate but deeply threatening. When she had poured and doctored her tea, she suggested that perhaps it would be wise not to talk about Mr Dermody when our father was present. She took a deep breath.

'Your father was on a jury that convicted Mr Dermody of a lewd act in a van.'

For some reason, the mention of the van set Hilary off and she set me off, the two of us going out to the scullery and closing the door so my father wouldn't hear our hilarity. When we had calmed down, we came back to find Mamma quietly finishing her first cup of refreshed tea and moving to the second.

'What's a lewd act?'

'You don't need to know.'

'Ah, Mamma, she really does,' Hilary said.

'Fine. *You* tell her, then.'

'Sex.'

'But sex isn't illegal.'

Silence.

'Is it that it was in a van?'

'No, it was that it was with a man.'

For a second, it sounded as if she was playing a rhyming game with me.

'How could a man have sex with a man?'

'To tell you the truth,' my mother said, mostly addressing the tea cosy, 'I wouldn't be very clear on that. It's called homosexuality. And people have other words for it. It's illegal and … and your father would have strong religious feelings about it.'

I looked at Hilary, who shrugged. My mother said something about St Paul, of whom my father was a big fan and my mother not. Ma thought St Paul was a one-hit wonder. Once he'd come out with that riff about love, he should have packed it in was her view.

'Dadda disapproves of it?'

'I'm not sure "disapprove" – he absolutely hates homosexuality and by inference homosexuals.'

'Do you hate them?'

'Oscar Wilde was one, so I would be loath to.'

(Even before I got to do dramatic solos taken from Wildean plays, Mamma had enthralled us by reading us Wilde's fairy tales.)

'Your father was concerned about this man having a bad influence on you,' Mamma went on.

'Talking crotches,' Hilary said helpfully.

'In the acting classes,' my mother corrected, and a wave of cold ran across the back of my neck at the possibility that I might have to leave the School of Acting. 'I did point out to him,' she went on, 'that if Mr Dermody was inclined to – to – be attracted to men, this might, in a sense, be a protective factor for the girls in the class, and your father agrees.'

The relief was enormous, although having to censor what I was saying at home was a pain. The word 'gay' hadn't been invented then. Máire Geoghegan-Quinn's de-criminalisation of homosexual acts was decades in the future, as was the work I did with members of the gay community, media-prepping them for programmes like *The Late Late Show*. It was a time of pejorative terms and careers imperilled, a time of public toilets and fleeting pleasures taken from and given to strangers, a time of biblical condemnations and medieval terrors. And, of course, women didn't figure at all. Even when lesbianism was addressed, it was done so in such obscure terms – witness Radclyffe

Hall's *The Well of Loneliness* – as to leave all but the already initiated perplexed, on the last page, as to what all that had been about.

Over time, it became obvious from side-references that everybody but me had known about Dermody's sexuality. His stories about Micheál Mac Líammóir and Hilton Edwards should have made it obvious. Mac Líammóir and Edwards were sufficiently overt about their partnership to make Dubliners feel liberal and in the know. Neither ever, during their lifetime, actually 'outed' themselves. They would have been fools to do it, given the laws and attitudes of the time. Being flagrantly camp, as Mac Líammóir was, didn't amount to an announcement of status, but rather a reversal into cherished oddity. Mac Líammóir's entire backstory was a fiction he maintained with a creativity as admirable as his seminal one-man show about Oscar Wilde. He was also one of the most vicious verbal abusers of his time, telling actor Coralie Carmichael in rehearsal that he hoped her womb would fester and fall out. Dermody had learned his viciousness from masters. The difference was that they were geniuses and he wasn't. He was simply cruel.

None of us believed that we were receiving a RADA-type dramatic education. However, just as evolution happens, some of the students began to grow in confidence and competence. Niall Buggy, Bosco Hogan and Joe Dowling speedily crossed the barrier between the School of Acting and the theatre company, helped by an unwritten policy that the school existed to feed the unpaid or underpaid into the system where they should be bloody grateful they had been given the chance to be onstage with their elders and betters.

Mostly, the School of Acting was like one of those medieval maps where, at the bottom, was inscribed *Hic sunt dracones*. Even the apparently simple exercises Frank Dermody created to stretch our creative muscles carried their own dangers. For one of those exercises, we were split into pairs. I always hated that, because, too often, I ended up with guys who were shorter and slighter than me and who looked at me as if I were a hippo come to take tea with them. This particular exercise consisted of a boy and girl fighting and improvising dialogue around a set theme. The boy was to grab the girl's arm and yell 'Tell me!' The girl, predictably, was to say, 'I won't.' Back and forth this went on for some time, with the fighters endeavouring to give the impression that the boy was half-killing the girl, who eventually had to cry that she was being hurt. One couple did this for ages, to Dermody's rising discontent.

'You're hurting me!' the girl cried piteously.

'Ah, for chrithaketh, thath not convinthing!' Dermody hissed, and she tried harder, meeting with more contempt.

'*You're hurting me!*' she eventually bellowed. Dermody said that was 'even worth'.

At this point, the girl slid to the floor in a dead faint, which was theatrically satisfying until we found out it was caused by a dislocated elbow. Her partner in the exercise really *had* been hurting her.

The worst thing about Dermody was his capacity to scar young people for life, which didn't reside in sexual predation but in raucous, vicious public humiliation. We were mocked for being fat, for being ugly, for having no talent. Sometimes we were mocked in a way that made no particular sense but still humiliated us, as in the case of the unfortunate young actor who had to walk across the stage as a news-paper seller in a period play, calling out '*Freeman's Journal, Freeman's Journal.*' At the dress rehearsal, which was traditionally attended by nuns and priests who were not otherwise supposed to go to the theatre, Dermody erupted from the stalls, bellowing: 'Ah, Freeman'th Tethticleth!' The only straw the poor young actor could grasp at was the possibility that his tormenter's weird pronunciation might have meant that the religious present hadn't understood him. Of all the bright, talented and ambitious young actors who were members of that school at the time, only one ever walked out. Only one. She walked knowing what was ahead of her: work in a dry cleaners and a mother who was proud of her dignity but distraught over the end of her acting career.

We heaved a collective sigh of relief when someone else appeared to give a day's relief from Dermody. Some of the permanent and pensionable actors within the Abbey would turn up to give us their expertise. Bill Foley, a quiet man, taught us how to breathe and project, this being a time before actors wore microphones on stage and had to be heard, unaided, in the back row of the gods, the topmost cheap seats in old-fashioned four-level theatres like the Queen's. The challenge was complicated in the new Abbey, into which we had moved, by an architectural and aural oddity which meant that in some seats it seemed impossible to hear anything that was happening on the stage.

Bill Foley had a fifty-six-inch chest because he was so committed to his breathing exercises. We students passed this bit of information among ourselves with reverence, ignoring the fact that it distorted his physique and seemed to have done nothing to promote his career, which left him in the middle ranks as no more than a reliable supporting performer.

Geoffrey Golden, one of two brothers in the Rep (the other was the ambassadorially handsome Eddie), gave classes in make-up. He had, as part of his own development, been trained as a theatrical and film make-up artist, and his classes were a delight. Long before contouring was a twenty-first-century thing, Geoff Golden taught us contouring and I briefly convinced myself that by using pale greasepaint sticks on my forehead, down the middle of my nose and chin, then deploying much darker sticks at the side of my nose, face and under my chin, I would persuade audiences that I didn't have a big fat face. Geoff taught us how to prevent a shine developing and was ruthless with some of the guys whose hair was already beginning to recede. They had to deal with realities, he told them, and that meant powdering their scalp if they didn't want the stage lights to reflect off it and provide a deadly distraction. We spent whole days making ourselves up to look seventy when we were seventeen. We looked like kids in a school concert pretending to be grandmothers or grandfathers, but we learned how to simulate scars and mix colour to fabricate a black eye. By way of a freebie, Geoffrey showed us how to conceal an *actual* black eye, which, given the drinking habits and pugnacity of some of the students, was probably of more practical value.

Ray McAnally, the actor who starred as Christy Brown's father in *My Left Foot*, not infrequently turned up to give us training. McAnally was rare, not to say unique, among Irish actors of his time in his deep dive into the theory and technicalities of the trade, which led him to write a weekly column for one of the newspapers about diction and projection, of which I never understood a word. He was a big, handsome talker, and unusual among actors in not needing to be liked. He wanted to be listened to, but popularity wasn't an objective. It was McAnally who hammered home the need for actors to take care of their own accessories, rather than blindly trusting in the 'props man', as even women in charge of these tools were called at the time. One of the students asked him about his recent stint in England in 'the Scottish play'. We all self-consciously called *Macbeth* that, the way neophyte broadcasters call their headphones 'cans' to prove they belong to an elite. The most scary moment, he said, was when the button came off one actor's sword without him noticing, so that in the onstage swordplay, when he was supposed to give the impression that he was running his fellow actor through, in fact he wounded him, although not severely, and the play continued to its conclusion.

Improvisation was pretty improvisational in its early days. It did not have rules that would control the situation and allow student actors to develop the fluency of thought to get themselves out of a difficult situation on stage. Our tutors would set up a scenario. We would perform it. They would point out the essential issue we had missed and we would be breathless in awe at what was – in hindsight – little more than entrapment. But of course we learned key lessons in the process. Like when McAnally arrived one day into the rehearsal room, the very presence of him stilled the pre-lesson chat. Cue reconfiguration of entire room to face him as he outlined his first requirement, which did not involve the lads. Cue slightly resentful relaxation on the part of all the lads present. McAnally required only the girls to do an improvisation. No words. He just wanted each of us to act the part of a very beautiful woman. Got that? Nods all around. The rehearsal room came alive with noise and movement as students, led by the redundant boys, pulled their chairs to the walls, leaving the central space free for performance.

One by one, then, the girls shimmied across that central space. One girl slowly smoothed imaginary clingy satin over her hips and managed to look like a sex worker having a bad day. Another girl, who was genuinely beautiful, tossed back her hair and consulted a non-existent mirror. Between improvisations, I kept my head down, trying to postpone the awful moment when this fat freckled redhead would have to pretend knowledge of a condition – beauty – of which she had no experience. Eventually, however, no other girl was available, so I pranced to a forgotten couch and flounced onto it as if the other pieces of furniture weren't up to me at all. Then, as if I was doing an ad for tights, I examined my high heels, crossing and uncrossing my legs until I ended in the classic pose, all in the hope that my tolerably good legs would distract from the rest of me. When I had risen from the couch and returned, red-faced, to the group, the old man of the theatre let us all down gently.

'A very beautiful woman doesn't get out of bed in the morning and preen,' he told us. 'Her beauty isn't a surprise to her. It's a given. An *assumption.*' For most of us, it was the first time we encountered the notion of acting as an internal truth, rather than an outward-directed duplicity. Acting is not about conveying something false. It is about sharing fundamental truths with audiences so they understand the world in a different way, having been moved to tears or laughter as the truth is revealed. The better the actor, the less likely it is that you will notice their technique, because you will believe in the character they're playing.

That was one of McAnally's recurring themes. Later, when prompting a truly godawful Lady Gregory play entitled *Devorgilla*, about the treacherous Irishwoman who took up with Diarmuid, the traitor who brought the Normans to Ireland, I was sitting in the prompter's seat in the wings, script in front of me, illuminated by a small bright light, watching the lead actor, the wonderfully witty Joan O'Hara, as she knelt alone on stage in the last minutes of the show.

The dire consequences of her actions now clear to her, she mourned her life, a single spotlight revealing the tears rolling down her cheeks. I watched reverently, wondering if I would ever be able to cry on stage on demand. McAnally, coming into the wings beside me, leaned down, gently taking me by the shoulders and pointing me towards the audience.

'Are *they* crying?' he whispered.

I looked at them, shocked to observe that they were not. They were doing what I had been doing: marvelling at the technical skill of the actor. But it moved them not. McAnally's lesson was that when the audience is consciously admiring what you do on stage, it means that they do not care about the character you're playing. Their minds may be engaged, but their hearts are not. A subsidiary lesson was that the real deal is an actor who doesn't produce any tears themselves but leaves the audience red-eyed and sodden.

Most of the actors in the rep visited the rehearsal room at one time or another and got to know at least some of the wannabe actors. Some, like Deirdre Purcell and Maire O'Neill, went out of their way to be helpful. Only one never appeared, and when we began to go on stage as extras, he went out of his way to humiliate us. This was Donal McCann, arguably the greatest actor ever produced by this country. He once said, 'I don't belong anywhere where celebrity equals merit or money means talent or wealth proves achievement.' Which is a high-minded trope unrelated to the unremitting nastiness of his inter-action with human beings, alive and dead. Any mention of his father, John McCann, whose formulaic middle-class plays had contributed to keeping the Abbey financially afloat in earlier years, would provoke him to searing denigration. Donal McCann was the personification of the actor who is real only from the moment the curtain rises until its fringed edges whisperingly meet the stage floor at the end of a perfor-mance. On stage, a thrilling genius. Off stage, a man poisoned by his own venom.

The oldest performer who was taxied in to meet us was May Craig, then in her mid-seventies and so frail that it was difficult to imagine her performing before the cameras in *Girl with Green Eyes*, released just the year before. May Craig had toured the United States six times with the Abbey. She served as a reminder of the great days of the theatre's past. She didn't lecture us or get us to do exercises; she simply sat in an armchair and took whatever questions we put to her. We found ourselves in a collective hushed crouch as we tried to capture her answers. One of the students, pointing out that understudies were a relatively recent development in theatre, wondered what it had been like to act in an era when nobody could step into your role, word-perfect, at short notice. Had anything like this ever happened Miss Craig?

'My dear', she said slowly, 'I went on the night my husband died. I went on the night my baby died. And in both cases, the play was a comedy.'

7

AN EXPLOSIVE SUMMER JOB

*T*een Talk opened up all sorts of possibilities for me. One night, for example, I had a phone call from a woman who asked if I would care to be interviewed on a programme that ITV was making about southern Ireland. When I said yes, she explained that they had already made and broadcast a look at Northern Ireland and were now planning to do one south of the border, which would be shown on Telefís Éireann and ITV. The producer, John Hutchinson, had already gone around the streets of Belfast asking the people what they thought of southern Ireland, evoking an impression of the Republic as priest-ridden. The Irish language emerged as a major barrier to unifying North and South. So they did some street interviews south of the border before interviewing Dr Garret FitzGerald and me. The filming happened in a room in the Standard Hotel, Harcourt Street, where I met Garret for the first time and I was paid £2. Cash. The two issues were equally important to me at the time.

Then Bunny Carr landed the editorship of the junior pages of the *Evening Press*, Tony Butler having moved to the *Evening Herald*. Bunny asked me to write an opinion piece, which I did, with so much prompting and sub-editing from my mother that it took on a magisterial tone quite unlike me. It essentially condemned everything about the modern world and suggested that we all deserved the atomic bomb. When it was published, the results, according to my diary, were startling. 'Nuncio didn't speak to me for weeks, people looked at my parents pityingly, and a priest from St Paul's told Dad he should send me to Patrician meetings, that I might learn something about life.' I knew nothing of Patrician meetings. Nor do I to this day.

Then another phone call came, this time from *The Late Late Show*, which had regular panellists like Ulick O'Connor and Ted Bonner who could be relied on to speak and even be entertaining if a guest tanked. Few guests tanked when Gay Byrne was in charge of them, but having panellists around allowed wider play and gave viewers a chance to line up and hate or adore them. The caller was researcher Pan Collins, who wanted to know if I would like to be a panellist the following Saturday. I said I would and my mother brought me to Brown Thomas to invest in a spectacular dress, on the basis that a panellist on *The Late Late* was seen right down to their feet in some shots, which demanded attention to below the waist. Not that I had a waist.

When I arrived at Montrose, Pan, a tiny, tubby woman with a beautiful voice, who was the determinative researcher – always seeing around corners, always on the watch for good contributors, always possessed of a Plan B – led me to a dressing room with a star and my name on the door. She outlined the sequence of the programme, told me I would be called to make-up in due course, and disappeared. I sat there, dying to eat the triangular sandwiches on a doily on a plate, but controlled by knowing that the BT dress was tight enough as it was. Eventually, someone brought me to be made up, after which I was returned to the dressing room, on which, within seconds, came a crisp knock.

'Come in?'

Gay Byrne stepped inside and briskly told me that during the programme I needed to be a self-starter. I should not wait for him to call me in. Or postpone a comment. I was to say what I wanted to say when I wanted to say it. I nodded and off he went. No comforting noises about managing nerves. No flattery. Just a clear-eyed, cool statement of his expectations: perform, take the initiative, and we'll all be happy.

Three days later, he sent one of his classic notes – witty, short, handwritten sideways on a personal compliment slip. The sort of note you could not but keep, while you hoped for another appearance on the programme, if only to watch him warm up the audience, so that by the time the signature tune played, half of them adored him and the other half wanted to belt him. His mastery of a studio was unimaginably good. He would know that in row three to the left was a woman who, given a little nudge, would share some tragic secret, and that over to the right near the front was a man who knew nothing about anything but who, if he ever started to talk, would be impossible to reverse into silence.

Writing for newspapers and appearing on radio and TV fitted around school and the Abbey Theatre School of Acting, which gradually became what any close-knit bunch of teenage creatives becomes: a hotbed of illicit sex, tightly delineated conspiracies, friends and enemies. Best of the friends was a beautiful blonde who had worked for Joe Walsh Tours and knew Eugene Magee, a dear pal who was their courier in Rome. Hearing of her former job, one member of the group implied that charter flight holidays were not safe. Fionnuala Kenny told of months of fending off worried phone calls from prospective holiday-makers who had seen the Joe Walsh plane and didn't fancy the look of it. Every day, sometimes more than once a day, Fionnuala would listen to their worries and assure them that the jet was trustworthy. It was fortunately the last day of the holiday season when the jet arrived in Dublin, landed, and had a door fall onto the runway.

Fionnuala and I watched the others, shared secrets and warned each other about love affairs between Acting School members and powerful figures in the theatre. I wasn't good at spotting them and had a big mouth on me, so I needed these warnings to survive. It was Fionnuala who covered up for me when I commented, in a big group, about how the two youngest children birthed by a particular Abbey actress closely resembled an actor in the company. Fionnuala explained gently that I was not inaccurate in my observation but that everybody but me knew the reason was that the two younger children had been fathered by that actor, although the actress never left her husband.

Then came the girls who wanted to be friends with me because they knew I was no threat when it came to pulling lads. I had to work hard not to become that stereotypical fat friend in whom boys *and* girls confide their love for someone else and receive the wise counsel of the profoundly inexperienced. I watched Aideen O'Kelly, pushing forty but playing twenty, effortlessly entrance every male actor around. I watched Maire O'Neill make up her nacreous skin, looking into the lightbulb-framed mirror in a terrified daily search for wrinkles.

Deirdre Purcell, who went on to be a journalist and bestselling novelist, fascinated me because she analysed performances better than anybody else. I always thought she should have headed up the school. Most actors fail as directors and trainers because they want the actor to *do it this way*. They know how they would play the part and just want the actor who actually has to play the part to imitate them, which never works. Deirdre could take the helicopter view and if she made a comment to one of us, it was a comment designed to break us through to the naked simplicity of acting. She was also the first person I ever met who washed her hair every day. I copied her, despite my mother's view that if I tidied my bedroom and concentrated less on my hair, we'd all be safer and healthier.

After the Dermody episode my father was silent as far as the Abbey School of Acting was concerned, and I kept out of his way as much as I could. Hilary went through a phase when, according to my diary, she saw me as 'selfish, a dodger, a sneak, and an underhanded little bitch'. Since Hilary is notably generous towards other people and accurate to boot, I figure she had me nailed. It didn't mean that I liked being nailed, as my detailed diarised whines recall:

Yesterday, because I couldn't stop sucking in my lower lip to stop me from something worse, Mamma said I looked like a rat in a corner. I wouldn't mind but the fight happened where dishes were left unwashed. I shifted Hilary's newly washed slacks in order to wash the dishes and she thumped me. Once. Twice. Third time, I scooped up a handful of sudsy water and gave it to her right in the face. Told me to clean the floor. I refused, dried my hands and walked out into the hall and up the stairs. I was on the fourth step when she leaped at me and dragged me down and I fell into the hall. Then Dad, who had heard HER version gave out to me ... PS It blew over but I'm still scarred.

Hilary, despite the brief physicality of our relationship in my teens, did her level best to help me with maths, at which she was superb. Every 'tutorial' ended with Hilary red in the face, ready to hit me for what she perceived as obduracy but which was, in fact, cast-iron, certified stupidity.

Fortunately, my summer jobs didn't call for much mathematical ability. I got a Saturday and Sunday job as a hat-checker in Dublin airport, sitting in a cubbyhole with a book while visitors ate in the half-moon-shaped dining room in the first airport headquarters, overlooking the runways. I would take their coats and issue them with half a ticket, the other half of the ticket being carefully pinned to their garment. I quickly learned who would be a good tipper and who wouldn't, since the airport didn't pay anything for the service, although you did get to eat a free lunch with the rest of the catering staff. The waiters' gossip was wonderful. They knew which famous person was having lunch or dinner with their mistress in the airport because the celebrity could always claim, if spotted, that they were just coming off a flight when they encountered her and felt they had to buy her something to eat, she looked so hungry.

Because the airport had a permanent hat-checker for the weekdays, I couldn't extend my service in that direction. Then Dad said that if I wanted a job in the Dublin Gas Company I should come in the next day for an interview, having first filled this in, he added, setting a big brown envelope on the kitchen table. In it were three copies of a two-page, four-sided questionnaire, which I filled in. What age I was, where I went to school, any prizes I had won. That last required a bit of squeezing, because the art competitions, the Father Mathew Feis, Feis Ceoil and essay contests had all generated wins. I had almost finished when my mother insisted on a scrutiny. I waited, sure she would find a misspelling or some other minor error, but happy that she at least got to the fourth page before her breathing changed. It was when she breathed only through her nose you knew you were in trouble. In this instance, she breathed like a dragon in full flame, folded the form along its central pleat and tore it in half.

'Epilepsy?' she demanded, as if it was a sexually transmitted disease. '*Epilepsy?*'

The form asked for details of any diseases that ran in the applicant's family, and Dad had epilepsy. Ma then made a speech punctuated with closed eyes and deep breaths. The burden of her tune was that although epilepsy was a random condition and not your fault, it was not seen as random by certain people. Certain people saw it in a negative way and as a result would extrapolate that negativity to a general judgement of you and your family. I was guessing at the meaning of 'extrapolate', but was gamely hanging in. I was at liberty, she informed me, to tell anybody to whom it was relevant that asthma ran in my family, but *epilepsy?* Never. It was not that *we* were ashamed of it, she told me, tight-lipped; it was that ignorant people thought badly of those with epilepsy and made outrageous judgements as a result and it was foolhardy to invite those judgements by excessive openness. I pointed out that I hadn't claimed to suffer from it, just be mildly related to it and anyway my father had never, to my knowledge, had a fit, thanks to the little pink pills he took each morning.

All that was irrelevant. I was never to use that word again. If I ever had to refer to it, it was a seizure. I was to fill out another form, leaving out any reference to epilepsy.

But that, I timidly suggested, would make the completed form a lie. It had an italicised printed sentence up at the top that didn't quite enjoin you to tell the truth, the whole truth and nothing but the truth, so help you God, although it came close. My mother added a stricture: only in court with your hand on the Bible were you required to be so comprehensively truthful. A commercial firm had no right to inquire into your health when you were applying for an eight-week job, and I should learn a little discretion. I went fishing in the brown envelope for a second blank version of the form, reflecting on how well my father knew his wife and daughter. Bringing home three copies of the questionnaire ensured that misspellings, errors and unacceptable truths about inheritable diseases would be removed before the final fair copy was signed.

The next day I dressed neatly, stood for inspection and tweaking in the hall and set off with my father, who left me in the ground floor showroom of the Dublin Gas Company, which occupied the middle of D'Olier Street and had art deco lettering on the outside. Inside, white cookers occupied the ground floor, with a central staircase leading up to a U-shaped customer care area. For some reason, the doors inside the gas company were shaped like coffins. Everybody commented on it. Nobody could explain it.

In the showroom, I sat watching salesmen direct conditional enthusiasm at potential customers. Their enthusiasm started off in a pure form, but became conditional when logistical questions were asked. The cookers were wonders of engineering and design. The only issue was how soon the customer's chosen cooker would 'come in', how soon after that they could 'get it out to you', with the added wrinkle that the guy who delivered it – with some reluctance, it seemed – was not the guy who would join it up to the mains and get it working, and it might be a while before the latter – a fitter – became available. When asked to define 'a while', the salesman invariably suggested the customer should sit while he fetched his boss, who, when he arrived, would go through the same palaver as the salesman. If the customer turned crabby and told them she had wanted an electric cooker all the time, it was just that her mother said gas was so much better for baking, the manager would hang his head and shake it, as if he was at a funeral. I was riveted by this and would love to have continued to be the audience, but, as my diary recorded, it was time for me to defend my thesis: the non-epileptic form.

I was led through *miles* of offices to a little glass-walled room, shaped like a narrow triangle. There was just room for a cupboard, two chairs, a table and a man. The latter rose as I came in, and by dint of moving around the cupboard, managed to add me to the room. He was tall and thin and he had a little bald patch with dark brown hair growing quite thickly around it. He had a nice handshake. Anyway, he addressed me as Miss Prone, which I found hilarious, and asked me what 'grade' I was in at school. Well, I told him and he inquired if I had done my Inter. Then he asked me how I thought I had done in the Inter. I told him I preferred not to think of the Inter at all but that I thought I had passed at least. He laughed in a faintly lah-di-dah way, so I fell in love with him there and then. Honestly, he was adorable. He could look supercilious and shy at the same time.

I added that I would undoubtedly get a great mark in English, because I was up to here in Shakespearean sonnets. The manager, named Frank Maye, muttered that the school method of teaching Shakespeare would make anyone dislike the Bard. He then asked me what modern playwrights I liked, and I said Ibsen, O'Casey and Shaw. Turned out he was a big fan of Ibsen, so we happily wasted time comparing notes on the idiocy of the hero in *A Doll's House*. After this, he produced an intelligence test and said he'd be back soon.

When I was on the last question but one, he came back and away flowed my domination of the room. He told me I had the job without ever looking at the intelligence test, which proves it had been only a formality and why they had it at all, I failed to see. A three-year-old halfwit could pass it. He said I would start at nine the following morning, we shook hands and did the little kowtowing required, and I set off to tell Dad. He was very pleased, but rather startled by the suddenness of it.

'Where did Frank Maye say you'd be?'

'The printing room.'

'I'd better bring you to see Paddy Tighe, then.'

Paddy Tighe – my new, albeit, as it turned out, temporary boss – wasn't just a lovely man, but a super photographer who managed to run his own substantial photography business as a nixer while officially working for the Gas Company. He later did the photographs for my wedding. His underlings were trained to manage his frequent absences by claiming Paddy had 'just stepped out' and would be 'back in just a sec' and in the meantime, how could they help? Everybody shook their heads while slowly exhaling in reverence at the predictability of his effrontery and everybody went along with it because who was going to shop a sweetheart like Paddy Tighe?

Before I left that day, I was introduced to the time clock in the corridor and shown how to use it. Not that I stood a chance of ever being late. My father made punctuality such a fine art that my mother credited him with my sister's chronic lateness as an inevitable reaction. Thesis. Antithesis. Synthesis. In this case, Hilary was Antithesis, forever arriving a bit late. She was so notorious, it made her success in the Department of Education in her first job amazing. The *Irish Times* of 10 July 1964 had a photograph of Hilary beaming at Dr Hillery while extending a hand to switch on an ICT data processing unit. 'The tabulator, an ICT 915', read the report, 'is the most powerful in Ireland and has a dual feed to produce cheques and payroll simultaneously.' The caption described Hilary as 'a member of the planning team', although my memory is that the planning team was singular and she was it. She might not always have been on time, but she was invariably worth waiting for.

Because of my father's punctuality, and also because the CIÉ bus landed us close to the Abbey Theatre at just the right time to allow a brisk walk across to the other side of the Liffey, on my first day I arrived in the printing room, time-clock serviced, before anybody else. I wandered around, loving the smell of paper and ink, examining, at a careful distance, the various machines. The one most to be respected,

I had been told, was the guillotine, which allowed you to slice chunks of pages into smaller sizes, and which now operated only when the newly installed safety guard had been clicked into place. Before then, you could put one hand in to adjust the paper and accidentally engage the power button with the other hand, which had caused a young summer jobber the previous year to amputate his left hand. He was rushed to Jervis Street Hospital, holding the severed hand in the unsevered hand. The Gas Company employee who brought him to casualty stayed long enough to hear a registrar give out hell to him for not putting the loose hand in a plastic bag, which was (and I think still is) the standard advice if you happen to lop off a body part. According to legend, the young man's hand, surgically reapplied, 'took' reasonably well, although he never quite had the dexterity he'd had before his encounter with the printing room technology. Nobody, back then, thought of compensation or of suing the Gas Company for failure in their duty of care. Indeed, the feeling was that the owners had been generous in paying the young man's medical bills.

On that first morning, I had the red warning signs on the various machines more or less learned off by heart before the three women who worked in the printing room arrived, along with the boss, who set me a filing task and disappeared to take pictures at a wedding. None of the girls was particularly friendly to me, which surprised me a bit; I had been brought up to believe that you had to do something to someone for them to dislike you. Fortunately, the printing room was divided up like a library with floor-to-ceiling shelving units, and each of the three seemed to have an allocated corner which meant that none of them could see one another and I couldn't see anybody. It was purely by accident that, just before our much-yearned-for morning tea break, I happened upon the girl named Betty reading a book and when she made a frantic fumbling attempt to hide it, said 'Don't mind me. I'll warn you when anyone comes.' She promptly gave me to understand that we were friends to the grave. Betty also promised to lend me the book as soon as she had finished it, showing me the cover to make me appreciate the value of this offer. I didn't come upon the phrase 'bodice-ripper' until later, but the cover of *Angelique* would give a clue, with its heroine producing enough boob to threaten the structural integrity of the bodice of her tight-laced dress.

The Gas Company had its own subsidised canteen, which my father avoided by going home by bus every lunchtime. Because I was a temp, I had sixty minutes for lunch, as opposed to the ninety minutes he got, so it was the canteen for me. The first day there, when I'd selected what I wanted, which of course included chips, a woman with white hair parted in the middle and in a bun at the back came over to our table with a jug of mint sauce. She cocked her head.

'You're new, aren't you?'

Betty piped up: 'She's Mr Prone's daughter.'

'Mr *Prone's* daughter? No!' She stood well back. 'Did your father ever tell you about me? Lizzie.'

Fortunately, he had, so I said yes and she was pleased

If you ate quickly, the slot between one and two was a wonderland of opportunity. At lunchtime Betty always went to the Amusements on the Quays, which was a riot of light bulbs and noisy machines, because, she said, Italians worked there. I went to Eason's second-hand section, and to Greene's, Hanna's and Webb's. Then I hit on the Banba bookshop in Tara Street, which dealt exclusively in second-hand paperbacks and for me served as a library with benefits: I would buy five books at a time for five pence each, read them within a couple of days, find shelf-space for perhaps two (some of which I still have) and bring the other three back to earn a discount on my next purchases. The women running the shop would beam when they saw me arriving and would produce from under the counter a couple of titles they figured I would like, because someone they noticed had similar tastes to me had liked them. They introduced me to a rake of writers I might never otherwise have read.

Tea breaks in the Gas Company were often taken in the 'girls' room', a kind of anteroom attached to the ladies' toilets. It had a few chairs and was cosier than the canteen, so many of the female employees tended to grab their tea or coffee and biscuits and retreat there. One day, having used the loo, I was coming through that outer room when the coffin-shaped door to the corridor outside burst open and a woman I had never seen before rushed in, banged it behind her, and stood with her back to it, shaking and swearing.

'That *bastard* Prone,' she hissed, straight into my face, because I happened to be directly in front of her. 'I mean, that total *bastard*.'

I stood silently while she favoured me and everybody in the room with an account of something my father had said at the end of some argument she had been having with him. Most people in the room, with the exception of this woman, knew me to be Brendan Prone's daughter, which froze them into silence and allowed her to repeat, with added emphasis, the essentials of her tale of outrage.

'He'll be extra nice to you tomorrow, though,' I told her. 'He always is.'

'How would *you* know?' she snarled.

Everybody in the room told her why I would know, and I did a palms-in-the-air gesture indicative of being related to him but not responsible for him, at which point she burst into tears and pleaded with me not to tell him anything of what she had said. Betty unexpectedly intervened to assure her that I never would; I wasn't that sort. (This was presumably extrapolated from us collaborating to conceal *Angelique* from the Gas Company management.) I nodded confirmation of my *omertà* skill and fled back down to the printing room.

My father never asked me about the goings-on in my summer job circle. As long as I didn't do something that disgraced him, he was happy to sit at his massive desk, working away with his impeccably neat script, a cigarette always on the go. Indeed, I got the impression that, as long as what I did qualified as revolutionary in some small way, he could have lived with being disgraced. Or at least more disliked. Somewhere in a working past before my arrival on the scene, he had made the decision to live with being disliked. Unpopularity was for him a validation. Other people measure themselves by the number of their friends. My father measured himself by the number of enemies he accrued, each of them, in his view, representing the fallen in a principled fight on his part against the unprincipled and venal. The best of his friendships majored on correspondence because the other party lived outside Ireland. So when Gerry Marrinan was sent by the Columban Fathers to serve in Korea, their friendship was sustained by hundreds of letters carefully crafted on airmail paper or in air letters, the careful crafting necessitated by the cost of overseas postage.

Dad's close friends tended to become my mother's, too. Like Father Gerry. And like Lily Keane, the nurse who was in charge of my father during his lengthy hospital stay as a result of breaking his leg for the second time in a rugby match. Broken legs, back then, were managed by something called 'traction', which entailed the broken limb being elevated and stretched using a weight and pulley system. This was supposed to ensure that the bone knitted correctly and that the limb was the same length after the months of traction as it had been before, although in my father's case this didn't work out – perhaps because it was a second break — and he was left with a limp, later mimicked with much affection by his adoring grandson Anton.

Bed-bound by the collapse of a scrum, my father was at his rattiest, and Lily Keane, the tiny-waisted wisp of a nurse taking care of him, might have been as intimidated by him as the Gas Company women who worked with him, were it not for the fact that nobody ever intimidated Lily Keane. She could pretend to be intimidated, if pretence were required, and so if a Jervis Street nun materialised and, running an accusatory index finger over a ward surface, found even a smidgen of dust, Lily could put in a creditable performance of personal regret, quickly followed, as the nun left the ward, by a tongue stuck out and thumbs inserted in ears to allow waving of fingers at the departing religious back view. The first time my father witnessed this, he was so surprised, he almost gave the game away by laughing out loud. From then on, he adored this lippy little west of Ireland woman, and for the most part would obey her instructions. Lily had a reputation as being a great bit of gas at a party. At the time, nurses and Guards held the franchise on throwing great parties. But Lily – even among nurses – was the outstanding example of the party-thrower. She was regarded as a girl who could party for Ireland. Despite being not much over five feet, she had the stamina of a yak, demonstrated one particular weekend when the craic was not just mighty but continuous. (My father, although he was out of hospital by this time, did not attend, him being a married teetotaller.)

On the Monday following the party, Lily Keane didn't go to work. Not because she was hungover, but because she was entering a religious order. Gobsmacked, her friends were, although they figured that Lily was never going to stick all that shave-your-head-and-bow-to-Reverend-Mother stuff. She wasn't the type. Sooner or later, she'd be over the wall. When she was professed, becoming a fully fledged nun, the grudging admiration was matched by a dread that Lily, now Sister Joseph Pius, would be wasted making tea for visiting bishops. Her Reverend Mother obviously thought the same, because she exported her to Africa where the Irish Sisters of Charity dispensed with the heavy black floor-length gown and the veil they wore at home, replacing them with a white floor-length gown and veil to deflect the tropical sun. Every now and then, pictures of Lily would arrive in our house, the mad merry eyes squinting against the brightness outside the hospital where she worked.

On one occasion, in a funny letter to my father, she announced that she had just been told she was to set up a new hospital in a particular location. Starting with finding the money. Then finding a site. Then negotiating with the government of the host country, which required the use of infinitely creative methods of facing down the standard requests for bribes. Then the little nursing sister from the west of Ireland had to find ways to truck supplies and artisans through rainforest, monsoons and tribal warfare. The mission was simple in its declared imperative: get the thing built. Hers was the responsibility to find out how to project manage a vastly complex enterprise and, when it was physically complete, to train nursing and other staff to the highest international standards. And then? In obedience to her holy superior, off to a new African country and a new hospital to be built and commissioned.

When Lily came back to Ireland for good, she should have retired, since Africa had been tough and she was now in her sixties. But her congregation was running out of nuns, so it was all hands to the pump. In her case, that meant running a hospital, which she did; and then, at an age when 99 per cent of the workforce would have retired, running a hospice in Cork.

At another time, women like Lily Keane would have been celebrated as definitive mná na hÉireann. They would have been on the covers of business magazines for the return – moral and monetary – they got out of investment, their faces as familiar as the faces of chairpeople and chief executives of today like Rose Hynes and Francesca McDonagh. But the ground-breaking work of Sister Joseph Pius and her colleagues happened when there wasn't much media interest and when women were supposed to be subservient, particularly if they were in a religious order. They went largely unappreciated and unadmired, except for faithful correspondents like my father.

The good and bad thing about families is that your own is your only model, so you work your way around any problems you encounter without precedents or rules. My father had ideas he believed in, and if you failed to uphold his beliefs or standards, you got the long and the short of it, particularly if you worked with him. He refused to be promoted into management in the Dublin Gas Company because it would have required giving up membership of the trade union, to which he was so passionately devoted that he brought me to a meeting of the union in the first week of my summer job. Long, tedious minute-reading was followed by ritual discussions of abstruse points with occasional irrelevant outbreaks. One old man close to where I was sitting would sporadically yell 'Wha' abou' our fopence?' On the way home, I asked my father what this meant and he said it was about a fourpenny concession agreed in 1934. I asked him why the old man was still barking about it and he started to explain and then abandoned it. It seemed that trade union meetings were like choral masses: of no great interest except to the deeply converted, of no immediate value to anybody, but affording those who needed to an opportunity to exercise a liturgy that made them feel better about their lousy position in the world.

Whenever I got bored in the printing room, which was often, I would sing. I was in full Julie Andrews mode on 'Show Me' from *My Fair Lady* when I realised a senior executive had been standing at the counter for some time. He had that louche, thrown-together look only highly educated, self-assured men have. He asked me about music and if I had heard Nicolai Gedda and I said no. I must, he said. Swedish tenor. Then he asked for his order, I found it, and off he went. A couple of days later, when I came home late from the Abbey, I found two LPs on the kitchen table with a pencilled note from my father to say the Gas Company manager had asked him to give them to me. When I tried them on the record player, my mother stood still in the hall as the first notes issued. 'The duet from *The Pearl Fishers*,' (sung with Robert Merrill) she said reverently. The two of us fell in love with Gedda and Hilary taped favourite tracks before I returned the records to the manager, who told me I could have kept them but thanked me for returning them. 'I hear you're moving,' he said, sliding the LPs down beside the leg of his desk.

'Moving where?'

'To the complaints department,' he said. 'Won't be much singing there.'

He was right. It was called the complaints department, rather than the customer service department, because the Dublin Gas Company created its own constant and sizeable supply of complaints by providing the most appalling service possible. No company until perhaps Ryanair was ever so hated by its customers, and at least Ryanair is cheap. The Dublin Gas Company's complaints department was a series of long desks fitted out with phones and headsets. Roughly the equivalent of a call centre today, with a similar staff turnover, mainly because young women, back then, worked until they married, and the complaints department was evenly split between girls flashing an engagement ring and counting down the days to their escape, and older women with the middle distance stare of lifers. Phyllis, one of the lifers, explained to me that first thing every morning I would clamp on a headset so the microphone was in front of my mouth, and the minute nine o'clock struck, I would press one of the lighted buttons in front of me and say 'Good morning, this is the Dublin Gas Company.' Then the customers would tell me their complaint and I would tell them we would do our best to fix it. If they weren't satisfied with me, I could ask them if they would like to talk to my supervisor and put them through to Phyllis. She showed me how the transfer system worked.

'What will *you* tell them?' I asked, figuring that if she had some secret code, I might as well use it to save her and the customer time.

'I'll tell them what you told them,' she said. 'You are expected to deal with at least ninety calls a day,' she added. 'So don't let them run on. Oh, and don't give them your name. Never, ever give them your name.'

I took that under advisement and sat down at my phone the following morning at 8.50. Because the panel of lights was already blinking, I put on the headset and was about to hit the first button when one of the engaged girls made a wild flailing gesture at me.

'We start at nine. Not one minute before.'

I waited until the big clunking clock on the back wall signalled nine o'clock, then hit that first button. Then I entered the fifth circle of hysteria hell. All the callers were furious. Some were desperate. Many cried. Several screamed. Every second one threatened to report me to the general manager if I cut them off like I had done the last time. Clearly, I was doing something wrong, because when I looked around me at the more than a dozen women working the phones, none of them seemed to have anything like the problems my customers had. Several of them were smoking, which I thought extremely cool, with Phyllis lighting one cigarette from the end of another. A couple of them smiled, rolled their eyes or winked at me, gesturing at the headset with a you-know-yourself complicity. I couldn't overhear any of them referring a caller to their supervisor, so I didn't, even when the level of customer desperation went well beyond my capacity to assuage. At tea break, one of the engaged girls asked me how I was doing.

'How do you *think* she's doing?' another muttered.

'She hasn't cried yet,' the first pointed out.

'Why would I cry?'

'Well, being called a Protestant wanker isn't exactly a great start to your day,' the first said.

'I'm not a Protestant.'

'The company is.'

'What's a wanker?' I asked, thoroughly confused, having been called nothing but Darling and Miss so far that morning.

'Ask your father,' one of the girls suggested.

The girl was immediately set upon by the other girls, who accused her of endangering me because of my innocence. Jesus, God, you didn't ask Mr Prone something like that. You'd never survive, even if you were his daughter. He was so religious, even when he'd be bawling you out, he wouldn't use the F word. I went back to my headset even more confused, because I couldn't see what using the F word had to do with being religious and I still didn't know what a wanker was. I hit the first flashing light and the woman who came on demanded to know if I was doing this deliberately to her. I suggested she take me through the problem and she burst into tears. I waited. She had five children, she told me, and her husband worked hard and they all needed to be *fed*. Was that too much to ask?

'Definitely not,' I said decidedly, and a couple of my colleagues looked at me, assuming this was the beginning of a fight.

'Well, eighteen months ago, the handle broke off my oven door,' she said. '*Eighteen months ago.*'

I wrote this down in capital letters as she recounted how she had telephoned the Gas Company and it had taken three months for them to get the handle to her. But the guy who delivered the handle said he had nothing to do with fitting it and after he was gone she had to ring the company to set up an appointment with a fitter, but a fitter didn't become available for another four months and when he arrived, did I know what he said? He said, she sobbed, that it was the wrong handle for that model of cooker and there was nothing he could do about it.

'Dear God', I said, 'that must have been awful. What did you do?'

Weeping hopelessly, she told me about ringing the Gas Company, going so far as to offer to bring the wrong handle into D'Olier Street on the bus herself, having her offer refused, and having to wait for a week for the wrong one to be picked up and another five weeks for the right one to be delivered. All the time, she had kept the door of the oven closed by blocking it with a kitchen chair. Without a handle, she ended up burning herself on the door whenever she had to open it, and was terrified that one of her children would 'burn the hand off themselves'. She added that her husband wanted to fit the handle himself – when the allegedly correct one arrived – but she was afraid that if he did, that would break the law. The two of us discussed this for a while and since she confessed that her husband wasn't actually the handiest, agreed that maybe it would be better if he didn't try DIY on the oven door. Then she thanked me warmly for listening to her and asked my name. I gave it to her, and even with the headset on, could hear the shocked indrawn breath of a whole line of colleagues beside me.

At lunchtime, in the canteen, my mortal sin became a social event. Strangers came to hear the story of me giving out my name. I had been warned, the newcomers were told. I asked why the fitters didn't bring the handles with them and do the two jobs at once. The man who had lent me the Nicolai Gedda records, who had been leaning up against one of the pillars that punctuated the canteen, shook his head, laughing.

'Never question the system,' he told me, over the heads of the seated eaters. 'First rule of survival. Never question the system.'

He wandered away, watched by the complaints girls.

'And don't be letting that randy old bastard near you, either,' muttered one of the older women.

'What's randy?' I asked my sister that night as she washed the dishes and I dried.

'Jesus, would you keep your voice down?' was the reply, as she turfed out the dirty water and glanced at our parents in the kitchen to see if they had heard me.

'Is it good or bad?'

'Depends,' she said and went off into the hall to answer a phone call.

That first week in Complaints, I realised that what customers actually needed from the women answering the phones were two things: advocacy and listening. Advocacy had to be done sparingly, with a quiet word to one of the guys who scheduled fitter visits and a description of how nice the caller was. It had to be done sparingly because if you went too often to the same scheduler he'd get fed up with you, and if you were too successful the other girls would be irritated. What the callers needed more than anything else was to be listened to. Listening I could do in spades. I could react sympathetically without selling the company down the river, though if ever a company needed selling down the river, it was the Dublin Gas Company.

'You're not *serious?*' I would put in at the end of a narrative of outrage, although a quiet sympathetic moan or 'go on?' were just as good. I was the equivalent of the doctors then heedlessly prescribing Valium and Librium to ill, abused and desperate housewives: Mother's Little Helper. I could at best marginally improve the realities of the situation inflicted on these women by the Dublin Gas Company, but I found that if I listened hard enough, and made sure they knew, before the end of the call, that I had registered the details of their misery, they went away one notch better on the scale of upset. Just being allowed to tell their story, uninterrupted, from start to finish, to someone who understood their deprivation, seemed to help. Giving them my name became my habit. Because I never promised anything, the customer could never accuse me of failing them, and because I had been reasonably civil to them, they decided I was their friend. Every now and again, I would be told that a customer was looking for me by name, and when I picked up, the customer would tell me that the fitter had just left and the cooker was working perfectly and they were so grateful to me. The customers whose problems had been solved just knew in their hearts that I had done it for them – sure hadn't I even given them my name?

Making nice to desperate people could go only so far, however, and Friday mornings inevitably stretched it. Friday morning was when a

hairdresser found that none of her geysers was working, so she had no
hot water to wash her customers' hair in preparation for that night's
'hop'. Even worse was the Friday morning when the first six customers
were all soaped up before the water went cold. That was when the
screaming began.

The only thing that generated actual corrective action within the
company, and speedily at that, was a leak or an explosion. For either
of those, we had a red form and instructions to bring it immediately
to a particular manager, pausing only to instruct the customer not to
go searching for the gassy smell with a lit match and to turn off the
gas at the mains. I was guiltily thrilled when one Monday morning call
required me to reach for a red emergency form. The woman on the
other end of the phone told me that a smell of gas was everywhere in
the neighbourhood. I wrote down 'All pervasive' for which I later got
hell, but it seemed a useful shorthand at the time. How long had the
smell been present, I asked.

'Since the 'splosion,' I was told.

'Sorry? Explosion? Wh–?'

'Friday night was the 'splosion. In number twenty-eight. Around
tea-time, it was.'

'Did it do any damage?'

'Blew the roof off and broke two of the woman's legs.'

I was distracted for a minute by the phraseology, which suggested
this unfortunate woman had more than two legs, but my reporter had
moved on and was explaining that the bang hadn't blown the main
roof off the house, just the flat roof off the kitchen extension. The
woman with the broken legs was in hospital and the issue now was
the smell of gas, which must have been compelling, since the cooker
had blown up late on Friday and gas had been flowing freely into the
neighbourhood since then. Neighbours had rung for an ambulance,
but it didn't seem to have struck any of them that ringing the Guards
or the Dublin Gas Company might be an idea. At this stage, I had
developed quite an audience in the complaints department and one of
the girls went to get an expert, who stood over me and read the red

form, visibly paling as he did so. He started to write questions down for me to ask the woman, who was beginning to tire of the exercise, so as soon as I had the information he needed, I gestured for him to pay attention to what I was going to say to her.

'Look, Mrs –', I began, flailing for him to give me back the red form with her name on it. 'You're actually in a dangerous situation. Don't light a match. Don't turn on your cooker. Don't even switch on a light. Go out and ask your neighbours not to smoke or cook or anything until the Gas Company gets there. They'll be with you very soon.'

At that, the expert left at a run, and the rest of us took a tea break, a little early, in the canteen, where we knew we had a bigger audience. Soon, historic famous accidents were being recounted, most of them resulting in scorched eyebrows and shock rather than death.

'Tell her about the suicide man,' someone said, and Phyllis, who had caught that particular call, told of a man who had organised his own suicide right down to the note and the towels rolled and pushed against the doors. The complicating factor was that the gas nauseated him and caused him to throw up before he had fully lost consciousness, and having to clean himself up had apparently made him think twice about what he was doing. He tore up the note he had left for his mother, not knowing that, bothered by his depression during recent visits, she had decided to drop in on him and arrived at just that moment. She pressed the doorbell, which created a spark, which generated an explosion, which killed the man and gravely injured his unfortunate mother. The woman next door had rung the Gas Company. 'It's always the women who make those phone calls,' Phyllis said.

I never found out how quickly the woman in my explosion got out of hospital. That was the curse and blessing of working in the complaints department of the Gas Company. You encountered people in their moment of greatest distress or agony, failed to solve their problem despite your best efforts, and rarely if ever found out what happened afterwards. The only assumption we all made was that it was great marketing for the ESB.

By the end of the summer, I had enough money to go on a high-tech typing course. The 'high-tech' part was a motorised voice demanding that you press a particular letter on a typewriter with blanked-out keys, with smaller and smaller intervals between the barked instructions. Inevitably, all twenty-eight of the participants were women. Just as inevitably, the barking voice was male. It didn't matter. At the end of the course, which took place somewhere in Aungier Street, I could touch-type. I was never going to do it speedily enough to get a job in a typing pool, but then a typing pool was up there with a pea-canning factory as a career to be avoided. Learning to type meant that I could be telephoned at home by an editor, produce clean copy and get on a bus within an hour to deliver it to the newspaper offices, where a typesetter would turn it into printable strips of words. Perhaps five hours from the start of the process to the end. The same task I now do in half an hour without leaving my home.

8

Interviewing a Seal

$\mathcal{N}$iall Buggy was such a great mimic, it had to be him who had rung that afternoon, putting on a whispery Cork accent and claiming to be Donncha Ó Dúlaing, head of Features and Current Affairs in RTÉ Radio. It was a riotous mimicry, so I delivered the required laughter and invited him to tell me the real reason he had called. Irritatingly, he continued to pretend to be the Cork man, even when I told him I knew who he was. Eventually, and still in role, he sighed and asked me if I had a pen and paper. Of course I had. Every hall in every decent home at the time had a telephone table with a velvet-cushioned seat, a place to store the telephone book and the Golden Pages, and a top section where the ultra-modern cream phone sat, together with a pad and tethered pencil for the taking of notes.

'Take down this number,' the caller said. 'It's the main RTÉ number in Henry Street. If you ask at the switch for Donncha Ó Dúlaing, they'll put you through to me.'

I backed down and apologised without telling him why I had got it so wrong. He wanted to meet me to discuss my presenting a new radio programme, since radio was about to go around the clock. Could we meet for lunch in the restaurant above the Metropole in O'Connell Street the following day at 12.45? Of course we could, I replied, as if I was accustomed to invitations to lunch, although this was my first ever. He would be accompanied by the producer, he said. I said I looked forward to meeting the two of them and tottered into the sitting room, where my mother was collating her market research reports, and asked her what 'going around the clock' meant for radio.

'You know how Radio Éireann closes down for a few hours in the morning and afternoon? The paper says that's going to stop and that programmes will be broadcast all the time, as happens with the BBC.'

'And Radio Luxembourg,' added my sister, earning herself a filthy look from Mamma, who disapproved of pirate radio stations, although it was less of an irritant now that Hilary had a good job and a social life to match and wasn't constantly imposing Gerry and the Pacemakers and Dave Dee, Dozy, Beaky, Mick and Tich on the rest of us from her bedroom.

Hair freshly washed, make-up carefully applied, wearing new kitten-heeled shoes branded 'The Young Idea', I was dropped off at the Metropole on the button of the appointed time and told by my mother not to go upstairs too quickly because it would look gauche if I arrived first. From the door of the restaurant, the maître d' pointed to two men with their backs to me and I took a chair on the opposite side of the table. Donncha Ó Dúlaing seemed delighted with everything. The producer, Howard Kinlay, did not. He looked furiously at me from under a shelf of blond hair and growled a greeting. The waiter hovered and we ordered. Now, here's the thing. I can remember what I ate and what shoes I wore at every important event in my life. I have to look up the serious stuff, but you can't fault me on food and feet. In this instance, I had Chicken Maryland and was completely distracted to find two slices of pineapple with the chicken breast. It was like finding a prima ballerina in a mud-wrestling contest. It tasted so wonderful that I had to force myself to concentrate on what Donncha Ó Dúlaing was saying, which was that a new programme for teenagers was planned to start simultaneously with round-the-clock radio. It would go on the air every Thursday at 4.30 in the afternoon. Howard would produce and I would present. Maybe, I thought, my being imposed on him without choice was what had Howard Kinlay raging. However, I did nothing but nod, ask questions and listen. After a while, Donncha went off to the Gents and, as the waiter cleared the table and asked us for our dessert choices (banana fritters for both of us), the producer looked across the table, smiled and said, 'That was pretty fucking impressive.'

I was stuck to the chair. I hadn't heard the F word often, but when it happened, it tended to coincide with rage. In this instance, it seemed to be expressive of good humour. I also wondered if his voice was permanently that hoarse. (It was.)

'What was?'

'You interviewing our new boss. Even got the budget out of him. Shhh.'

Donncha, rejoining us, said the new programme would be called *The Young Idea*. The coincidence with my black patent leather shoes was so astonishing, I was tempted to tell the two of them, but Donncha was now explaining why Howard was the perfect choice as producer. He was new to RTÉ, but – Ó Dúlaing suggested – must be well known to me. I apologised for not knowing who he was and Kinlay shook his head violently. Apparently he was a radical student leader in university. I had no idea what 'radical' meant, but widened my eyes at Howard to indicate how impressed I might be if I *did* know. He was also a folk singer, Ó Dúlaing went on. I must have seen him on TV with his guitar and his girlfriend? I explained that my parents had banned TV from our house until the previous month, and even still regarded it as the spawn of Satan, at which Howard became interested and asked what religion I was. He seemed slightly disappointed when I said I was Catholic.

'Why? What religion are you?' I asked. 'And what's it to do with television?'

He was an atheist, he told me. Ó Dúlaing winced. But, Howard went on, he had been brought up in the Plymouth Brethren. He started to explain, using words like 'low Church' and 'nonconformist'. Donncha concentrated on getting and paying the bill. I concentrated on the banana fritters, never having had one before. I got the impression that the Plymouth Brethren were extremely Protestant and had no priests. They also seemed to disapprove of frivolity, and TV counted as frivolity. I considered my father might have missed his vocation and that he probably should have been a Plymouth Brother because TV was redeemed for him only by a series called *The World at War*. The only TV I really liked was *Telefís Feirme*, presented by Justin Keating, who did the most phenomenal job of explaining things like how to help a cow deliver a calf, using graphics of such childlike simplicity that to this day I nurture the notion that I could, if called upon, midwife an expectant bovine.

Donncha headed back to Henry Street, having ordered coffee for Howard and me so that, he said, we could have our production meeting. Another first for me: an actual meeting. I took out the notebook and pen I had brought with me and sat poised for the producer to produce. He looked across the table at me in a threatening silence and then roared laughing, gesturing at my pen and pad.

'You think *I* know how to do this!'

'You're the producer. Mr Ó Dúlaing said they trained you.'

The only thing he remembered from the training, he told me, was that if anything went wrong during a programme, the producer had to write an immediate report – called a discrepancy report – and send it up the line. Oh, and that it was always useful to have something on tape in cased a contributor didn't turn up for a live broadcast. I knew that only death would prevent me from turning up, but made a note of the need for a pre-recorded item. He added that I might as well come up with the ideas because Henry Street was scared stiff of him because they thought he was a revolutionary. Was he? I asked. He shrugged and said more an anarchist. This was the story of my life: people explaining things in a way that left me confused at a higher level. I asked him if he was radical and he said anybody with a conscience and a brain had to be, but the point is what items were we going to cover? What would people of my age like to hear? People my age, he shrugged, were cool and groovy. People his age had already been subsumed into the establishment. I didn't tell him I was the least cool and groovy person he'd ever met, but I did announce that I knew nothing about sport and didn't plan to learn. That might be a problem, he said, because he knew nothing about sport, either, but we could address that later. What *did* I know about? I listed them off: school, competitions, theatre, radio, singing, books, knitting, horses (I knew all about horses in theory, had a library about them and went to the Horse Show every year to watch President de Valera fumbling his short-sighted way around horses' heads to present the Aga Khan trophy, but I had never actually been close to a real horse), art competitions, poetry. He looked more depressed than ever. Then I had an inspiration. I started to make a list, directly cribbed from my memory of the Contents page in Hilary's *Girl* annual. The list went like this:

Pets

Poetry competition

Famous people

Books

Hobbies

Places to visit.

I suggested that if we had one item per slot per week, of roughly five minutes each, that would fill a thirty-minute programme. Howard immediately clicked with this and suggested other categories. Some would happen each week, some only once a fortnight. Agreed? Agreed. Plus, he pointed out, beginning to create a grid, we had music at the top and bottom and announcements about the people like the sound engineers, and that would take at least two minutes, so we really had to fill only 28 minutes. We began to put the names of people we knew into the blank spaces and by the time the waiters began to hover, devoutly wishing us elsewhere, we had outlined and peopled four programmes.

'Those are great ideas,' Howard said, as we went down the stairs to O'Connell Street. 'How did you come up with them?'

I stole them, I told him, explaining about the *Girl* annual.

'Nah,' he said, with the simple certitude people bring to not believing truths they don't want to.

The next time I was in the Abbey, I asked all the students for ideas and indicated that I would want to exploit them as guests. Only one – Fionnuala Kenny – came up with ideas. All the others either wanted to insert drama or pop music. I was apologetic about asking them to appear on the programme because the budget allowed for only derisory guest fees, but most of them would have taken my arm off to do it, with or without a fee. It was the first time I had encountered the ferocious lure of the open mic. Most of the actors and actors-in-training I invited appeared only once. Howard and I learned quickly that the wonderful lines actors get to articulate on stage and screen create an aura of intelligent thoughtfulness around them which is mostly false. The best actors are pure conduits.

In the middle of our preparations, I was invited to a reception in RTÉ Donnybrook to announce round-the-clock radio. I wore the Young Idea shoes and my first cocktail dress, a gorgeous A-line streaming from a round sequined collar. Also at that reception was Bunny Carr, surrounded by a circle of admirers, creating laughter. When we briefly found ourselves in a twosome with a waiter offering flutes of champagne, each of us took one.

'You know', Bunny said with his characteristic gurgle of laughter, 'you're planning to work in the two trades – journalism and broadcasting – where you can be an alcoholic for free.'

I put the glass back on the tray, untouched. Even the most minuscule self-awareness suggested that if I could get addicted to relatively benign things like books and food, my chances of *not* becoming addicted to alcohol were non-existent, especially if it was free and frequent.

Howard and I got ready for our first programme, filled with the confidence of our ignorance. We did enough advance studio work for me to establish that being too close to the microphone shared my every wheeze with the listeners. Other than that, we were on our own. Or rather, as Bunny had said at the champagne reception, *I* was on my own.

'Doesn't matter what the programme is called', he said, 'it's heard by listeners as the Bunny Carr programme or the Gay Byrne programme or the Terry Prone programme. The producers and directors matter, but not to the listeners. It's *you* who gets blamed if anything goes wrong.'

He also talked to me about interviewing. Questions needed to be short and open. 'How do you react to that?' rather than 'Do you feel that you shouldn't have said what you said on that particular occasion, given the consequences that ensued for everybody involved and the damage done to the reputation of yourself and everybody else?' Questions had to emerge from what the person in front of you was saying, not from a list prepared in advance. But what, I asked, if the interviewer got a blank?

'You simply say "Go on", and they always do.'

Bunny observed and coached. Gay Byrne performed. Everybody in RTÉ, even back then, talked of Gay Byrne as the legendary crisis manager when things went wrong, and credited it to his appreciation – his deliberately learned, hard-won appreciation – of the role of every member of the crew. He knew everybody by name and skill and treated crew on the floor with a respect he could never muster for the suits in management, even though he was frightened by the power those managers had. His theory was that if airline pilots can sound cool and unworried while in the middle of a flight crisis, knowing that they and others might die if they don't get it right, a broadcaster can certainly do it. I began to read everything I could get my hands on about air crashes and the black box, and found out that the final words of the pilot in almost all fatal crashes are the same: 'Oh, shit.' Or 'Oh, fuck.' That's what they say when, having gone through all the procedures and protocols, they find themselves facing the mountain and destruction. Up to then, anything they say to the passengers is calm, almost bored. Good broadcasters have to do the same. One of television's newsreaders, Jim Sherwin, who was also a continuity announcer linking the last programme to the next, had distinguished himself when he announced a programme and nothing happened, other than the Bakelite phone on his desk ringing. He lifted it, listened silently and put down the receiver, assuring viewers that normal service would resume in a few minutes. For the next eleven minutes, with a silent phone and a copy of the *RTÉ Guide*, he talked in a casually unhurried way about upcoming programmes, including a thoughtful critique of the movie *The Diary of Anne Frank*. Then the phone rang, he listened, turned to the camera and led into the next show as if nothing had happened.

Research and rehearsal for the new round-the-clock radio shows went on against a backdrop of publicity. For the first time, I became the subject of media interviews, along with the other newcomers. Pat Ingoldsby came to talk to me directly after interviewing the slightly older and infinitely better-educated Pat Kenny, who was also a studio newcomer. I said whatever I thought wouldn't get me fired, and the result was a flowing feature with shots of me and Pat Kenny, and a date with the writer. Another interviewer duly reported me to be dating a 'dashing' journalist, although that may be the only time the sweet-natured and gentle Ingoldsby, a vox pop genius and poet, was so described.

The Young Idea went on the air among a flurry of new programmes, including a magazine in the morning presented by Freda McGough. Up to that point, radio had been so sporadic, with so few broadcasters involved, it had, as far as newspapers were concerned, been little more than an extension of the civil service. Now, however, newspapers reacted to the new schedule by installing radio critics and every broadcaster lived in dread of what they might say. Howard and I were relieved to find what I knew to be my incoherence interpreted by the new critics as charming enthusiasm. The *Irish Times*'s Mary Leland, on more than one occasion, praised me for breathlessness.

We also learned that we had to fend off the helpful. Although everybody in Henry Street knew somebody they felt would be perfect on the show, in the main, the people they wanted to offer were adults, whereas we were on the hunt for young people. We stole – or perhaps borrowed – anybody I knew and liked from *Teen Talk*. But then a critical mass began to develop. Teenagers started to send us poems and scripts and when we went looking for prizes from potential sponsors, they would listen and come back saying, yes, they would give us a book or a gift token. And invariably suggest their son or daughter as a contributor. We tried everybody, with varying degrees of success. The lesson from *Teen Talk*, warmly hammered home by Bunny Carr and Denis O'Grady, applied every time: the world is full of nice, polite people and if you want to make great radio, you need to avoid them.

Howard and I learned to use a Uher, which we were repeatedly reminded cost more than a car. It was a reel-to-reel German tape recorder that was allegedly portable, although it weighed so much you needed to be in the whole of your health before trying to carry it anywhere. But we were young, strong and decidedly in the whole of our health, so we jumped at the chance to do interviews out of the studio. Quite early in the run, we decided to go to Dublin Zoo, always the go-to place for broadcasters at a loose end, since every one of the staff loves what they do and is eager to involve listeners in the importance of breeding rare animals.

Howard persuaded one of the keepers to let me get high up on the rocks above the pond where the sea elephant seal was kept, and handed me the microphone, which fortunately had a long lead. When he gave me the signal to go, I read some details about the sea elephant seal from the notice on the fence, described the scale of it and then, because it had climbed up the rocks to see what I was doing, asked it what kind of a day it was having. It heaved a satisfyingly audible sigh suggesting that it wasn't doing so well, in the process immersing me in a cloud of the most spectacular halitosis I had ever experienced. 'Oh, Jesus,' I said, 'the smell of him.' The sea elephant seal obligingly belly-flopped back into his pool, creating another great sound effect.

Howard was on his ear with delight as he drove us back to Henry Street. Radio Éireann was on the top floor of the GPO before it moved out to Donnybrook where the TV block was already in operation. It had one of the longest corridors I have ever walked, punctuated by door after door, behind each of which lurked producers and department heads. The producers shared offices, two by two. The department heads had their own offices to themselves. Close to the end, on the left, as you walked to the studios, was the office of the controller of programmes. This was a man named Roibeárd Ó Faracháin, who had started in the thirties as talks officer and gone on to found the repertory company in the station while at the same time publishing fine Irish language poetry and prose. Howard had developed the habit of shying like a nervous horse whenever he passed Ó Faracháin's door, because, even early on, he had been keelhauled several times by the controller for lack of judgment, which was Ó Faracháin's blanket term to cover anything of which he instinctively disapproved. And he instinctively disapproved of everything about Howard. Howard, with years of student politics behind him in one of the most vivid third-level decades in Ireland, fought his corner and promoted new thinking as best he could. He invariably lost and needed to go out into Henry Street to smoke one of his hand-rolled cigarettes to recover, because, although he was an intellectual revolutionary, he hated fighting with people. He would often offer me a puff of his cigarette when I went down to find how he was doing. I thought this strange until he explained that sharing was a key aspect of marijuana culture. Howard thought my life would be immeasurably improved by smoking hash. I would be calm and happy, he promised me. I pointed out that I was reasonably happy anyway and that, since I never drew the controller on me, I didn't have the same therapeutic need for weed he had.

In the edit suite after the visit to the Dublin Zoo, we played back the interview with the sea elephant seal, laughing so much that others were attracted in to hear it played again and again. (Whenever you could, you propped open the door of an edit suite, in order not to suffocate: the GPO lacked air-conditioning.) Padraic O'Neill (Paddy O'Brien), the greyhound racing commentator, stood in the doorway, silhouetted against the brighter corridor light, and when the laughter had died down, muttered something to the effect of it being a shame we couldn't broadcast it. O'Neill was second in command to Michael Littleton, a terrifying senior producer.

Howard bristled. Of course we were going to broadcast it. Why on earth wouldn't we? Paddy heaved himself up off the lintel and got serious. 'Jesus' was not ever broadcast, he explained. It was broadcast every Sunday morning in the RC Mass, Howard retorted. Different context, Paddy said. So? Howard asked. One context is respectful, the other not. Not true, Howard said. Terry was calling on a higher power to give her the strength to cope with the bad breath coming at her from the animal. Mammal, someone suggested. Paddy smiled the world-weary smile of the institutional lifer and shrugged: your decision, your career. We cut the sentence.

When the task was complete, Howard sat back and beamed at me. 'I really like working with you. You know that?' he said. I burbled in embarrassment. I was a fat sixteen-year-old without much experience of compliments. True, one of my mother's bits of advice had always been that when someone compliments you, you must never contradict them but accept the compliment graciously. I knew the rule all right; I just couldn't get the behaviour in place. Howard watched my floundering with some amusement, then got serious.

'Whenever you like someone, or whenever you find you love someone,' he growled, 'tell them. Tell them right then and there. Don't put it off, don't tell other people but not tell them. You know why? Because life is awful short and someone could die without knowing you admired them. Or like them. Or loved them.' I thought I would never get out of that control room, between compliments and advice on how to prevent someone dying unconsoled by the knowledge that I was fond of them. But then I started to do it, discovering, in the process, that it usually comes as a welcome surprise to the recipient. We're great at telling people about what they're doing wrong. We're fantastic, we Irish, especially with a couple of pints or a modicum of grievance in us, at telling people they're the scum of the earth, come from a long line of bastards and shouldn't be allowed to live. But telling people we like them, admire them or love them is a risky proposition that can make us look seriously uncool, so we don't do it.

Howard and I trusted each other and relied on each other totally. When I told him that poems sent in by one young male listener showed him to be a young Yeats, Howard said to make that comment on the air. I hadn't yet done my Leaving Cert, but was being determinative about writers even younger than I was. In that particular instance, I got lucky. The thirteen-year-old sent me a long thrilled handwritten letter, thanking me for giving him confidence. In 2000, Katie Donovan wrote in the *Irish Times*, 'Although Terry Prone broadcast some of his earliest poems on *The Young Idea* radio show, [Dennis] O'Driscoll's stern "inner critic" prevented him from sending work for publication until 1977.' After that, as Eileen Battersby of the same paper put it, he became 'the lyric equivalent of William Trevor'.

I wrote back to every young listener who submitted prose or poetry for our consideration, my letters neatly typed in Howard's office when he wasn't *in situ*, which was frequently, partly because he continued to be involved in student and left-wing politics despite being told he wasn't allowed to be, and partly because he was producing other programmes. One of them was an experiment for Saturday nights, which was dreamed up by Bunny. The idea was that, at the end of *The Late Late Show*, Gay Byrne would turn to the camera and say something along the lines of 'Hope you've enjoyed tonight's show, and if you have, make sure to tune into Radio Éireann, where, on *Later than Late*, the topics will continue to be discussed by Bunny Carr's panel.' Bunny later said that Gay had 'misgivings about it', which was Bunny being positive. Gay hated the idea, fought it to the wire, and made the requisite announcement with the enthusiasm you'd bring to an invitation for a quick swim in a cesspool. Chilling the relationship between Gay and Bunny for the year it ran, it was one of Bunny's few mistakes. Most viewers of *The Late Late Show* tottered upstairs to bed as soon as it was over, satisfied that Uncle Gaybo had taken each discussion as far as was productive. Within months, the radio programme had become a more general late night chat show with whoever was willing to come into town late on a Saturday night. I was pulled in by Howard as assistant producer. That sounded better than it was, which was doing what he normally did when he couldn't be bothered. I learned to work the desk, direct the presenter, get the timing of commercials right; although, given the paucity of advertising at that time of night, we weren't much troubled by ad breaks. Northern Ireland was heading into the ghastly decades of what became known as the Troubles, and so I also learned how to reach Northern politicians and persuade them to go into the BBC's Belfast studios to join in. The Northern Ireland situation and the fact that the show went out live and was going to include phone calls late at night when listeners might have a few drinks in them prompted management to instruct that we use new technology which effectively recorded the programme and broadcast it seven seconds later. In theory, this meant that if someone uttered a profanity or a libel, the sound engineer could cut off the recording and go instead to the live feed, removing the offending words. Which was fine until the night a caller cordially greeted Bunny before telling the nation that one of the panellists, Labour Party politician Ruairi Quinn, was a pervert and a prick. Instantly, Bunny gestured at the sound man and Howard yelled at the same lad to cut to the live feed. The sound man had no muscle memory of cutting to live in a panic, and dithered just long enough for the comment to go out on the air. Bunny turned to Ruairi Quinn and invited him to agree that such a ridiculous comment was of no significance and did an established, respected politician like himself no damage. Ruairi, knowing Bunny was backfilling against the possibility of a libel suit, smiled and agreed – out loud, which was vital – and everybody in the control room wilted over the desk like their bones had melted. A few days later, Howard showed Bunny his two-page discrepancy report before sending it to the controller of programmes. Bunny read it through twice before telling Howard it was an admirably thorough piece of work. Howard was halfway to the door when he stopped and came back.

'Okay, Bun, what's wrong with it?'

Bunny told him that there was nothing wrong with it, but that if such a long document arrived on Roibeárd Ó Faracháin's desk, the controller might logically take the view that this was a grave matter demanding his concentrated attention. Howard nodded, puzzled.

'Howie, think about it,' Bunny said. 'Is that the reaction you *want* from the Controller?'

Howard tore up the two pages, sat down at the typewriter again and a few minutes later presented Bunny with a discrepancy report that ran to three sentences, none of them long. Bunny read it and gave the producer one of his rib-threatening sideways hugs. The Ruairi Quinn incident was absorbed into the mythology of bad moments nobody of importance noticed.

While Roibeárd Ó Faracháin's attention was distracted by what were essentially viewed as offences against middle-class Ireland, the Pronunciation Unit's concerns were narrower. Narrower and sharper, like a scalpel. The unit comprised two women, Brigid Kilfeather and Una Sheehy, adored by professionals like Gay Byrne who always wanted to know the correct pronunciation of any word before broadcasting it, but feared by the rest of us. To be brought in for remedial teaching by Brigid or Una meant you had brought the station into disrepute, since the summons was always retrospective: a consequence of your crime. One of the most chilling moments was the day I walked out of studio, having read a short story by P.G. Wodehouse live on air during the mid-morning programme at short notice because some planned item had fallen through. I was on a high, having got through the reading without a slip. Or so I believed. I knew to the differ the minute I saw the two of them. They were kind and credited me with a highly professional read. I waited for the other shoe to fall. Una compassionately offered that I was awfully young, and this might explain why I had mispronounced this name. She advanced a pad on which was written 'Cholmondeley.' I had pronounced it precisely as it was spelled. In fact, she gently pointed out, it was pronounced Chumly. I thanked them and promised I would never make the same error a second time, thinking that this wouldn't be that hard, since I was never likely to encounter the name again, on or off air.

Perhaps because I was less threatening than Una and Brigid, the adorable Larry Gogan, he of the encyclopaedic pop music knowledge and the mop of black hair, used to accost me in the corridor and get me to pronounce names and words in ads he was about to read on air. The two of us would say 'L'Oréal' at each other until he was happy he had it nailed, and off he would go, ridiculously grateful to a teenager to whom he was the definition of fame. Larry was a solid gold human being, with the humility and self-deprecation of a newcomer all his life.

The big new arrival into RTÉ Radio at that time was Liam Nolan, a former BBC broadcaster my mother thought was the best boxing commentator since Eamonn Andrews. It was announced that Liam Nolan would be doing a news- and current affairs-based programme in the slot previously occupied by Freda McGough. A bevy of producers were allocated to the show, including John Keogh (musician with the Greenbeats), Pat McInerney, whose real name was Tom McInerney and who was a Jesuit priest in civvies, and Liam Ó Lonargáin, who was easy-going and good-humoured. Howard was kept away from what became *The Liam Nolan Hour* for the most part, no doubt because of the whiff of radical sulphur he carried about him. I became 'the girl reporter' on the show. Even before Liam Nolan actually arrived, the ten regulars on the team had an ill-concealed conviction that it was going to be the most important force in modern broadcasting. Once he was on microphone, with his impeccable diction and preternatural calm under pressure, we were sure of it.

We were surprised to find that someone who had returned from long years working in London was much more religious than any of the rest of us, including the Jesuit, but the producers gently pushed a fine broadcaster towards the more liberal Ireland they saw around the corner. Indeed, for the most part, we believed we were already living in that more liberal Ireland, leaving behind the days when a girl having a baby without benefit of clergy might as well have had a brand on her forehead. That's what we believed. Events would prove us to have been optimistic and ignorant in equal measure.

But at the end of the 1970s, it was all excitement and risk and kicking over of traces. Women's Liberation was emerging and its proponents – Mary Kenny, Mary Maher, Nell McCafferty, Janet Martin, Máirín de Burca and Mary Anderson – were a constant vivid presence on radio and television. Liam looked horrified at free-form discussion of vaginas and contraception, but questioned them with curiosity and courtesy.

Not that curiosity and courtesy were always enough. On one occasion, five minutes before the Angelus break at noon, Liam was told, with great excitement, that the team had snagged two members of the Chinese table tennis Olympic team as guests for the show. He wound up the interview he was doing, and turned to the two young athletes, welcoming them and asking them to pronounce their names, which they pleasantly did. He then asked the older player a question about training. Were they doing much of it? Oh, yes, thank you, the young man told him. Even this far in advance of the Games? Oh, yes, thank you. Did they believe they would take home a gold medal? Oh, yes. The fifth identical reply forced Liam to realise, in concert with the horrified crew in the control room, that this was as far as the linguistic competence of the guests went. With four minutes to go, he asked longer and more information-laden questions until the interview became a monologue with affirmations. While the researcher who had landed this dud item on him was appropriately apologetic, it became something the entire team liked to quote to prove just how good their man was. And he was very good indeed, as demonstrated by the day John Keogh got smart with the seagulls.

Liam was reading a lengthy script and about to do a live phone interview when John noticed a clatter of seagulls on the flat roof outside the window of the studio. He went into the office and retrieved a discarded sandwich from a wastepaper basket, breaking it into bite-sized segments before tiptoeing back into the studio with it. He created a Y-shaped path of crumbs, starting at the window, then separating and running on either side of Liam's chair. Liam was too preoccupied with his script to pay any attention to him. John then carefully opened the sash window and threw out the remaining crumbs. The seagulls followed his carefully set trail and soon Liam was interviewing someone in London about apartheid while surrounded by seagulls in studio. His rage was interesting to watch, as soon as the

Angelus struck, but John Keogh was so puckish in his delight, nobody could stay mad at him for long.

Working on that programme taught complex and contradictory lessons about the position of women in journalism. Nobody thought it a matter for official complaint when one of the male continuity announcers developed the occasional habit of quietly letting himself into a radio studio where a woman was live on air and removing his clothes below the waist. This form of flashing was regarded as just the way he was, and he never did it twice to the same woman. The women warned one another never to get into the lift with another producer (although they did the warnings *sotto voce*, because he was married to a senior producer nobody believed should be humiliated by his behaviour). The warning was delivered to every newcomer: if you get into the lift with him, he will push the button for the basement, lock the mechanism and grope you for as long as he thinks it's safe to have the lift in the one spot. Inevitably, I *did* get into the lift with this man, and when he never laid a hand on me, had a brief sense of let-down, so skewed were the sensibilities of even a confident teenage girl at the time.

Sex, most of it illicit, ran beneath every aspect of my life at the time, never touching me, but ever present, like drizzle. In the Abbey Theatre, Fionnuala and I registered as a reality the fact that a couple of girls in our class were shagging producers. Having sex with actors, even married actors, was regarded as kind of normal. But sex with a producer was seen as sleeping your way to the top, a conviction never dented by the fact that some of these girls didn't sleep themselves to the middle, never mind the top. What was interesting, though, was that nobody blamed the producers for using their power to have sex with much younger women who were, by any standards, more attractive than anyone the producers could have hoped to get close to were they not in such a disproportionately strong position. That was life. If I thought about it at all, it was as one of the choices from which I was spared by being unattractive and fat. Nobody ever came on to me, nobody ever tried to get me to go away on a dirty weekend, and the only designs Howard had on me were to introduce me to marijuana.

I was, however, increasingly resistant to the 'girl reporter' stuff in *The Liam Nolan Hour*, constantly protesting about the bilge I was handed and being gently warned by male producer 'friends' that I wasn't on staff and therefore should be careful about biting the hand that fed me. On one particular morning when I arrived in, I was told I was interviewing the linoleum buyer of Guiney's, who was retiring that week. I lost my temper and yelled that they could stick their patronising subjects and that once I had done the professional job I had to do with the linoleum buyer from Guiney's, I was out of there. I then went into the studio to start a four-minute interview with a dapper old man, who turned out to be riveting. He believed in lino like it was a religion with science thrown in. He explained that the constituent elements making up linoleum were all natural and that, in combination, they ate germs, which meant that all hospitals should use lino, rather than the inert vinyl, to cover their floors. About three minutes in, I glanced up, and saw the producer in the control room doing the expanding concertina gesture that means 'keep it going'. Four minutes became nine, and when I left the studio, members of the *Liam Nolan Hour* production crew congratulated me on getting so much out of the retiring linoleum buyer.

9

The Problem with the Leaving Cert

*C*oming up on seventeen, I was presenting a weekly radio programme, assisting on a weekend programme, doing interviews on a daily show, attending the Abbey Theatre School of Acting and appearing onstage there in small roles. Between radio, TV and print journalism, I was making a decent living, partly thanks to Seán McCann, features editor on the *Evening Press* and father of Colum, one of Ireland's great novelists and maybe the most sweet-natured writer alive. But I had to go to university, so I was studying like crazy too. I was away from school much more than I was present and never went to art classes because I was sure of an easy honour in that subject and also because I hated Miss Mayne, who hated Hilary. Hilary, working in the Department of Education, had probably forgotten whatever had caused Miss Mayne's enmity towards her, but, while I don't hold grudges for myself, I never let go of the grudges of those I love.

On the first day of the exam, I watched other girls crying and being hugged by their parents and being told that, whatever the result was, all would be well, which I thought idiotic. What on earth were all these years of repetitive boredom inflicted on us for, if we didn't prove something at the end of it? I also knew that criers always get it soft and regarded them as having suckers for parents. When I said this to Hilary after the first day of exams, she pointed out, in a saintly way, that they might be genuinely stressed by the exam process. Yeah, I said, and how were they going to manage careers like airline pilots if they couldn't handle a bit of exam stress? Hilary's lips tightened, because she had wanted to be a pilot, but no woman had ever been permitted to fly a plane back then because – cue all the guff about women losing their capacity to reason and react during their periods. My mother had been markedly unsympathetic when Hilary voiced the certainty of rejection as a putative pilot, indicating that if she wanted it badly enough she would fight for it. In fact, Hilary, even if she'd been a man, wouldn't have qualified as a pilot, since her eyesight was so bad (as was mine) that the two of us had sat across the aisle from each other on the 44A bus for one trip and didn't recognise each other.

Everything worked according to plan and I was set for university. I couldn't wait for the mind-opening promise of academia. University College Dublin was situated in what is now the National Concert Hall, which seemed right and proper for an institution where young intellectuals would gather to explore ideas, hopes and dreams. The first day knocked that notion on the head. Earlsfort Terrace was Heuston Station without the trains, filled with teenagers smoking, rushing, lingering and conveying 'I could take you' mutual arrogance (the lads) and 'Oh, look at you in your wrong jacket' mutual hostility (the girls).

The problem was me. I didn't make the effort to get to know people or to be helpful to people. I projected onto others my failure to adapt to the college. I didn't join anything. My parents were somewhat surprised that I didn't join the Literary and Historical Society, but I wasn't that much of a fool. I might, in secondary school, have got away with completely disconnected thought processes decorated with the random 'shinies' – clever, compelling comments – of an autodidact, but it was going to be prohibitively difficult to achieve the same at third level and would have simply added another misery to the pile. I had chosen to do history, Irish, English and philosophy, only to discover that one of the history lecturers was always going on about the 'Owsthrians rewolting'. Just as in school, history was about men and battles and remembering dates. That said, at least I understood it, whereas, from the first class, I was lost when it came to philosophy. I could understand the individual words in each sentence, but, put together, they amounted to a terrifying confusion. It was like trying to knit a jumper using cooked spaghetti – all slither and shame. I asked for explanations and helpful tutors gave them and I sat, earlobes purpling with the humiliation of not understanding the explanation, while nodding appreciatively. All the diligence in the world could not substitute for the brain cells I didn't have.

In the Abbey, I was moving from minor roles to more solid character parts, although progress was bumpy. Treasa Pron figured as Ropin in an Irish-language version of Behan's *The Hostage (An Giall)*. 'Na stri-opaigh' – the prostitutes – was how the girls were described in the programme, which meant a short tight dress, fishnet stockings and totteringly high heels. I also had to smoke throughout, and was supplied with a yellow packet of Sweet Afton, described by the many smokers among my colleagues as made from the sweepings of the factory floor. The smokers taught me how to draw smoke into my mouth, hold it there while I breathed through my nose, and then expel it towards the ceiling in a way they swore would look authentic. Within a day, my tongue had the texture of a doormat. Frank Dermody directed and was in his element, ordering teenagers dressed up as slappers to walk around the huge shell-shaped stage of the new Abbey in a way that conveyed their desire to sell their bodies.

On the first night the theatre was half full. Dermody had ordered us to 'paper the house' by giving free tickets to our relatives and friends, but, for the most part, they resisted this suspect largesse. By night three, we peeped out before the house lights went down, and counted thirteen people scattered throughout the stalls. Someone went out on stage and suggested they huddle together in the middle. They did and seemed quite pleased with the arrangement, even sharing their sweets.

Some plays I regarded myself as well out of, like *The Playboy of the Western World*, with Vincent Dowling as the Playboy, Máire Ní Dhómhnaill as the Widow Quin and Aideen O'Kelly as Pegeen Mike. A great cast, and my friend Fionnuala figured in the crowd. I was glad to be out of it, firstly because most of the cast were barefoot throughout, and naked feet I loathe. Once humans are older than three, their feet are unspeakably awful, and in plays like *Riders to the Sea* or *Playboy*, you had stiletto-shoe-warped city feet letting on to be free-range country feet and filthy with it. I also hated Synge, his claimed love for the peasants of the west of Ireland given the lie by making them talk a stagey poetry they never spoke in real life. Lady Gregory, always looked down on as producing lesser plays, at least bothered to watch and listen to the peasants about whom she wrote.

The disaster of *An Giall* was spectacularly outweighed within a short period of time by another play adapted from the same writer. Nobody had any idea that *Borstal Boy*, Brendan Behan's account of his time in a British youth prison resulting from participation in IRA bombings in England, would be a hit. What was apparent, though, was that the variegated levels of the stage were going to provide director Tomás Mac Anna with a dreamscape on which to deploy his actors, with minimal scenery, in one fast-moving scene after another. Mac Anna was a big, bombastic, long-haired man who co-wrote the play with Frank McMahon. He could see in his head a production of the book that moved between time and place, creating, from the bleakness of an uncluttered stage, a series of ineradicable images in the imagination of the audience. This allowed a brilliant cast, which included Joe Dowling, Bobby Carlisle, Alan Devlin, Jim Bartley, Bosco Hogan and John Kavanagh, to be on the move all the time in a fast and musical play that veered between low comedy and high drama. *Borstal Boy* was structured so that much of the narrative was carried by 'the elder Behan,' played by Niall Toibin, who slumped, dishevelled and looking astonishingly like Behan himself, at the side of the stage, watching the younger version of himself and making the odd encouraging, cynical or regretful comment about what had happened in his past.

The 'younger Behan' was created by Frank Grimes, the boy who had laid the barstool on its side to represent the dead Julius Caesar at his audition. From a working-class Dublin family, he had obvious affinities with the young Behan. But what Mac Anna evoked from him was a portrayal of Behan at his panicked, naive, courageous best. It was a performance that never became studied. Never became ironic. Never became self-regarding. The combination of the sure-footed Tobin and the raw genius of Grimes was so thrilling that actors who had done their bit for the evening would stand at the back of the stalls to see it unfold, night after night.

My role, fourth in the cast list because she appeared so early in the play, was that of Mrs Gildea, a woman with an apron around her and a headscarf over her curlers, who is brought to the front door of her house by a knock. The door was just that: a door within a frame, the whole thing on wheels. I would open it in character, be told my son had just been blown up while planting a bomb for the IRA, and scream. No words, just the loudest screams any human being could produce before two neighbours appeared and pulled me gently away from the door, which was immediately rolled off, in full view of the audience. The door and I were done for the night, and I would go up to the light box, high above the audience seated in the balcony, where I would watch the rest of the performance, whispering the lines as the two versions of the playwright spoke them, right down to the stutter each brought to their role as the stammering Brendan Behan. Waiting for the last moments, as the young Behan looks out from the deck of the ship returning him to Ireland after he has served his sentence, and Behan the elder follows the direction of his gaze, identifying landmarks. No matter how often I saw it, I had tears in my eyes at the end.

As the summer 1968 run of *Borstal Boy* progressed, Mac Anna got together with Fergus Linehan of the *Irish Times*, who was married to Rosaleen Linehan, to create a show for the Peacock Theatre called *The Sound of the Gong*. 'It is something new for the Abbey to put on a review and in fact poke fun at itself and at its history,' wrote

Mac Anna. 'The show itself traces the founding of the theatre and the earlier trials and tribulations of the founders in ballads and parodies.'

I was cast in *The Sound of the Gong* while still in *Borstal Boy*. The transition from the screaming Mrs Gildea upstairs and the mini-skirted teenager downstairs having a lark had to happen so quickly each night that on one occasion, I arrived out onto the central circular stage in the Peacock and opened confidently with one of my songs. Half a verse into it, I realised that I had made a mistake. I flagged down Éamonn Ó Gallchobhair at the piano and, in the sudden silence, looked at my colleague Niall Buggy.

'I'm singing the wrong song,' I told him. 'What song should I be singing?'

'Jesus, I don't know,' came the terrified response. 'It's *your* song.' Although *The Sound of the Gong* always got many laughs each night, this was the biggest we ever got. We considered doing it deliberately, but decided it would never work. The minute you touch natural stupidity, the bloom is gone. On that particular night, Ó Gallchobhair hammered out the melodic introduction to the proper song, and off I went.

Because I could sing and mimic others, when Joan O'Hara became pregnant before the Abbey was due to take a production of Boucicault's *The Shaughraun* to London's West End, I was given her role as the Keener, performed on the London stage, stayed in Dame Sybil Thorndike's beautiful apartment with her granddaughter, Bronwen Casson, actor and designer, and got to explore Swinging London, coming back with a purple cloak and pink platform boots.

The West End has to be a notch on the career of any teenager, but – like everything in the Abbey – it was two steps forward, one step back. Came the day I encountered a camera-laden photographer leaving the rehearsal room, as I arrived back from some errand. I held the door open for him and his paraphernalia and then joined the group who were having coffee. 'Photographer?' I asked. Yeah, someone explained. He was from a newspaper. *Evening Press*, actually. Took pictures of six of the School of Acting girls for a photo feature about the Abbey's next generation of actresses. The story would appear that very afternoon. Really? Rictus smile affixed, let joy be tight contained. As the rehearsal progressed, I beamed particularly warmly at the six, wondering how to avenge the elaborately deliberate exclusion.

When the solution came to me, it merited a finger snap at chest level, but I restrained myself. Of course. Tony Butler over in the *Evening Press* right across the Liffey. Big fan since I first sent him paragraphs and sketches for his 'Junior Press' page. I came up with an excuse to leave the rehearsal room and took myself over to the *Irish Press*, asked to see Tony and told him I had a story for him. Probably for the front page. About myself. Go on, he said. 'Well, I open *Borstal Boy* every night as a woman in her fifties and then run downstairs to the Peacock, taking off wig and costume as I go, to sing the first song in *The Sound of the Gong*, the revue at the Peacock, in a mini skirt, where I'm a teenager.'

Tony laughed, called a photographer and the photographer brought me outside to take pictures of me leaning on the wall by the Liffey. Then a junior reporter took notes and I ran back to the Abbey and rejoined the rehearsal. Someone went out at lunchtime to buy several copies of the first edition of the *Evening Press*, where the six heroines were to star. As indeed they did, in a small way, on an inside page. Me, I had page one.

Evening Press, August 1968
Middle-aged to Teenager in Minutes!

Eighteen-year-old Terry Prone's life seems to resemble a time machine at the moment, for actress Terry is a middle-aged lady and a young girl all within the space of a few minutes.

Terry, from Clontarf, is with the Abbey Players on a probationary basis, having attended the Abbey School for the past four years. She is at present playing in both the plays running currently in the Abbey and in the Peacock.

Coming offstage as a middle-aged woman in *Borstal Boy* in the Abbey, Terry rushes down the three flights of stairs to the Peacock, furiously scrubbing off her make-up with a towel and make-up remover. By the time she has reached the Peacock, she has taken off her overall, turban and sloppy sandals and put on the costume she wears as a fifteen-year-old girl in *The Sound of the Gong.*

Terry, who is taking an arts degree in UCD, had to miss her exams this summer because she had signed the contract with the Abbey.

Everybody wanted to know how I had achieved this, and I produced half-sentences that added up to nothing in particular. Mac Anna didn't react at all, but then he never again excluded me from a photo opportunity, and so in December 1968 the same paper carried a short of 'Nineteen-year-old Terry Prone, made up for her part as Síle in *An Baile Seo 'Gainne* at the Abbey.' Also, without Abbey permission, I played a role with the RTÉ repertory in *Tarry Flynn*, an adaptation of Patrick Kavanagh's novel. The role involved sex in the grass and I was enthralled to see a sound effects man running his fingers through a basket filled with discarded audio tape directly under a second microphone in order to convey the right noise. I couldn't believe the authenticity of it when it was broadcast. Until relatively recently, I would receive minuscule cheques from RTÉ when they replayed that production of *Tarry Flynn.*

Borstal Boy was a breakout success and shortly thereafter went on tour. Limerick was one of the cities visited and I got barred from a hotel there. I could have appealed the sentence because I was innocent of the charges, but I couldn't see myself ever going back to what was then a depressed and depressing city, hungering for the architectural and social refurbishment soon to come. One of the actors, Donal Cox, remarked during the tour that the only thing to do was cavort for as long as you were able, fall into bed jaded and batter the time away. One way to 'batter the time away' on any tour is for actors to pair off, whether that was their pre-tour intention or not, and this meant that I had to spend time wandering the corridors of the hotel having been turfed out of shared rooms by girls who required those rooms for fell purposes. On the final night, I ended up in the refuge bed of a sweet, bearded set designer and painter named Eddie Doyle, who behaved like a father or brother, tucking me in before sleeping on the other side of the bed. On that night, several of the cast, dominated as it was by young men, got spectacularly drunk, along with their visiting permanent girlfriends or temporary girlfriends, and trashed several rooms. Hence the general barring of members of the Abbey company from that hotel.

I never did anything to deserve being barred. Lack of opportunity, rather than virtue; even though I was in the middle of it, I missed the Swinging Sixties almost completely. I was, however, increasingly aware of the Troubles in the North. On one occasion, a major address to the nation on TV and a mass protest outside the GPO coincided with Bunny's late-night radio programme. Getting the guests in through the protestors and the phalanx of Guards put in Henry Street to prevent them from getting into the national broadcaster's radio headquarters was in itself difficult, but then Howard Kinlay sheepishly told the presenter that he – Howard – was one of the speakers slated to address the crowd outside and would have to leave me in charge. Bunny suggested that it would make our lives simpler if he left right then, which he did.

Typically, Bunny's first question after the show was, 'So how good was Howie's speech?' Good enough, as it turned out, to land him in the controller of programme's office for an epic confrontation and a three-month suspension – which was shortened by eleven weeks when it became apparent, even to outraged management, that, given the unravelling north of the border, the national broadcaster needed all its personnel.

One frequent guest on Bunny's programme was Mary Kenny, who had come home from London to become women's editor of the *Irish Press*. Mary was all short skirts, sexiness and breathless excitement, personifying the Mary Quant-dressed woman of the sixties, and she created a maelstrom of controversy and outrage. I was at home one day when the phone rang. 'Dahling,' said Mary, 'I want you to be my fashion correspondent.' I laughed. 'Mary, have you *looked* at me? I know the sum total of shag all about fashion.' 'Oh, I don't want you to know anything about it. Fashion, written seriously, is so *boring*. I want you to write in a funny way about fashion. Make it different.' Floored, I was thinking about this when another thought struck her. 'And beauty. I want you to be our beauty correspondent, too. You know all about make-up from the theatre.'

I would write a weekly fashion column and attend fashion shows, although Mary wasn't sure she could persuade Tim Pat Coogan to stump up for trips to the London and Paris collections. I should drop into the *Irish Press* offices now and again to pick up copies of WWD. 'WWD?' I asked. '*Women's Wear Daily*,' Mary said airily. Freelancers like me depended on this American fashion daily newspaper to tell us if the midi would ever reach the popularity of the maxi and whether stacked heels were or were not essential for Fall. I started to write for Mary the following Friday, bussing my copy into Burgh Quay and often joining an impromptu meeting with other freelances, including Linda Kavanagh, Mavis Arnold and Anne Harris, who later went on to edit the *Sunday Independent*. I grievously offended Anne Harris on one occasion when Mary was waxing lyrical about sit-ins in RTÉ, where one of the dissident leaders was Eoghan Harris, then a charismatic left-of-centre figure. Knowing that Howard Kinlay was involved in the sit-ins and fearful for his future, I had limited patience for Mary's extravagant praise of Eoghan Harris. 'Mary, let me tell you what's going to happen in RTÉ,' I said. 'When the dust settles, several young idealists will lose their jobs and be unemployable, and Eoghan Harris will be promoted.' The frozen silence that ensued seemed more weighted than the blurt deserved. 'Terry, you do know that Anne here is married to Eoghan?' Mary asked. Of course I didn't and I told Anne that I was sorry for saying it in front of her. She said not a word, then or ever, but I never got the impression that I had been forgiven. Nor should I have been. I believed it then and still do.

Working for Mary was like going to the circus every day. All colour. Big brass bands. Excitement and tension. Sudden bellowing of big beasts – like when I annoyed designer Clodagh with some criticism and she went directly to Tim Pat to demand that he fire me. Mary and I ended up together in the editor's office, trying to explain to him how chiffon frays and the wonders of a serrated scissors. Once he knew the paper couldn't be sued, he lost interest, in an amused way.

Mary took her small team on trains around Ireland, where I found clothes to write about and Mavis, Anne and Linda Kavanagh explored the city or town until they located a story. At this time, Women's Liberation was beginning, and Mary was out in front of many of the events, particularly the contraceptives train. I was on the panel of *The Late Late Show* that night, and, when Mary came on, demonstrated my capacity to get the facts straight while missing the essential point. The essential point was that Ireland was changing in deep and permanent ways, particularly when it came to women, and the symbolism of the train was important. I nit-picked about the girls not knowing that buying the Pill north of the border would require a doctor's prescription. Since they had no prescription, they had bought silvery blister packs of over-the-counter painkillers, waving them in front of the cameras very quickly so that viewers would not be able to read the word 'Aspirin'. I also told Mary, my beloved boss, in front of the nation, that being rude to customs men wasn't much in the way of revolutionary behaviour. Good television, because Mary looked so hurt. Did she hold it against me? Mary Kenny didn't hold anything against anybody.

Much later, when she converted back to religious belief and practice, Mary Kenny was mystified when the *Irish Times*'s Mary Maher blanked her. She genuinely believed friendship could bridge even the most pronounced differences in stance. Those of us who worked for her, all too briefly, adored her, learned from her, were sneakily scandalised by her and were grateful for the excitement she brought to our lives. I also tried to imitate her, but, although I was a good mimic, I could never quite 'get' Mary's soaring posh delivery, which, as someone later said, had the ring of her auditioning for a role as a Royal in a TV series.

Once I started to work for Mary, I was part of a group of women tidal-waving into journalism in the late sixties everywhere in the Western world. In New York, Gloria Steinem, Letty Cottin Pogrebin and others founded *Ms.* magazine to address issues, starting with abortion, never up to that point countenanced by mainstream media. In Ireland, the (then) three national papers, the *Irish Times*, the *Irish Press* and the *Irish Independent*, all unselfconsciously created or enlarged their women's pages and hired writers like Nell McCafferty, Mary Cummins and Mary Maher (*Irish Times*), Janet Martin, Marianne Heron and Mary Anderson (*Irish Independent*) as well as Mary Kenny and her crew on the *Irish Press*. What a time for a woman journalist to be alive. Male editors enthusiastically bought into controversial handling of previously taboo topics. It was box office. It sold newspapers, and, for the first time, the amplification effect of radio and TV was measurably in play. Mary Kenny, Nell and Janet were all good radio and TV performers and their presence on electronic media drove readers to pick up the newspapers in which they appeared.

I worked for all three papers under different names. It wouldn't be possible now, when every byline is accompanied by a passport photograph, but back then people like Janet Martin didn't care if I chose to call myself Geraldine Desmond in her pages, any more than Maeve Binchy cared if I called myself something else. Or several somethings else. On one occasion, I provided three different columns taking three different viewpoints on 'The Other Woman', on the same page on the same day in the *Irish Times*.

Feminists were not the only women journalists making their mark around then. Maeve Binchy's self-deprecatory style, best exemplified by her account of her time working in an Israeli kibbutz school, where she started by telling the boys to take off their caps and then asked for everybody's Christian name, made her adored by readers long before she became a best-selling novelist. Terry Keane became a household name gossip columnist who was big friends with June Levine, a researcher on *The Late Late Show* without, as far as the rest of us could tell, having anything in common. Rita O'Kelly in the *RTÉ Guide*, married to the *Irish Times*'s Dick Walsh, was powerful, although not as formidable as Caroline Mitchell, known professionally as Barbara Dickson.

Barbara would arrive, sit, accept a glass of red wine, pull the sugar bowl over, transfer six spoonfuls to her glass, stir briskly, and consume. I envied this because one of the reasons I didn't drink was the taste of wine and I figured that much sugar added to it had to improve it. It did not seem to dilute the impact of the wine and so any of us who were reasonably big and strong tended to have to link arms with Barbara to get her down the stairs of the Shelbourne and into a waiting group taxi. Once, when in this condition, she looked at the doll-like Clare Boylan (who edited a women's magazine while secretly storing up the material for her later elegant fiction) and warned her against getting old, because, she told Clare, she would end up looking like Barbara: 'an old, peeled wall' shocking herself in the mirror. (Clare died of cancer before reaching the age Barbara was when she offered this advice.)

Collectively, the women journalists, according to Kevin Myers, were 'the Witches Coven, a gang of old crones whose gossip went from charitable ill-will, pausing to linger lovingly over the m-words – malicious, malevolent, malignant and malign – before hastening on to intravenous polonium. They were invited to everything, because *not* inviting them would be a disaster for any PR consultant.'

I wish, in the interests of female solidarity, that I could contradict Myers, but he's not completely wrong. Some of the older women were particularly bitchy to public relations people. They could kill a product or service by a negative review and so PR, in its infancy in Dublin, concentrated on a form of bribery unacknowledged as such by either side. The journalists were taken to lunch or dinner in gorgeous venues, flattered and plámásed and sent home with enough samples of whatever was the item seeking publicity to supply the Red Army for a year. Some of them stayed bought. Some of them, however, maintained their sense of self-worth by taking the samples and then rubbishing them in print.

Many of the products were so essentially domestic in purpose that, in retrospect, it seems weird that women's pages largely devoted to exploring the outré would have sent their journalists to cover them. But a free lunch, or a trip to London, had its merits. I remember being taken to a Marks & Spencer premises to learn about the testing processes to which they subjected their products, including knickers. They had a machine for pummelling knickers to simulate the stress delivered by the average woman wearing and washing a pair for a year. That trip was organised by the woman usually described as 'the doyenne of public relations,' Mary Finan. (I say 'usually' because some male editors covertly called her 'Mary Fine Thing' because she was so good-looking, well-dressed and charming.)

One of her outstanding PR trips was a journey to nowhere on one of the brand-new Boeing 747s. It was a rite of passage to national adulthood when Aer Lingus bought its two 747s. A move away from the inward-looking years when we told ourselves that we liked Tintawn, a form of carpeting closely related to wire wool and just as attractive. With the jumbo jets, however, we were suddenly cool and outward-looking. Their arrival had such a momentous impact on the nation that Mary Finan knew she was on to something when she hired one of them for a fashion show. The hacks arrived, trying to look unimpressed. (That's an early lesson journalists learn: never look impressed or you'll be seen as naive, and even if you *are* naive, you don't want to be outed for it.) Maeve Binchy, surveying the oh-so-casual heavyweights of female journalism walking down the aisle of the plane, was heard to remark that if this one went down in the drink, a lot of great jobs would become available. We casually sauntered onto this gigantic plane, took our seats, and off it flew. Once the plane reached cruising height, models wearing the creations of some designer – perhaps Thomas Wolfangel, a power in haute couture at the time – walked between the rows of passengers while we ate a delicious lunch and made the occasional note before the plane landed again in Dublin airport. Mary Finan was way ahead of her time; that notion of a flight to nowhere came back into fashion during the Coronavirus pandemic, with a few airlines providing flights, food and a short period in the sky for those suffering aviation withdrawal symptoms. The fliers landed at the same airport from which they had taken off, which meant they didn't have to quarantine. But they didn't get a fashion show.

Then came a letter from a publication in the US.

July 1 1969

Dear Miss Prone:

From time to time *Seventeen* invites outstanding teens from other lands to be our guest in the United States. We have done this with French and German girls; now we would like you to come and represent Ireland.

I can give you only tentative dates at this point, but this is what we have in mind. You would fly here on Saturday, October 4 for several days of sightseeing and fun; then there would be an Irish party on Tuesday, October 7 at Bergdorf-Goodman, an outstanding New York department store, where high school editors from the metropolitan New York area would quiz you on Irish fads and fancies among young people. Then we would take you to Washington and possibly one other American city. You would return home around Monday, October 13.

Naturally we would try to see that you see what you want and that you meet people of your own age and tour new boutiques, Greenwich Village, attend theater — in short, have fun!

I am sure you know the reputation of *Seventeen* — it is read by one out of every two of America's 12.9 million girls …

I had never heard of *Seventeen* and couldn't for the life of me imagine why they had picked me to represent Irish teenagers. It wasn't that I had imposter syndrome; it was that I knew I was no typical teenager and would have to take remedial teaching in how to think or act like one. The day after the letter arrived, the Industrial Development Authority rang to say that this was part of an Irish sportswear promotion they were organizing with *Seventeen* magazine, involving shooting beautiful photographs in the west of Ireland. It was the IDA that had nominated me as Ireland's Outstanding Teenager.

The plan, they explained, was that my mother could accompany me and I would appear on radio and TV. Had I been to the States before? No? Oh, I would have a great time. I immediately started to mentally run through my clothes, the highlight of which was a trouser suit in pink, double-breasted and with knee breeches. This, with silver-buckled shoes made me, I believed, look like a regency dandy. Beau Brummell had nothing on me. The IDA told me I would not be packing any of my own clothes, because an entire wardrobe would be provided for me by Irish designers. The IDA appointed a liaison officer, who set up fitting appointments with the various designers, one of whom kindly told me to stop sucking in my stomach because they needed genuine measurements. Within a few weeks I had a hand-knitted oyster suit by Cyril Cullen, a Jimmy Hourihan coat, and a wonderful full-length crocheted red-hooded evening cloak, which I still have.

When the plane landed in New York, and the door was opened, four men, two of them armed and in uniform, two clearly armed but in civvies, came on board and talked to the woman leading the Aer Lingus cabin crew. All wore crew cuts, in sharp contrast to the majority of men of their age, who wore their hair long. We watched the conversation, which ended with her leading them down the aisle. They stopped at my seat, the two uniformed guys moving slightly beyond it, the two in civvies facing me.

'Miss Prone? Please accompany us,' one of them said, indicating to my mother that she should stay put. That she put up no opposition speaks to how impressively authoritarian these guys were. I unbuckled and started to reach for the overhead bin. Uh uh, I was told. That would be taken care of. The first two men led me off the plane and into a room where I was instructed to sit, and the two of them sat opposite me, while one of the uniforms stood outside and one inside the door.

The two men sitting on the other side of the table simultaneously produced cards identifying them as agents of the Federal Bureau of Investigation. Adrenalin surged through me. Also terror. They told me they understood I was going to be interviewed by Barbara Walters on national television. What did I plan to tell her? one of them asked. I hadn't a clue, I truthfully said, since I hadn't known she was going to interview me. The second agent got impatient and indicated that I knew I was going to be interviewed by more than one TV personality, and could I tell them what I planned to say, in a general way? I said I would maybe talk about what it was like to act with Ireland's national theatre company, how it felt to be a regular presenter of radio programmes and what fun it was to write for newspapers. The first guy's eyes narrowed and he asked me about controversial topics. What about Northern Ireland, he demanded. What about it? I asked. How frequently was I there? He inquired. Never, I told him.

'You've never been in Northern Ireland?'

'Well, once when I was thirteen. On an educational tour.'

I explained that it was considered educational to get on a bus with your classmates, sing Elvis Presley songs, cross the border, see pavements painted red, white and blue and also red pillar boxes. The armed uniform smiled at me but then unsmiled his face. The two in front of me looked at each other and at me. The one on the left took a deep breath and asked me if I knew Bernadette Devlin. By reputation, yes, I said. Personally, no. Their two voices crossed so I wasn't sure what either was saying, but the general drift seemed to be that it was not possible, surely, for me, as a famous teenager, not to know Bernadette Devlin, who was only a few years older, when she lived only a hundred miles away. I gaped at them and suddenly got it.

'Oh, you think a hundred miles is *close*,' I said. 'In America, maybe. But in Ireland, it's – well – *miles*. Why are you worried about me knowing Bernie Devlin, anyway?'

One of them turned over a copy of the *New York Times* lying on the desk and showed me the picture on the front page of Wee Bernie being carried shoulder high at some protest in Washington.

'Are you going to agree with what she says?'

'I don't know enough about Northern Ireland to agree or disagree.'

'But what will you say if you're asked on TV?'

'I will plead ignorance and move on to talk about something I know about. I know about a lot of things – quite interesting things. Why would anybody want to know if I agree with someone I've never met, in a different – different –'

'Jurisdiction?' suggested the smiley man, earning himself a blinder from both FBI agents.

'Jurisdiction. Precisely. Thank you.'

The two lads wanted a cast-iron guarantee that I wouldn't do inflammatory anti-British talk to Barbara Walters.

'*If* it's Barbara Walters,' I said, never having heard of her. 'It says on the sheet it's Dave Garroway.'

At that, one of them laughed and seemed convinced that I wasn't a danger to homeland security or likely to create a diplomatic incident, and they walked me out to rejoin my mother, giving me handshakes that nearly crippled me and wishing me a great time in the US. My mother had been unworried by this intervention, on the basis that I hadn't been in the US long enough to have committed a crime.

From then on, it was go, go, go. I was brought to two kosher restaurants side by side to learn that Jewish orthodoxy separated milk and its products from meat, so they were served in separate restaurants. I was brought to discos and press conferences and TV/radio studios. I met Barbara Walters, the most successful TV presenter of her time, which stretched right into 2015, when her final interview was with Donald Trump. She interviewed me on national television the morning after *Seventeen* magazine brought me to a disco in a place called the Electric Circus. Walters never so much as nodded to me as I was slid into the chair, reading her first question – something about contrasts between

New York and Ireland, for a teenager — off the autocue. 'Oh, such contrasts,' I smiled. 'You'd never see artwork in an Irish disco like I saw last night in the Electric Circus. People having sex with animals is not something an Irish teenager would often see on the walls of discos.' It was downhill from there and she was clearly glad to see the back of me.

The newspapers that covered the visit, like, for example, the *Standard-Star* in New Rochelle, New York state, touched on how the word 'groovy' hadn't made it to Ireland at that point, but moved swiftly on to more serious issues, like Ireland's strict Catholicism.

Most of the interviewers brought up Bernadette Devlin, and I made careful responses which, coming from a teenager with no political or civil rights experience, were ridiculously pompous. But as far as I was concerned, the main audience was the FBI and the main objective was to keep them happy.

Outside of ensuring Barbara Walters would never want me back, I performed creditably on countless radio and TV programmes, although it took me several days to realise that I didn't have to have something fresh for each interview, since each station had its own geographical area and didn't overlap with the next. The magazine rejected all the clothes I'd brought and gave me a new wardrobe. I got to meet Helen Gurley Brown, seminal editor of *Cosmopolitan*, who told me that Barbra Streisand had a sister who also sang and was overweight. Much later I realised that Gurley Brown, who made every day of her life a battle against gaining weight, may have been warning me. I went with my mother to the hit Broadway show *Hair*, about which my diary notes, 'I was dead worried the nude scene would put Mamma off her feed. At the end of it, she left the theatre with a face on her. "What did you think of the nude scene?" I asked. "The nude scene", she said austerely, "was the most decent thing in it."'

The day we boarded the flight home, my mother told me I had done well, but it would be wise not to believe the publicity about myself. I had no interest in the publicity. I had discovered New York, with

Gimbels and Korvettes, the automat, the Waldorf-Astoria with its famous phone number (Glenn Miller's 'Pennsylvania 6-500'), cheese-cake and Tab. I had bought myself a maxi coat with a dashing military air. Set for life, I was.

10

YOU'LL NEVER WORK IN THIS THEATRE AGAIN

I knew Bunny Carr, yet I didn't know him at all. I knew him as a voice on the phone, a deadly handsome presence in a TV studio, a man it was fun to write for, work with. I knew he was married to Joan, a former physiotherapist and tennis champion, who was in a wheelchair, having had polio, and that they had three children. I knew he was the most *loved* TV presenter, although Gay Byrne was the most admired. I knew he had a weird memory, which enabled him to memorise the names of 120 audience members and get them right whenever he had to call on one of them, yet evaporated immediately thereafter, so if he met any of them the following day he had no idea who they were. Bunny's quiz programme *Quicksilver*, with organist Norman Metcalfe providing contestants with whimsical and sometimes just plain bonkers musical clues, was a phenomenal success, inserting several phrases including 'Stop the lights' into popular culture.

Then the head of the IDA, Ireland's most glamorous organisation at the time, head-hunted Bunny, wooing him away from television. Bunny later revealed that he had hoped that one, even one, person in management in RTÉ would ask him not to leave. Nobody did. They saw him as a lightweight and didn't bother to hide it from him. That, plus the extra money and security the job offered – important, in view of Joan's disability and a growing family – made him decide to go, much as he would miss television. The IDA job required Bunny to charm the boots off millionaires and entrepreneurs and seduce them into setting up parts of their businesses in Ireland. 'Crazy hurtling jaunts that had me in every country in the continent except Norway, inside the first eight months. One day I awoke in Milan, had lunch in Zurich and dinner in Vienna.'

After Bunny donned his trench coat and grabbed his briefcase, I met him only once, when he came to Henry Street to be interviewed by Michael Littleton, then RTÉ's head of features. 'I would gladly have swapped my beautiful office, my two telephones and my expense account,' Bunny later said, 'for his battered backless chair in that Henry Street studio in which I had so often sweated through a dull programme, and occasionally steered a good one.'

My own life included a weekly column for the *Evening Herald*, where the editor was a lovely man named Brian Quinn. I was earning a decent living from journalism, but my ambitions still lay with the stage. That speedily changed when I was told that the artistic director of the Abbey, Hugh Hunt, wished to see me in his office. I had never exchanged as much as a nod with Hugh, so I climbed the rubber-edged stairs to the management corridor with trepidation. He told me I was unarguably the most talented actress of my generation. It was all I could do not to fold foetally in response. When someone in authority says something like that to you, you know the blow that follows will be heavy. It was. He sighed, the sigh suggesting that this communication hurt him more than it hurt me, and explained that, in the past year, I had consistently played character roles and played them superbly. So, he went on, steepling his fingers, he had something of an *embarras de richesses* of middle-aged character actresses to play those parts. What he needed was brilliant young performers to play roles like Juliet. And – forgive his bluntness – none of his producers was ever going to cast me as Juliet because I was so fat. It would thus be incredible to cast me as an ingénue. Now, of course, I was a valued member of the Abbey Theatre Company, and that would continue. But he wished to give me some advice, in my own interest. I needed to lose at least two stone and lose it permanently or else get out of the theatre, because the current situation, extended over my career, would lead to frustration. He didn't say where the frustration would sit. I looked at him, thinking that while my good friend Joe Dowling was already directing productions, nobody had never come to me with an offer of directing. But then, I was a girl. It wouldn't occur to them.

He stood up, reached across the desk and limply shook my hand. He was seated again and going through papers before I left his room. I stood in the corridor, trying to work out how to avoid going into the rehearsal room and face the questions about what he'd said to me, when from around the corner I could hear someone calling me. I walked towards the voice, face empurpled and bloated with shame, swallowing down the exigent need to weep. One of the School of Acting people had fainted and needed to be taken to Jervis Street Hospital. Since I had a car, would I take her? Of course I would, I said, letting on I was her solution when in fact she was mine. (I suspect, in retrospect, she was anorexic and anaemic.) By the time normal service resumed, any interest in my having been in the artistic director's office had faded, so I never had to tell any of them what he had said. Nor did I ever weep, much as I wanted to. No point.

Hunt's suggestion that I lose weight and keep it off seemed predicated on an assumption that this would be easy. But from my mid-teens, I had been trying to do precisely that, and failing every time. So much so that the class year book ran a humorous caption under my picture announcing that I knew the calorie count of every foodstuff known to humanity and every scientific principle attached to losing weight. I could lose two dress sizes and frequently did. I was riven with the self-contempt every fat girl experiences – and remember, this was fifty years before 'fat' got switched to 'big' and self-contempt, in theory, morphed into body confidence. Hunt was right and I'd been deceiving myself with all the blather about it being fun to play bothered oul' wans.

I had a multiplicity of other possibilities I needed to concentrate on and invest in. Starting with buying an electric typewriter. My current machine was a portable Brother manual. The following day I dropped into the showroom of an office supply company and fell in love with an electric machine with several daisy wheels carrying different fonts. How much? £160. Done, I said and took it home with me. When I found I could produce more work that looked better in half the time, I made it a personal rule: I would always be what was later dubbed an 'early adopter'. I would invest in technology I couldn't afford long before I needed it.

A fast typing speed did have one disadvantage, which I found out about one day when I was in Mary Kenny's office in the *Irish Press* and a man walked in to drop something on her desk. 'Terry, this is John Spain,' Mary told me. 'He is the wonderful, *wonderful* sub-editor – he and John Boland – who keeps us all out of jail.' The man leaned over to shake hands with me and halfway through, froze. '*You're* the one with the bendy last lines,' he said. It took me a minute to realise what he was talking about. 'Mary said never to carry a sentence from one page to another,' I explained, daunted by his ferocity. 'But since I got the electric typewriter, it goes so fast, I suddenly find myself at the end of the page and I have to sort of hold it in position in order to finish the sentence.'

Spain put a sheet of A4 paper in front of me, took a pencil, and put a big X two inches from the bottom of the page, then rolled the page into a typewriter and showed me how it would surface in plenty of time to warn me to finish the sentence I was on.

'And then I can rub it out later?' I asked. 'That's *so* clever. Thank you.' He tore the sheet out of the machine, crunched it into a ball, tossed it at Mary's overflowing wastepaper basket and left the room. Mary giggled into the phone call she was pretending to have.

My maternal grandparents

First Holy Communion – the only girl in brown shoes

My father's mother – who once, my mother contemptuously remembered, took two buses to the Northside to learn a new knitting stitch

Hil and me, summer holidays, Laytown

Moira Colfer – my mother

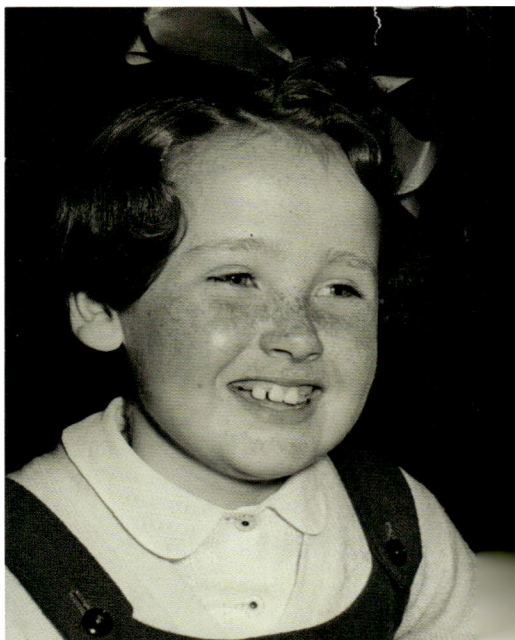

First picture in a newspaper, after
Feis win

Ireland's Outstanding Teenager
on Broadway

First – and only – time a bridesmaid,
for my big sister, Hilary

Studio shot for portfolio at 16

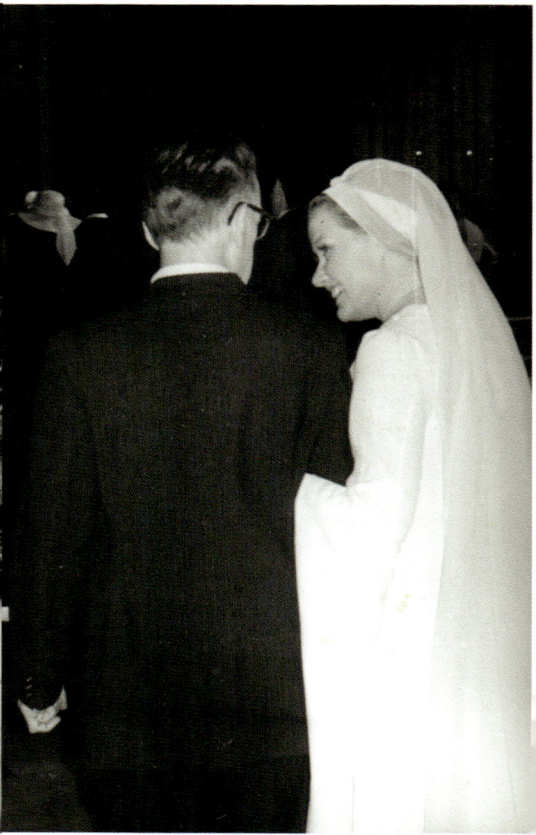

Reconciled – my father walks me up the aisle

Fr Tom Savage, left, ignoring visiting Taoiseach Seán Lemass at the Catholic Communications Centre

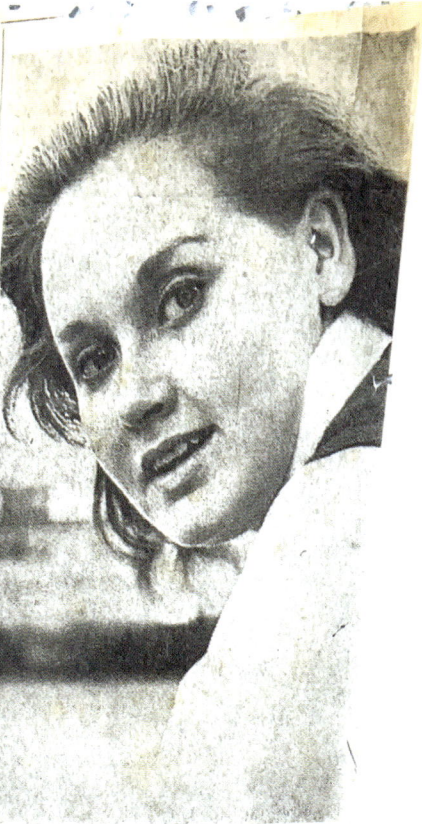

The guy at the back, supervising me, Beatles haircut and ever-present cigarette

Middle-aged to teenager in minutes!

Eighteen-year-old Terry Phone's life seems to resemble a time machine at the moment, for actress Terry is a middle-aged lady and a young girl all within the space of a few minutes.

Terry, from Clontarf, is with the Abbey Players on a probationary basis, having attended the Abbey School for the last four years. She is at present playing in both the plays running currently in the Abbey and in the Peacock.

Coming off stage as a middle-aged woman in "Borstal Boy," in the Abbey, Terry rushes down the three flights of stairs to the Peacock, furiously scrubbing off her make-up with a towel soaked in make-up remover. By the time she has reached the Peacock she has taken off her overall, turban and sloppy sandals and put on the costume she wears as a 15-year-old girl in "The Sound of the Gang."

Terry, who is taking an arts degree in U.C.D., had to miss her exams this summer because she had signed the contract with the Abbey.

Five boys escape from Daingean

A search got under way today for five boys, all aged under 17, who escaped from Daingean Reformatory, Offaly, last night.

The boys, three from Galway and two from Cork, are all thought to be wearing civilian clothes. They scaled the prison wall last night at about 10.30 and it is expected that they will make for their homes.

A Garda spokesman said that he thought that they would be picked up trying to get a lift. They had got very little money with them and no food.

The boys used a ladder to escape from the reformatory farm yard.

Struck by motorcycle

Gardai in Dublin refused to release the name of a 50-year-old woman injured last night when struck by a motorcycle in Middle Abbey Street, Dublin.

A hospital spokesman said the woman's condition was "comfortable."

Front page story I placed in a rage over being left out of an Abbey Theatre photo op of young and promising actors

Tom with the red Fiat that I was driving the day of the Dublin bombings

Hilary, me and Anne Sheehy

Wedding day – 3 April 1975

Tom – always reading

Anton being scary with a
rubber alligator

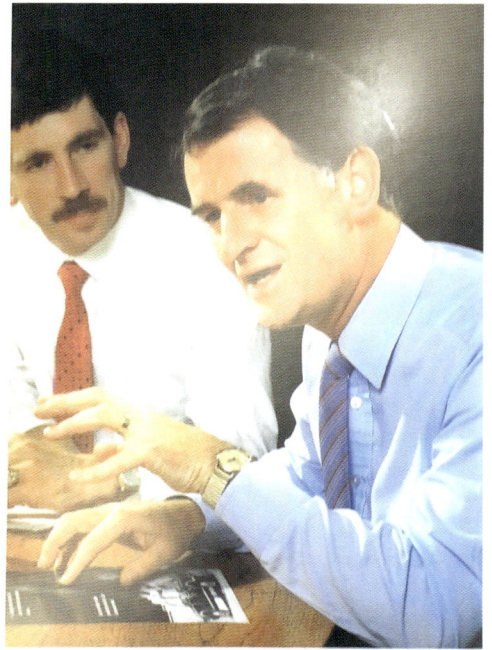

Top left: Tom – after my car crash and before his cancer

Top right: Tom – the quintessential trainer

Middle: First form a family – the three of us in Baldoyle

Bottom: Anton and Tom

Top left: Classic Tom – whistling and swinging jacket

Top right: That's Dr, actually …

Bottom: Anton tidying me up before I was conferred as a Doctor of Letters in University of Limerick, 2023

I headed over to the Abbey, where I dropped in a resignation letter to the general manager's office, indicating that the freelance option suited me better. The general manager, Phil O'Kelly, rivalled Ernest Blythe in his corporate meanness, so the letter probably made his day; one less salary to pay.

One Thursday in August I had a phone call from Tomás Mac Anna, who got straight to it. I knew Bríd Ní Loinsigh was playing the mother in Liam Lynch's *Soldier?* Yes. Well, Bríd had fainted at the end of the show the previous night and was in hospital. She would not get better, ever, he said, and would never leave the hospital, so advanced and ubiquitous was the cancer from which she was suffering. Since I had done the reading of the role a few months previously, I must be reasonably familiar with the dialogue, so would I go on in her place that night? They would make an announcement at the outset, offering everybody present their money back if they wanted it, and explaining that I was not an understudy, but had – had … He petered out. I thought fast. First of all, nobody would ask for their money back. Although Bríd Ní Loinsigh was a respected veteran performer, she was not a crowd-puller. Anybody who had bought a ticket for *Soldier* would not be riled by a replacement. In fact, audiences being audiences, they'd be slightly thrilled by the drama. I said I was willing. Okay, he said, could I telephone Phil O'Kelly, sort out the money and then as soon as possible get into the theatre. I suggested he give me a couple of hours to work on the script, which I still had from the reading, which would mean the walk-through rehearsal would be more productive. He was delighted and rang off.

I picked a sum out of the air and rang the general manager, who thanked me, indicated that if it went okay, a three-week engagement would follow, and told me I would be paid £12 a week. I said I'd need £50, which would be worth about €800 today. He laughed as if I was trying it on. I allowed silence to pressure him into repeating his offer before restating what I required with the resolute calm of someone who doesn't care about the outcome and knows the other side does. He was getting madder by the minute, but worked his way up to £20.

This I parried with a repetition of the original demand. I didn't argue or justify. I just waited, and after a furious, heavy-breathing silence, he conceded, with the threat that as long as he was general manager of the Abbey, I would never work there again. 'I'll tell Tomás what we agreed,' I said. Mac Anna couldn't have cared less, but the promise to tell him would reduce the chance of Kelly backsliding.

I then went through the play out loud four times before driving to the Abbey, where the cast were gathering. Mac Anna positioned me and we were off, me with the script in my hand, looking at it whenever another character had a speech. The words created the choreography, leading me to move in ways that for the most part matched the blocking (on-stage movements) laid down. We went through it twice. After that, it was into the dressing room, rhyming off the lines until the very last minute, when I sat onstage in the dark, listening to the announcement about Bríd's illness and me replacing her.

The lights dimmed. Then the stage lights came up and it was like crowd-surfing, the experience of being buoyed up by good actors determined to keep me afloat. Handed from one to the other, their performances thrillingly ordinary as we slipped into the groove of character and time and place. On several occasions, what I said was only an approximation of the proper lines, but the sense was right and the other actors came in on cue, even where I failed to deliver that cue. And then a lifting, thrilling, spinning emotion took hold of us and of our audience and it was better than real, harsher than performance, sweet and painful in the honesty of it. Liam Lynch's words came out of us in accents that became our own, the pain of wasted heroism became real and present for us and for those who watched us, and when the end came, silence followed. Then thunder as the audience rose to us for curtain call after curtain call.

While some of the applause acknowledged the professionalism of a short-notice stand-in, the surging energy of it was for a great little play and a superb cast. That was the joy of it, and it got better every night for the remainder of the run, because the other actors had to concentrate less on watching out for me faulting a jump, so their performances were purer. I still have the programme the Abbey ran off to cover me appearing until the end of the run, and although I was impressed at the time by the speed with which it was produced, a glance at it today establishes that it was one notch better than a photocopy. A few weeks after she fell ill, Bríd Ní Loinsigh died.

That was the end of theatre for me. Done, dusted and no regrets. No regrets because of 'the thing with feathers'. Hope fluttered around for years. Hope that a director who had seen me and who needed a Lady Bracknell would call me out of retirement. But it wasn't a painful hope, like the hope that drives cancer sufferers into despair and desperation in the determination to try one more thing that might lead to survival. It was a sweet eyebrows-raised hope with more feathers coming off it with every passing year so that when it finally died, I didn't notice.

Bunny Carr and I abandoned careers at the same time, but acting was less determinative of my life than broadcasting was of his. He missed it fiercely, but would probably have stayed with the IDA were it not for a tall, distant man with a hard-boned face named Father Joseph Dunn. Joe Dunn was the last man you'd ever put on a television programme, but he was, almost single-handedly, the force that pushed the Irish Church into – briefly – coming to terms with that newly powerful medium. Joe Dunn petitioned his archbishop to send him to the United States to learn how to make television programmes. Archbishop John Charles McQuaid agreed. Dunn came back to Ireland fired with the urge to evangelise for this medium and persuaded the hierarchy that they needed to set up a centre in which to make television shows and also to train nuns, priests and brothers in how to survive on screen. The result was the Catholic Communications Centre at the top of Booterstown Avenue. Dunn staffed this television production division – Radharc – with talents like Father Peter Lemass, an unaffected and skilful presenter of the documentaries Radharc made and provided to RTÉ at a time when independent TV production was embryonic. No doubt RTÉ wouldn't have bought the documentaries – invariably about some Church-related topic – were it not for the powerful influence then wielded by the Church, but whatever the rationale, the religious and the faithful around the country got to see new topics and a new set of skills in action. The Radharc team knew how to research and write for television. They had contacts right across Africa. They were passionate about what they did. Even today, clips from Radharc documentaries that turn up on *Reeling in the Years* show Peter Lemass and others talking to a camera worked by Dunn, on location in Kenya or Congo, without technological assistance like autocue, with confident ease and authority.

But Joe Dunn's vision for the Catholic Communications Centre was much bigger than Radharc. In the main building, he set up a fully broadcast-quality TV studio and control room. In another building out the back, a broadcast quality radio studio was where Father Pat Ahern, the Kerryman who created *Siamsa*, the folk theatre, crafted radio programmes broadcast on RTÉ radio. (This was before local radio, other than a few pop music pirate stations.)

Father Dunn had encountered Bunny Carr a couple of years earlier, was familiar with Bunny's work and knew he made no secret of being 'a staunch supporter of the One True Church.' Dunn sold him on becoming the director of the Catholic Communications Centre, 'to equip priests and religious, particularly those going to work abroad, to make some contribution to radio or television'. It wasn't that hard a sell. Bunny was working twelve hours a day in a job which, according to his wife, had sucked the happiness out of him. Running the Catholic Communications Centre looked 'like holidays with pay', even if it meant a substantial cut in salary. The tacit understanding was that he could also present programmes on RTÉ, if that came about. It did.

Along with Barry Baker, a former BBC producer, Bunny started to craft courses for clergy and the religious. Courses in presentation to camera for priests who might be called on to do *Outlook*, the five-minute televised reflection to end the day; interviewing and scripting for those who might, as missionaries, make programmes in the country to which they were sent by their order or congregation. Some courses – led by Father Brian D'Arcy – were in writing skills for newspapers and magazines. Some were in writing sermons. Everything was based on the premise that the Church was coming out of the media dark ages and that its brightest and best needed to be comfortable and competent in studio and on location, although the hierarchy showed only a sporadic and half-hearted commitment to the enterprise, which some of them saw as an expensive investment in ephemerality. Joe Dunn, however, was resilient and relentless and so the entity flourished, becoming a focus for liberation theology.

I had but the sketchiest appreciation of any of this when Bunny rang me one day, suggesting that I spend a couple of days in the centre training parish priests to improve their sermons. 'I know shag all about sermons other than being bored by them on Sundays. I'd say something completely wrong and get you fired,' I told him. Not possible, he said. He would put one of his senior lecturers in the room to make sure I didn't cross any red lines. The following Tuesday, I arrived half an hour early to find the place abuzz with men in black and a fair few religious sisters, too. Bunny brought me into his office for coffee. A balding Englishman appeared, clutching one of those oblong bottles labelled Cork Dry Gin. Bunny introduced him as Barry Baker from RTÉ, who had 'lowered himself to share his Protestant insights with the Catholic clergy'.

'What's in the bottle?' I asked Bunny when Barry had left.

'What would you expect in a bottle labelled Cork Dry Gin?'

'Gin, maybe?'

'This is why you're paid so much. You can read the signs.'

'Yeah, but why is Barry carrying it around at half eight in the morning?'

'Because it gives him a good start on his obligation to transfer its contents to the inside of Barry before quitting time.'

Barry was a high-functioning alcoholic who carried his fix with him at all times, consuming the contents of the big bottle in neat sips throughout the day, so he managed never to be drunk while always avoiding the threat of sobriety. Nobody seemed to find this odd. Not that I cared, that first morning, fearful as I was of failing the parish priests lined up classroom-style in the conference room. One of the two young laymen who worked for Bunny was to do filming and playback. Following Bunny's guidance that if I concentrated on each individual at the beginning of the day, finding out something memorable about each, I would not require name plates in front of them, I bantered to and fro with the twelve of them. I was young, as famous as one could easily be in one-channel land, and the only woman in the room.

Six of the twelve participants came to the podium, one after another, to deliver their prepared sermon to the large camera and to their colleagues. Halfway through the recordings, another man slipped in at the back. Decades younger than the parish priests, with a Beatles haircut, he made a half-gesture – 'Don't greet me' – and sat down without being noticed by most of the group. At the end of the recordings, the first cassette – an enormous block of plastic – was put into the machine and the centre staffer asked me if I wanted him to start the playback. I didn't know what I wanted, so, to test my name recognition, I asked the man who had been recorded after all the others if he could recall what the first had said. The last man looked at the first man as if something in his appearance would clue him in to what the first man had talked about. Someone prompted. I shook my head. The last man, mortified, admitted that he couldn't remember anything his colleague had said. Why? I asked. The unfortunate whose face was filling the TV screen laughingly suggested that it might be because his sermon had been so boring.

'Might be other factors involved,' one man said.

'Like?'

'Like that none of us knew which order the recording was going to be in', he said resentfully, 'so we were all anxious that we might be next. It distracted us.'

Several of the priests laughed and nodded, although the man whose recording was about to be played back murmured that members of a congregation had all sorts of things going on in their lives that might distract them. But, someone else responded, why would they go to church if they weren't going to listen to the sermon? Mightn't have much choice, most of them, came the response. Eventually the group came to a vague consensus that capturing and keeping the attention of a congregation might be just as hard as being memorable to their peers. I gestured for the playback to start and within forty-five boring seconds, the man watching himself in the black and white recording asked that it be paused.

'I've been twenty years ordained,' he said. 'I've had twenty years reading the best communications lessons. And I never noticed what they were telling me. The parables? Jesus preached in stories. Stories our of the lives of the people he was talking to. Fishermen. Farmers. "A sower went out to sow his seed …" I didn't have to be hammering home lessons. People draw their own conclusions from the parables. I should have been talking about them, not interpreting eschatological questions for them.'

The man, throughout the rest of the playback, fumbled his way to a truth he had never before realised: that simplicity is difficult, that illustration is essential, that being in a pulpit forces on the preacher an extra obligation not to bore or intimidate the congregation. The priests present also made notes, although one of them queried if I didn't have 'television advice, like'. I promised to deal with peripherals like grooming, stance and gesture later, then moved on to the next man in the sequence, who had delivered his sermon with a fear-inducing fury. When I stopped the tape, I was thrown for a second by the way the observer priest at the back was watching me, his head tilted forward so the deep-sunk eyes of him were almost hidden. Then I asked the group for comments. They nudged around as if asked to play handball with a boiling hot ball.

'Father, before we get to content,' I said, 'let's look at delivery. Do you always take so … so robust an approach to a congregation?'

Some of the others began to laugh, but I waved them down. The man looked as if he was being inflated from inside, he was so furious.

'The good Lord told us to be shepherds of his flock,' he snapped.

'True,' I said. 'But not sheepdogs.'

For twenty seconds, he stared me down, and then raised his hands.

'All right,' he said. 'Teach me how not to be a sheepdog, because I've been one for a long time.'

The observer priest quietly stood up and left the room, leaving me with a sinking heart and the terrified realisation that I must help a man free himself from the habit of decades, even though I didn't know how. I played another minute of the tape and asked him to explain it to me as if I was a bright, willing newcomer to the church. He began to talk, to hesitate and to be surprised as some of the other priests made helpful suggestions. He made notes and men who had been afraid of him were flattered. I suggested we had learned all we needed to learn from the first few minutes of playback, and if it was okay with him, we wouldn't play back the rest. He told me he would be extremely grateful if the rest wasn't inflicted on him or on anybody else and that he sincerely hoped it was coffee time because he needed a coffee and a smoke to recover. The staff member who was with me nodded and everybody trooped out to the big room where coffee was served, while I knocked on Bunny's door and was invited in.

'I'm sorry,' I said. 'Your guy left at an awful point in that session. What did he say about me?'

'He said you were playing a blinder and that he didn't need to be wasting his time watching you.'

'You're kidding?'

'He specifically praised the way you got them all talking at the beginning and then assessing each other. We always want the trainees to do eighty per cent of the talking. It's one of the things Tom is very strong on.'

'Tom who?'

'Tom Savage. Father Tom Savage. My senior lecturer.'

Back in session, the playback for one of the priests was problematic. He had begun his sermon with the statement, 'Last week I was driving from Dublin to Galway, and I decided I might be bored, so I picked up a young man.'

Despite now knowing that I should get the men to talk, rather than talking at them, I could not figure a way to use them to help a middle-aged innocent come to terms with what his congregation might read into that statement, I decided I had to be anecdotal.

'Before we start on this one,' I said to the group, 'I want to talk about an interview I did on radio a few months back. You all know about St Audeon's Cathedral?' Nods all round. 'Well, the organist from the cathedral came in to be interviewed, and I made a crucial mistake very early on. I asked him about his organ.'

I closed my eyes at the memory. Some of them laughed immediately, some after a double-take two seconds. Some stared at me, perplexed, including the man who had picked up the young man because he was bored.

'I asked him if his organ was dilapidated because of age,' I went on. 'I asked him if it was affected by damp. I asked him if his organ was capable of as many variations as it used to be.'

I told them how, when the time allocated for the interview ran out, I sought in vain for instruction, looking through the glass separating the control room from the studio, to find the control room apparently empty, although in fact all five of the crew were still there, just lying on the floor, helpless with laughter and not wanting to share something with their presenter that might cause an on-air problem.

'Okay,' I said, when the eye-mopping had finished. 'Father Larkin has given us a parallel example of someone endangered by not having a properly dirty mind, and you gentlemen are going to work out how the story – the good story – central to his sermon can be told without laughter in the house.'

Not unexpectedly, the key thing most of the priests wanted was a foolproof way of preventing nerves. I remembered the story of the legendary Abbey actor F.J. McCormick, who was so religious that the Abbey had to seek permission from the Archdiocese of Dublin for him to use the holy name onstage in an O'Casey play, because he wouldn't do it otherwise. McCormick never swore, never used the holy name. Except in one situation.

'If another actor ever spoke to him when he was standing in the wings, ready to go onstage,' I recounted, 'he would swear. "Christ" this and "Jesus" that. Because he was so nervous. *Rightly* nervous. He was going to go out in front of eight hundred strangers and try to move those strangers to laughter or to tears or both. Of course he was nervous, and he couldn't pretend to be casual with some actor who didn't understand. You're going to go into a pulpit and try to change someone's life, make them see things differently. Definitely, you're going to be nervous. You *should* be nervous. You just need to control the symptoms of nerves, like shaking hands and a dry mouth.'

I offered them some actors' methods of adrenalin management and they loved them. So much so that when I later encountered Barry Baker, clutching his bottle with about an inch of liquid left in it, I told him I was bothered that showbiz gimmickry wasn't half as important as some of the breakthroughs the guys had made, yet they seemed to value that gimmickry most.

'We are the fifth column of good communications, my dear,' Barry told me. 'We find ways to give them what they need by convincing them we are giving them what they want.'

He knocked on Bunny's door, used the gin bottle to gesture me in ahead of him, and ushered Father Lemass in after me. Bunny was already launched on a story to Father Billy Fitzgerald, an administrative staffer in the centre, about a young priest in his group who had chosen to be questioned about a three-month stint in New York, where, he said, he had seen 'murder, rape and pillage'. Impressed, Bunny had asked him about being an eyewitness to murder. The young man talked about the murders that had happened while he was there and Bunny gently summed up: 'So you didn't actually witness a murder. But what about the rape?' The priest admitted he hadn't seen any rape, but he had certainly witnessed pillage. 'What sort of pillage?' Bunny asked. The unfortunate exemplified witnessing pillage as having seen with his own eyes the theft of a bicycle.

The next day, as I walked into the centre, this time excited to be there, a burst of singing came from the conference room. Three-part harmony. 'Lord of the Dance.' Soaring, confident voices. I slid up to the open door to see Dominic McNamara, one of the young laymen who worked for Bunny, another priest who was a stranger to me and Father Tom Savage, who was conducting with his eyes closed. When they came to the end, he did a conductor's cut-off gesture and opened his eyes, to spot me standing open-mouthed in the doorway. Dominic laughed and introduced the other priest. Father Savage nodded towards Dom and told me he had been a cantor in Maynooth. 'Oh, like Al Jolson,' I nodded. Dom looked startled. 'Al Jolson was a cantor in his local synagogue,' I explained. Father Savage looked quizzically at Dominic and suggested this was a bit of information he would find it hard to make useful on a day-to-day basis, which I took as a reproof for offering irrelevancies. To hell with him. I moved into the room, set down my stuff and Dominic ordered the other two out.

As I recorded the second group, my heart lifted. All of them were better, although several of them were markedly more nervous, not having adopted any of the methods they had loved the previous day. Father Savage, who had come in at the back, talked about establishing habits, illustrated by reference to football and hurling, which made great sense to the group, although it left me stupefied. The burden of his song seemed to be that almost infinite disciplined repetition was required to inculcate a new habit.

'And another thing,' he said. 'Who're the golfers here? Harry? Yeah. Who else? Donal?'

Five of the men confessed to being golfers.

'Any of you ever go to the local professional to get your swing ironed out?'

Three heads nodded. He began to swing an imaginary golf club, two, three times.

'And you know what happened to you? For several weeks after you went to the pro, you were rubbish, every time you swung. Right? Why? Because you were no longer able to use the swing your muscles were used to, but you weren't yet comfortable – your muscles were not yet comfortable – with the new swing. That's what happens when you learn a new communications skill. And that's why most of you will show up on that screen today as improved, but at least half of you, a year from now, will have reverted.'

'And on that encouraging note …' I said, pushing the playback button to start what turned out to be a day of triumph for the participants. When we came to the end of the first playback, there was much back-thumping and praise. None of it, I noticed, came from the priest with the Beatles haircut, who sat at the back, engaged but uninvolved, watching to see what I would do. I told the group about the first night when Laurence Olivier played Richard III. The audience had risen in a standing ovation at the end of the play, yet other members of the cast were dismayed and baffled when, the moment the curtain finally came down, Olivier stormed off to his dressing room. One of his colleagues pointed out to him that he had been superb.

'I know I was good,' Olivier responded. 'But I don't know *how.*'

Knowing how to craft a sermon would, I pointed out, move them from guesswork and inspiration into competence. One of the parish priests, who had been on a training course in Britain, said that they should start every sermon by telling the congregation what they were going to tell them, then tell it to them, and at the end, say what they had told them. I listened to this, knowing instinctively it was wrong, but too appalled by the enthusiasm with which they were writing it down to intervene. Then, with fascinated curiosity, Father Savage addressed the priest who had offered the advice. 'Peter, tell me,' he said. 'Is that your approach to communication with your housekeeper?' The man laughed impatiently. Of course not. Father Savage pinched the bridge of his nose and nodded, reflectively. 'If you wouldn't communicate with one person in that way, why would you communicate with a few hundred people that way?'

Father Savage sent me a carefully typewritten letter of thanks the next day, telling me the centre would hope to use me regularly as a guest lecturer. Within days, Bunny's secretary, Kay Daly, called to see if I would do interviews and assessments on a media skills programme. In thrilling contrast to what I was doing on daily radio, this gave me the chance to do serious and in some cases aggressive interviews. Which in turn led to near mutiny before we began the playback. Asking the group for their reaction to the interview experience produced responses on a spectrum from resentful to furious. Some told me my 'rude' interruptions were typical of the way people like them were treated by the media. They then, collectively, performed the war dance I was to witness on almost every media skills course in every decade thereafter. Media people just cared about their ratings, not about the truth. With the exception of Bunny Carr and maybe Brian Farrell, all media interviewers were a disgrace.

I told them the interviewer had to be the voice of the person at home and express whatever the person at home was thinking at that particular moment. (The example of this in action, mentioned sniffily by one of the priests, was Gay Byrne, handed a baby monkey on TV, embracing it while asking its owner if it was likely to pee on him.) I dealt with the reason the interviewees were so frequently interrupted – long conceptual sentences nobody at home could get a grip on – and indicated the need for a small dose of humility. A media interview was not a lecture interspersed with acceptable questions presented in a docile tone. Nor, I told them, was it appropriate for them to pull rank with me, because in this context they had no rank. I was the expert. They were the trainees. So here, I finished, was the deal. If they were prepared to return after an early coffee break, ready to stop patronising me because I was young and female and concentrate instead on the wealth of wisdom I could offer them, I would see them back in the conference room in twenty minutes.

Twenty minutes later, Peter Lemass came out of the coffee room where the priests were, wanting to know if I would prefer to abandon the programme or have him sit in. I said no. I was intrigued by what had happened and intrigued also to see if I could dominate a group of men. It was a gamble. That I wasn't frightened seemed to be because it all fell into the performance model I was used to. This time I was the guy in *Twelve Angry Men* who moves the others in the jury room away from a flawed certitude. It was only in the car going home that I realised my shirt was damp with perspiration and that getting a bunch of older men to change long-embedded views while keeping them in relatively good humour had been tough going.

The Catholic Communications Centre was the highlight of my life at the time. Of course I had a boyfriend, and a clever, successful and decent boyfriend he was, too. I had two newspaper columns a week and was moving in a most interesting circle of women journalists. I had daily radio appearances, although I was growing more and more irritated about discrimination, and sharing that irritation with any journalist who interviewed me.

'They think we can only do soft stuff because they don't give us anything else,' I told journalist Donagh Buckley when he interviewed me for one of the Creation group's women's magazines. 'Do you think the people of Britain who listen to Jacky Gillott presenting current affairs programmes care less about the topics because she's a woman?'

The place where they talked ideas and knew they were on the cutting edge of a new version of a global entity was the Catholic Communications Centre, where you would be drawn into a debate, whether about celibacy, the fall-off in vocations, or the ethics of some recent newspaper story. On any given day, Brian D'Arcy, who ran basics of journalism courses, Desmond Forristal, one of the *Radharc* founders and a playwright, Billy Fitzgerald (an administrator) and any religious visiting the building would be standing around with Bunny or Barry, drinking coffee and chatting. On a Monday, the groups would be segregated by sport, the ones who loved it walking up and down the grounds explaining the iniquity of a referee's decision or the beauty of a try. The conversations were always civil, but often edgy, as when Desmond Forristal at some point responded to something one of the religious had said in such abstruse terms that the individual, who clearly didn't understand, took on the appearance of a chastened child.

'I must give you lessons in coping with Des,' Tom Savage said, raising his quiet voice in the way you do when your comment is aimed at someone other than the person you're ostensibly talking to. 'Des tosses an intellectual stone over a wall. Doesn't care whom it hits. Doesn't ever scale the wall and go after it. Right, Des?' Forristal looked at him from under his eyebrows, amused by the conceit while just slightly put out by it, and diverted the conversation into a question, directed at Savage, about the speed at which priests should read sermons. Savage looked surprised.

'You are *never* reading the sermon,' he said. 'You are *telling* people. The speed? The speed at which you move from one idea to another. You are not social workers or church builders or youth leaders or fundraisers. You are fulfilling a much more fundamental role. Liturgy is part of the crucial teaching role of the Church. We are opening people's minds so they see new possibilities in the familiar and relate those possibilities to themselves.'

Asked what he meant by 'the familiar', he gestured at the conference room. 'In there, yesterday, an old canon chose the Good Samaritan as his subject. Now *that's* familiar. But what made it interesting was – you know where the Samaritan hands over the money? The canon pointed out the instructions the Samaritan *didn't* give. He didn't say "Don't let him fill himself up with drink." He gave the money unconditionally. Each one of us was left to reflect on unconditional giving and how rarely we do it.'

'We're always looking out for the "deserving poor",' someone said.

'Gracious condescension and charitable dole are things of the past,' another offered. 'But we still want to offer pity, when we should be offering a service.'

'And we want an objective,' a third said, 'instead of just bloody *giving*.'

'That's one of the functions of a great sermon,' Tom Savage said, patting his pockets to make sure he had his cigarettes. 'To use the familiar, even the cliché, to unravel an unquestioned certainty.'

11

MY FIRST TELEVISION SERIES

*W*hen Denis O'Grady, the ex-BBC producer who had given me my first TV break, became head of religious programming in RTÉ television, he proposed that I present a series of half-hour interviews with people of faith who 'might be a bit unexpected', like Lord Longford, who had befriended Moors murderer Myra Hindley. The series aired in the summer of 1971 and television critic Brian Devenney said that it was 'one of those infrequent occasions when a prominent place on TV is conceded to a woman'. Another critic, Tom O'Dea, described the Lord Longford conversation as 'a textbook interview … it revealed a good deal without resort to badgering.'

I was lucky in that new jobs popped up serendipitously. One of the laypeople in the Communications Centre asked me one day if I could take photographs, because a Fleet Street Catholic weekly needed a 'stringer' in Dublin; someone who could write but also produce the pictures. I nodded. Leave it with him, he said. Ever optimistic, I bought an expensive professional camera, got used to it and within a fortnight he was back with a retainer. For three years, every week, I produced copy plus black and white photographs for that paper.

When photographing famous people, in common with the other snappers, I always looked for one of three shots: the Smiley;

the Serious; and the Holy Shit! That last was where you captured a troubled business executive or politician beneath a light that made them look like Lucifer or beside a sign advising the picking up of dogs' doodoo. These print interviews and photographs were fun, particularly when I bought my first portable word processor. 'Portable' was euphemistic. It was the size of a suitcase and weighed a ton. But it took floppy disks and was a lot faster than a typewriter.

Because I was so often in print, Father Brian D'Arcy frequently invited me to run basics of journalism courses, which attracted laypeople as well as clergy. Towards the end of the first week, a famous person came in to be interviewed and profiled by the trainees. On the face of it, a simple exercise. But not really. First of all, it required the trainees to observe how the celebrities acted when they were talking. Who they looked at. How they gestured. Second, it required that they interrogate their subject, which led to wild divergences, with some essentially asking the celebrity to tell them how wonderful he was, others wanting to know what he thought of Gay Byrne or the news-reader Charles Mitchel. On top of that, the trainees had to listen and make notes. Some of them, as they tackled that strand of the task, reminded me of myself in university, frantically trying to write down everything the philosophy lecturer had said, since my mind could not distinguish, in the moment, between the essential and the inessential. It was infinitely sad to see others rushing to get everything written, knowing they would not, afterwards, be able to read much of what they had noted. They would look wonderingly at the few trainees who, for the most part, just watched but made relatively few notes.

Post-interview, they had three hours to write their profiles to meet a specified word count. The next day, the profiles were swapped around so that each had one that they hadn't written. None of them had names on, so nobody could favour their best pal. Most of the profiles started with a description, simply because it was the first pillar on the chart, and the majority seemed heavily influenced by Garda missing person's notices on radio, describing people in terms like 'Of stout build with black hair going thin, wearing a brown jacket and corduroy trousers.' Occasionally, one would break through to the truth in a way you'd have to have reservations about. 'Father Fergal O'Connor has long brown teeth' was the opening line of one profile by a professional journalist, which led to some regrettable emulation by trainees. It had to be explained that while attracting and holding the reader's interest was paramount, doing it without egregiously wounding the subject might also be an objective. On the other hand, some awestruck affiliative trainees produced PR rather than journalism, especially when they saw the finish line in sight, lashing in a comment like 'And as Joe Bloggs walked away, I reflected on what a nice person he is in real life.'

Celebrities have a legend, a song they're used to singing about themselves; and unless the interviewer is trained to disrupt the legend, the song goes on being sung, repetitiously appearing in virtually identical versions. While it was possible to give interviewers a series of disruptive questions, it was better for them to identify for themselves when the legend song was being sung. One newcomer to journalism did it on the third course in which I was involved. She worried me, this newcomer, because although she took notes, she asked no questions until the celebrity was gathering his possessions ready to vamoose.

'Just one more question?'

He nodded, smiling at the timorous manner of approach.

'You've talked about your wife and children and your mother and your brother but you've never mentioned your father. Do you hate him?'

He looked at her for a long moment before putting down his belongings.

'I do hate him. I hated my father when he was alive and I hate him now that he is dead.'

He talked of abandonment and seeking his father out in his twenties only to be rejected in what amounted to double betrayal. The group wrote furiously and while they were writing, he took his stuff and, without a word, went to his car. Of course, the following day, that was the main theme informing each and every one of the profiles. When the assessment was complete, one of the guys asked if it was okay to submit corrected profiles for publication. Father D'Arcy said that each famous person who agreed to be interviewed had also agreed that people could seek to have the profiles published. Three days later, the profile written by the student who had asked the tough question appeared in a national newspaper.

Alan Bennett, in *Beyond the Fringe*, wrote a sketch about a vicar struggling to keep his sermon simple:

You know … life … life … it's rather like opening a tin of sardines. We are all of us looking for the key. Some of us – some of us – think we've found the key, don't we? We roll back the lid of the sardine tin of life, we reveal the sardines, the riches of life, therein, and we get them out, we enjoy them. But, you know, there's always a little piece in the corner that you can't get out. I wonder … I wonder, is there a little piece in the corner of your life? I know there is in mine.

Bunny, Tom, Barry and Aidan Meade trained young priests and sisters away from that kind of stuff. They operated along similar lines, but with interesting contrasts. Name plates were always banned, but whereas Bunny worked hard to get all the names learned off quickly as a method of relating properly to people, Tom Savage worked in a quite different way, worrying at names as a way of understanding their owners. On one course, when a novice gave her name as Paschaline, he sat back and washed his face with his hand – a characteristic gesture – before announcing 'Well, that tells us two things about you.' The young woman bridled and demanded to know the two things.

'You were born around Easter and your parents were Gospel-greedy,' Tom told her.

She nodded and laughed. In this introductory session, he would often tell the men present what sport they played. The set of a man's neck established him as a rugby player, the pallor of one hand identified a glove-wearing golfer. It was the entry point to learning more about them. They played prop forward, right? With Terenure? Okay,

was that where they lived? Oh, the family were blow-ins. Even if they
came from a tiny rural hamlet, he would invariably work out a degree
of connection: the Purcells across the river or the Colemans from the
lough. It was infuriating to try the same approach and have it fail
because, of course, Savage had travelled the country for years giving
retreats and, now, courses. When I mentioned it to him, he laughed
and told me I had missed out on the greatest connection of all: the
GAA. Next to the Catholic Church, he maintained, the GAA was
the greatest force for social cohesion in the state. The GAA created
communities, enemies, crises, solutions, and defined people in a
particular way. He shrugged about having been so defined himself.

'To a lot of older people in Cooley, where I come from, I'm the guy
who missed the penalty. Cooley got to the county final in sixty-nine
for the first time in years. Ten minutes to go, we're a point behind the
Blues. I miss the penalty. We lose the match – by a point. Next year I
had to leave Cooley to play for Ballymacnab, where I was stationed as
a priest. Landed a penalty perfectly and could hear the shout from the
sidelines: "You couldn't effing do it when you were needed to do it!"'

Bunny's charm and capacity to engage a group was breathtaking,
but it was Father Tom Savage who laid down rules for us. We were
not, for example, ever to make personality verdicts like 'abrasive' or
'emotional' or 'defensive'. We were never to identify flaws integral to
the man or woman in front of us. And we were always to remember
Barry Baker's key advice: 'Talk about what you know about, talk about
what you care about to people that you like.'

One morning when I was setting up the room for a basics of journalism course, I realised I had company: a priest in late middle age,
quietly reading his Office. Our eyes met and I did the 'I'm not here,
ignore me' head shake. Once I was set up with the right number of
pads on the desks, pens neatly lined up alongside, I went over to the
notice board to look at pictures randomly pinned to the cork board.
Yes, that was Bunny, the man he was greeting was Seán Lemass, then
the Taoiseach, the man in the foreground was Alpho O'Reilly, RTÉ's
head of design. Out of kilter with all the others was the figure on

the left, prowling towards the camera, unsmiling, ignoring the most powerful man in Ireland and the most powerful man in the Catholic Communications Centre. At which point I noticed the older priest was putting his battered prayer book in his briefcase, task complete. I went over to him and sat down.

'What would you normally be doing on mornings you're not here?'

He said he'd go out with a net outfit on him to his hives and let bees walk all over him. It was comforting, he said, the noise and the calm busyness of them. He wasn't good at small talk, he said, and bees didn't need it from him.

'Peter! I figured you were hiding somewhere.'

The older man stood up and embraced Tom Savage.

'This man is the future of the Irish Church, if it has a future,' Savage told me. 'He doesn't see poverty as something inflicted by God or Satan, to be coped with by prayer, but by social services. Peter Birch, Bishop of Ossory.'

'Your Eminence', I said, 'I'm sorry for not giving you your proper title.'

'He's not your eminence,' Savage laughed. 'He's not even your grace. You have to become a cardinal like Big Bill Conway before you become an eminence.'

Bishops often turned up at the Catholic Communications Centre on their way to another event. Some of Bunny's people believed they came to check up on how the hierarchy's money was being spent, but sometimes, it seemed, they came for a cup of coffee and a bit of gas. One of the most popular was Bishop John Kirby, a mathematician who always wore a grey suit, so he looked like a Protestant clergyman.

The first day Bishop Eamonn Casey came, I slid out through the group welcoming him. My parents regarded Casey as a come-all-ye singing self-publicist without merit, so I had no great interest in meeting him. Going outside, I sat at one of the picnic tables with a book. In the distance, Father Savage was walking up and down, smoking, the cigarette-holding hand swinging loose except when he was sucking in smoke. After a while, he came over, squashed the cigarette butt into an ashtray on the wood-planked table and sat down.

'You know Bishop Casey is visiting?' I asked him.

'Mmmm.'

'Do you know him?'

'Yes, I know Eamonn Casey. I know him for what he is and he would not be happy to see me appear in front of him'.

'Why?'

'Because he stole my scholarship and passed it off as his own.'

'What?'

Savage had, he told me, a graduate degree in sociology from Queen's University Belfast, having been the first Roman Catholic priest to attend that university. He had done research work in London into homelessness, this being the time of the TV programme *Cathy Come Home*. Father Eamonn Casey was referred to him because Casey was also interested in homelessness. Savage gave him a copy of the research and a few months later found himself reading about the ground-breaking work with the homeless done by the Kerryman. His original research had been claimed by Casey, who, he pointed out, had no sociological background.

He pulled a small book out of his pocket and found the Office for the day, so when the bishop came out of the Centre and drove away with explosive acceleration, Savage was a small shadow in the dark of the old broadleaf trees that constituted the boundary to the property.

Although the bishops flattered themselves on their advanced thinking in setting up the Catholic Communications Centre, they vitiated its potential by chronically under-funding it, forcing Bunny to go looking for laypeople to be trained by us. He thought he might get politicians, having been mesmerised, in the course of a weekly political TV programme, by how inadequate their media skills were. One man, at the end of a programme, elbow-nudged Bunny and told him, with some pride, 'Mind you, you didn't get much outa me, did you?' Bunny believed the time had come for politicians to be interesting, under-standable and memorable on TV and radio. The political parties did not share that belief. Nonetheless, a trickle of external commercial work began to boost the centre's finances just a bit. A monthly open presentation skills course was scheduled, with businesspeople and some clergy booking in. The target numbers were two groups of seven. Most months, if four people pitched up, it was accounted a success.

Brendan Bird, then deputy chief executive of the B&I shipping line, resentfully attended one of those courses at the behest of his chairman, Alex Spain, having instructed his personal assistant to ring our switchboard at noon to report that the shipping line was having a crisis. Since B&I was, at the time, engaged in one never-ending crisis, this wouldn't require her to lie and would get Bird out of the course before it became too painful, while allowing him to snow his chairman with scattered quotes from the course, or at least from the morning he had attended.

The six people in his group, including himself, were video-recorded by Tom Savage, each giving a five-minute presentation on a subject of their choice. The tutor started to play them back. Brendan Bird was restive enough during the first playback and assessment, which took forty-five minutes and brought the group up to coffee break. But restive turned into febrile during the playback after coffee. The entire recording (which overran its allotted five minutes by half) was replayed from start to finish. It was delivered by a senior partner in an accountancy firm. Let's call him Jake, because it's nothing like his real name. The B&I man watched Jake perform and began simmering. 'I decided the presentation was the greatest load of bullshit and if that guy in charge' – Tom Savage – 'didn't *tell* the accountant it was bullshit, I was out of there even before my PA's phone call was put through.'

Tom Savage languidly elicited responses from participants. People were not allowed to make judgements, good or bad. That cut off 90 per cent of the available reactions, because most people, having watched a talk, if the speaker who gave the talk is present, want to say something pleasant, like 'I found it interesting.' Or 'It could have been more punchy, but it was good.' Or even (starting to applaud) 'I really really liked that talk.' None of which advanced the state of communication one little bit. In this particular case, the tutor sought anecdotes or illustrations people remembered. None was offered, which mollified Brendan Bird a little but not much.

Tom Savage asked the speaker what he wanted his audience to do as a result of his talk. The accountant, who was braced for heavy artillery fire, began to relax and think before going on to explain. The priest, who had a habit of washing his lower face with his hand whenever he was listening intently, did a lot of face-washing while nudging the man into greater elaboration: 'Yeah? Why would that matter? And explain why X?' Jake began to lean forward in his chair, gesturing and becoming more animated. He also began, subliminally, as we all do in a group situation, to pick up and be boosted by the unconscious 'tells' of other participants, as they nodded at a point he was making or turned more to face him. When the man eventually ground to a halt, some of the other participants wanted to get in on the act. Tom Savage did another characteristic gesture: closing his eyes, pinching the bridge of his nose with his right hand, doing hushing gestures with the left. Silence fell. And continued for several seconds. Then Tom sat up and gestured at the monitor.

'Tell me something, Jake,' he said slowly. 'If you can be as interesting on this topic as you've been for' – he looked at his watch – 'the last ten minutes, why would you *ever* deliver a load of bullshit like you delivered up there on screen?'

On the face of it, that was insulting. But the man was laughing, because in fact he had been flattered. He had been told that when he was not pretending to be someone else, when he was seeking to explain something from his field of expertise, one-to-one, to someone he quite liked, he was interesting, but that something in the one-to-group situation ironed him into being boring. Brendan Bird, meanwhile, was watching in disbelief, thinking, 'He told him it was bullshit. He did. I swear to God, he told him it was a load of bullshit.' Then our receptionist knocked and came in.

'Tom, sorry to interrupt, but B&I have been on urgently for Mr Bird. There's a crisis and they need him ...'

Brendan waved her away. No, no, everything was grand. She stood, irresolute, for a moment, and then left, trying to work out whether it was B&I or its chief executive who was crazy. Brendan stayed for the rest of the two days, vacuuming up everything the tutor had to offer and becoming a friend for life in the process.

That same day, I came upon Tom Savage and Peter Lemass having an argument in the corridor. Peter gestured for me to join them.

'I am trying to persuade this man to present a Radharc documentary about the crisis in the priesthood – priests leaving, although not that many in Ireland – but vocations on a downward slope. You'd agree with me that he's the perfect man to do it?'

'Not doing it, Peter,' Tom said. 'No interest.'

'But you do *Outlook*,' I pointed out.

'Yeah, but now I have paid off my car, I don't need to any more.'

Two years earlier, a priest friend in Northern Ireland had asked Tom to do the UTV five-minute reflection. He initially refused, but changed his mind when the priest making the suggestion said it paid £10 a night.

'I was trying to buy a new car,' Tom Savage told Lemass and myself, 'and fifty quid at the time would get me over the line. But I won't do this documentary, Peter, and I'll tell you the real reason. The real reason is that the programme is asking the wrong question. The question is not why we have so few priests today and will have markedly fewer in the future. The question is why we had such a gross oversupply in previous generations.' Lemass looked as if he would argue further, but Tom was having none of it. I pointed to the picture thumb-tacked to the wall.

'That's so funny, you not paying a blind bit of attention to the VIPs.'

'Yeah and the bandy rickety legs that couldn't stop a pig in a lane.'

'How d'you mean, rickety? I asked, puzzled, because he was a big, hefty, muscular athlete.

'You've heard of rickets? That's one of the symptoms. Shorter, bowed legs. A teacher in the school in Armagh made that pig-in-a-lane-crack about me when I was about eleven. I stood up and told him if he made reference to my physical makeup ever again, I would report him to the dean.'

I wondered at the courage of the eleven-year-old and at the understanding the child had of how the system worked: that he had recourse to a higher officer and that what the teacher had done didn't conform with the rules. At eleven, I would have had no such understanding. At best, I would have known that my higher officer was my mother and that *she* knew the unwritten rules of the education system: what was permitted teacher behaviour and what wasn't.

I followed Tom out to the grounds and walked in step with him. He shifted the cigarette to his left hand and started to blow the smoke away from me, which I thought a pity because few smells are as wonderful as that of a freshly lit cigarette out of doors.

'How did you know what to do, when you were only a little boy?'

'I was clever.'

'Always a good thing.'

'Maybe in your life. Not in mine. I remember going back to school in Armagh at, what, twelve? thirteen? On a scholarship because I was clever. Last day of August. Top deck of the bus, looking down at lads digging a trench in the road, stripped to the waist, tanned, laughing, covered in sweat. Wishing to be down there with them, doing physical stuff. Just living. Going home in the evenings to people who loved them. Whereas I was on a bus back to a boarding school where I would be for three and a half months, never seeing my family, living from letter to letter, package to package. Because I was clever. I just wished I could have been born stupid. I hated being clever. Having so much expected of you, so much invested in you. Sport saved me. No sport I wasn't good at. I have an all-Ireland medal and a Sigerson Cup medal and ...'

'For what?'

'Football.'

'What kind? The kind with the egg-shaped ball or the other kind?'

He turned slowly to look at me the way you'd look at a new species of striped invasive mussel.

'You really are a sporting illiterate, aren't you? Mother of Jesus, the egg-shaped ball ...'

We were walking back into the building and he was telling the others about the question, shaking his head in wonderment, when we got swamped with the buzz of a course finishing. That was always the way. Courses, whether they lasted two or three days, ended on a Friday with wine and cheese. This offered the joy, for participants, of a continuum of the adrenalin and affection built up during the ups and downs of the training, for tutors to hold on to 'trainers' high' as long as possible, and, for Bunny, the chance to hold court. In hindsight, we have to be grateful that somebody with a few glasses of wine in them didn't kill themselves on their way home from the Catholic Communications Centre. On this particular day, one of the priests in Barry's group had excoriated divorce as the refuge of the shallow and the uncaring. Not surprisingly, given the period, this was met with general agreement from the other clerics present. Barry drank, bugle-style, from his Cork Dry Gin bottle and gently asked the priest if he had ever met someone who had been divorced. The man shook his head. 'Well, you have now, Father,' Barry said, grasping him warmly by the hand. 'I'm on my second marriage.' He was so kind about it that the priests tried explaining that they understood divorce was okay where he came from (London) but that he'd gradually see that Ireland was different.

Bunny, in another quadrant of the room, was listening to a man giving out about platitudes. Radio and TV were full of platitudes, he told Bunny furiously, and they were without merit. Any fool could think up a platitude. 'OK, think up one now,' Bunny suggested. The man eventually said 'Touché', earning himself the slightly muffled round of applause you get when people can only pat their free hand off their wine-holding forearm.

Unlike Bunny and Barry, who set themselves down in one place and became the nucleus of a group of circling atoms, Tom Savage wandered around the back of several groups, teasing, questioning and cueing those he knew to tell stories he'd previously heard them tell. One of them told a funny story about Cardinal Conway, whom he referred to as 'Plus William'. Tom leaned over to me and murmured that cardinals always sign official documents with a cross in front of their names, the cross looking like a plus sign and giving rise to the nickname. Someone asked Tom how he was getting along with Plus William. 'Other than the carpeting six weeks ago, great. He has yet to forgive Mr Carr for stealing me away from my role as head of social services in the Archdiocese of Armagh, but he'll get over it.'

The wine-drinkers wanted to know why Tom had been carpeted by his bishop. He invited them to share how most of them hated having children under four in their car, because the kids would maul everything, investigate the glove compartments, leave sweet papers everywhere. Well, Tom said, he knew two exceptions. Two-and-a-half and four. Boy and girl. The most mannerly you ever met. If you gave them sweets, they'd hold the wrappers in their little hands without a word unless you noticed and disposed of them. Their mother, Fiona, would sometimes sing on the longer drives, and the two little sprouts would be on the back seat, fast asleep in each other's arms. Fiona didn't do performance parenting, he said.

'Define "performance parenting",' Father Forristal asked, and Tom made the group laugh by mimicking parents who hissed out of the side of their mouth at their children while smiling at the visiting priest and held them that little bit too tightly by their wrists when they wouldn't behave. Performance parenting was when the parent saw the child as an accessory, rather than as an individual. Fiona Mulroney (not her real name) just plain loved her kids and they loved her right back. But someone had seen Tom driving her in his car and had reported him to his bishop, the cardinal. So he was summoned to Ara Coeli, the cardinal's residence, and asked to account for himself.

'Big Bill tells me I've been seen in the car with Fiona and I say "And her children."'

And he says the children aren't the point, and I ask what *is* the point and he just looks at me. "Oh, right", I say, "being seen in the car with a mother of two children, along with the two children, that's not the issue. The issue is that she's the local prostitute. She can't afford a car and the bus doesn't come at a great time and she is religious, Your Eminence, about getting her children to school on time."

"But what about those to whom your giving her a lift might give scandal, Father Savage?"

"Well, Your Eminence, if I stopped doing it, I'm sure they'd find another issue about which to be scandalised. And about which to report to you." And he says he's sure I'm right and he knows he can rely on me.'

Tom said this standoff reminded him of the time the goose took a run at him and the other kids in his family. His sister Teresa, then about eight, grabbed the goose by the neck, which effectively immobilised it. However, she then faced the consequent problem that she couldn't let go of the bird until an adult appeared, and the first adult – their mother – was not due for more than an hour. According to her brother, Teresa kept a grip on the goose for more than an hour. When it was released, the poor bird staggered away and bothered nobody for a long time.

'Teresa lives in Raheny, near you,' Tom said to me. 'I must stick you for a cup of tea next time I visit her.'

I nodded and forgot about it until one evening a couple of weeks later, when there was a knock at our front door at about seven, and he was on the doorstep, dressed as always in black formal clothes. I brought him into the sitting room, where my parents were watching television. When I introduced him, my mother directed me to where the better biscuits were kept. He shook his head and asked if it was possible to have white bread and butter. I made tea and brought a tray into the dining room, where the priest was looking at a framed newspaper shot of the painting of the scene from the movie *The Castaways* that had won me the chance to work with Harry Kernoff. I said I used to paint. Not any more.

'And you used to act and now you don't?'

I told him the reason and he absorbed it without comment, moving on to talk about Teresa and the former Christian Brother, Charles, to whom she was married. Charles was a bit like me, he told me: a decision-maker, a hard worker, always happy. He stood up and thanked me for the tea. Knocked on the sitting room door to say goodbye to my parents, and off with him to Raheny.

12

SPEAKING UP

*T*he *Liam Nolan Hour* arrived on RTÉ radio in February 1970 and I was asked to be 'the woman on the team'. This was not a gesture to diversity, but rather an expectation that items might have to be included that no self-respecting male could be expected to handle, because they were so expressly female as to bring any lad out in a cold sweat.

The more positive aspect of the job was that when Pat McInerney discovered that I was able and willing to fully read a book, produce an introduction to the author and make a list of questions overnight, he and the other producers used me as reader-in-chief. I got paid buttons for this extra task, but often got to keep the hardbacks and ask the authors to sign them. The best part, though, was the variety of reading; anything from a book on improving your own mental health to a tome about Ireland's tragic deforestation, from a solid history book to a Jilly Cooper bonkbuster. The best days were when something happened, in Ireland or overseas, while the programme was on the air. Not many experiences equal the thrill of being part of a group frantically working the phones to reach the friend of a dead former cabinet minister or an expert in earthquakes or skyscraper fires because the news on the wires needed to be explained by a real live person.

I usually went in to RTÉ early in the morning but on one particular morning I was on the road far later than was sensible, which explains why I drove straight up the exhaust pipe of the car in front of me on Annesley Bridge. I sat, stunned, knowing how guilty I was. What was most worrying was that the driver of the car ahead of me had obviously been so injured by the collision and had collapsed out of sight, because I could see nobody behind the steering wheel. Then the driver's door opened and out popped a tiny man. I recognized him immediately: Professor Charles McCarthy, one of the few people in the world who could make industrial relations interesting. He had, he always claimed, been a fine rugby player until the day another student on the pitch lifted him up and threw him away. It was only at that point that McCarthy came to terms with the fact that he had stopped growing rather earlier than he would have liked.

'Are you okay?' he asked, as I rolled down my window.

'More to the point, are *you* okay?' I responded, following this up with a flurry of apologies. He waved them away. The bumper of his car, back in the day when cars had bumpers, was already so dented that he maintained he couldn't identify the new ding I had caused and as long as I was sure I was feeling all right, it had been a pleasure to meet me and we should probably get moving and stop inconveniencing other drivers. I drove gratefully and shakily on, found a parking place on Henry Street and ran the length of the long corridor to the studios, where I was handed a brief and told I'd have to wing it because I had arrived so late. The double doors into the studio were opened, I slid in – and sat down opposite the man I had met earlier, Professor Charles McCarthy, who behaved as if we were engaged in a happy conspiracy to be kept secret from the listeners. Charles was the dream interviewee everybody hopes for: lucid, loquacious, expert, enthralled by his own subject and unsuspicious of the media interviewer in front of him.

That interview would have been the exception, in my five years in Features and Current Affairs, because I was The Daily Girl – the one who could be inserted as a filler between more serious, male-dominated items. It was standard at the time and it lasted way beyond its time. I remember the response of a newspaper editor – much later, perhaps around 2006 – when I asked him what tone he wanted in a column he was commissioning me to write. 'Light and frothy,' he told me. 'Like my girlfriends.'

If you were a woman in talk radio in the nineteen seventies, your specialities, in the line of interviewing, included talking to minor showbiz personalities, writers of new cookery books, and people with patented diets to prevent bed-wetting in young and old.

'At this stage,' I told *The Cross* Catholic magazine, in 1973, 'I feel that I should have an honorary medical degree and an honorary Montessori diploma because of my vast knowledge culled from interviewing. As a woman, you are not expected to interview on major political, religious or social items.'

Sometimes, if the regular male interviewer on your programme was unable to dash to an airport at short notice, you were sent instead. But it was a vicious circle: women didn't generally do 'hard' current affairs interviewing; ergo, women were perceived as *incapable* of doing that kind of broadcasting. Rather than fight this, most of the freelance women in radio worked around it. They accepted the 'Here's Miss X, and you should just see the pretty pink shoes she has on' slot into which male producers tended to put them. Female producers were few and far between (although Kathleen Kelleher had succeeded Howard as producer of *The Young Idea*) and a variant of the prejudice that applied to women broadcasters applied to women producers, who most of the time ended up working on arts programming.

Prejudices became dogma. It was a rule, for example, that women were not allowed to interview one another, on the basis that women picked up each other's tone of voice and so it would be impossible for listeners to differentiate between them. That was the justification for never having more than one woman in a panel discussion, although women in such discussions were rare at the best of times.

'The luxury of boring people is permitted to you if you are a government minister, a cleric, an educationalist, or a trade unionist', I told *The Cross*, 'but if you are a woman, you must be sparkling, memorable and, if possible, outrageous.' The connection between words and outcomes wasn't that evident in the interviews I gave. I seemed happy to forcefully make points, but not unduly disturbed if those points didn't bear fruit. If RTÉ management noticed, they seem to have seen it as deluded self-expression by the fat redhead. But then, half the time I was using a pseudonym, so they wouldn't have known, for example, that it was me, writing as Geraldine Desmond (homage to Hilary's two eldest sons, Gerard and Desmond), who wrote infuriated feminist pieces for the *Irish Press* women's page, edited by Liam Nolan after Mary Kenny high-tailed it back to the bright lights of London. A few of the female women's editors took a dim view of what they viewed as a retrograde step on Tim Pat Coogan's part in putting a man back in a role that Mary had made her own, and an overtly and traditionally Catholic man at that. But, although Liam was fiercely conventional about the family unit, he never let that limit the viewpoints on his page, consistently giving space for this sort of thing, which appeared on 1 November 1971:

'Big deal' is the bored reaction of most women in a position to assess clearly the findings of the recent commission on the status of women. Big deal that it should say that all women should receive equal pay for equal work. Big deal that the marriage bar should be condemned. Big deal that it should be found that Ireland will have to toe the EEC's line in regard to women. All these things were known before, at least by women. What is important is what relevance it has, how much notice will be taken of it, and to what degree it can be used as a weapon. This is where we women become just a little cynical. What happens if the findings of the commission are implemented? With personnel managers, middle managers and boards of directors laden with men, the overwhelming likelihood is that women will simply be second choices in the employment field. One of the first reactions came from the Minister for Industry and Commerce, and his words are surely significant: 'The report would be circulated to all departments' and he would be 'very surprised ... if action is not taken.' He may well be in for such a surprise ...

In his very first interview following the release of the report, the Minister covered one line of retreat very neatly. The economic position of the woman who opts for staying at home and minding her children, at present so much worse than that of the single man or woman, he said, will get even worse if the findings of the commission are implemented.

What we want is for women to have positions on company boards where their common sense would, hopefully, influence the introduction of staggered working hours, which would a) benefit those family women (DOWN with the word 'housewife') who could do a NON-nine-to-five job, and b) lessen traffic chaos at the current 'rush hours' ...

The likelihood of our getting these things is small with no political party actively fighting for the emancipation of women, and with our policy makers, men themselves, relying so much for guidance on foreign reports, produced by men like Kinsey, Buchanan, etc.

I didn't join any of the groups of women, whether unofficial – meeting in each other's homes to do consciousness-raising and vagina interrogation using mirrors – or official, like the ones meeting in Gaj's restaurant, generously fed by Mrs Gaj, or Nuala Fennell's Women's Aid. I helped, but never joined. Which saved me a lot of the misery those groups inflicted on their members as time went on. The repressed, in the early years of revolt, have a capacity to join like quicksilver and separate like quicksilver and be as mutually toxic to those joining and leaving as quicksilver. (It happened everywhere. Rita Mae Brown has written brilliantly about the exclusion forced at the time on America's working-class and lesbian feminists.)

Just as happened fifty years later, when 'politically correct' became the accusation of the establishment against the outsiders, I watched and listened as women leading the charge were dismissed or stereotyped.

Nell McCafferty was in great demand when she was writing about unfortunates in the District Court being talked down to and insulted by judges suffering from an over-supply of entitlement, but the demand faded as she became more militant. Other feminists came with a sort of inbuilt caveat. Mary Maher was very clever, but that American accent! Máirín de Burca was brilliant but a communist, probably. Mary Cummins was fine, but you couldn't be sure of her. Mary Anderson sounded English and was a bit strange. (Mary's strangeness eventually took the form of changing her name to Emerald O'Leary and running her own church in the United States.) Nuala Fennell was respected by feminists and broadcasters until she became a Fine Gael Minister of State and everything she had done up to that point was reinterpreted as selfish career-building, which it was not. Mavis Arnold was a good talker, but sounded terribly Protestant and, anyway, was married to Bruce Arnold. That last one caught me by surprise because many of the others who were dismissed, like Mary Maher, had husbands (in her case, at the time, trade unionist Des Geraghty), but the husbands didn't tend to be listed as disqualifiers. Bruce had two strikes against him in RTÉ. The first was that he always asked what he was to be paid when invited to participate in a programme either about art, in which he was an expert, or politics, his special niche in the *Irish Independent*. I once asked Bruce about this and he got quietly livid about what he perceived as RTÉ producers' habit of responding to a perfectly legitimate query about fee level with, 'Oh, we won't fall out about that.' Bruce proved them wrong on that one, early and often. The other reason he was mistrusted was an urban legend, rife at the time and impossible for him to disprove, that he was a member of MI5. Not that he was alone, at the time, in having such affiliations attributed to him. As far as Fianna Fáil and Fine Gael were concerned, half of RTÉ were card-carrying members of the 'Stickies', and as far as the Labour Party was concerned, the other half was made up of secret members of Opus Dei or the Knights.

The difference was that men like Bruce were well able to fight their own corner, and those producers and interviewers known to have 'Sticky' leanings were sufficiently subtle not to present management with evidence compelling enough to provoke their dismissal. The feminists, however, never coalesced into an overt or covert body powerful enough to spot and fight female stereotyping and exclusion from programming. It was simply assumed that all panel shows, from the Irish-language *Iar-Phroinn* to political debate programmes, were properly populated by men in dominant positions. Since women were not in prominent positions, that sorted that.

It sorted it so effectively that when Fine Gael's Gemma Hussey brought a group of women from the National Women's Council to the Catholic Communications Centre for training, several deep breaths were taken at the idea of making a video to challenge the exclusion of women from news and current affairs in RTÉ television. Who would present it? I gestured at the women present. They did everything except climb up the studio's cyclorama curtain at the idea, except for Gemma, who took it on. The video was made and shown. It got the coverage it was always going to get from the women's pages, but it also achieved coverage on the news pages. Within a year, a woman was reading the news on screen at the national broadcaster, and the assumptions that had solidified into self-reinforcing prophecies were falling away, one after another. I was never sure and am not now sure where cause and effect lay, believing at the time that gender equality was ineluctable. Whenever a major social change happens, campaigners claim credit and historians crystallise their actions as instrumental, because humans like a story that is not random, that speaks to human progress and the agency of inspired individuals, but time and again I have watched heroic and inspired leadership shown in situations where the result seemed inescapable, so that what appeared instrumental was more of an accompaniment.

Eavesdropping on men in power demonstrated a tangible disconnection between a feminist argument and a result, that disconnect happening whenever a man in relative power perceived the woman promulgating the point to be complaining or reproving. Much later, Barbra Streisand nailed the differences in the way women and men are viewed:

A man is commanding – a woman is demanding.
A man is forceful – a woman is pushy.
He's assertive – she's aggressive.
He strategises – she manipulates.
He shows leadership – she's controlling.
He's committed – she's obsessed.

But before Streisand articulated those truths, I realised that when a man patronised you on radio, it tended to work better if you smacked back in a good-humoured way, for example: 'Glossing over the misogyny in that comment, which I'm *sure* would never be intended by a modern politician like yourself …' The same applied when a course participant called me 'honey' or 'sweetheart'. Everybody else present would be neutral to positive about such endearments. I would stop dead, flag everybody down and say 'Sorry, I'm not sure I heard that. What did you say again?' Invariably, the comment would be repeated, shorn of the offensive term. A compliment to the offender on his capacity to edit on the fly and we'd have moved on before offence could be taken, while at the same time, everybody present grasped that it wouldn't be safe to try that again.

I also avoided being the coffee-maker and server. It still drives me nuts to see women in meetings taking on coffee-pouring duties. Back then, it was de rigueur and it took nerves of steel to stay seated when the trolley was brought in. But, just as someone always fills a silence, someone inevitably steps up to take on coffee-serving duties. It was noticeable, in the Catholic Communications Centre, that traditional roles applied when it came to washing up. Priests and brothers automatically ceded the washing and drying of coffee and tea paraphernalia to the nuns present, with the exception of Tom Savage, who was often in the kitchen, a tea towel thrown over his shoulder like an accessory, whistling to himself while he did the dishes. If one of the men wanted to talk to him, and they always did, whether it was about a training issue or (on a Monday) the lamentable performance of some football or hurling team, then they had to wash while he dried. He would tell them that his mother had worked all her life outside the home and had made sure that every one of her children had their own domestic chores, whether it was making beds or doing dishes. Her not being there to do those tasks didn't mean the tasks didn't have to be done. His mother seemed a formidable woman, cycling home at lunchtime when any of the children were babies to breastfeed them before returning to work.

Tom was embedded in his family to a degree I found unexpected, given his absence from the age of eleven at boarding school, and then seminary. Or perhaps that was why he was so willing to tell stories about them. Peter, the youngest and a ferocious combatant whose back came warm against his older brother's when the latter, refereeing a match, met with threats from the followers of a team against which he had made a ruling. Tom would cock his head, appreciating the memory of the much younger brother threatening death and destruction to a collection of men much bigger and older than he was. Tom talked of his little sister, Marnie, who was barely out of nappies before she learned to insist 'I go with the boys,' fearful of being left in the house to do domestic duties. Of Seamus, a brother who was then doing expert sports broadcasting on a pirate radio station. Of John, who, having elicited the meaning of a word of which he was learning the spelling, was heard going around the house murmuring 'C-O-S-Y snug' to himself.

Their father, a perfectionist stonemason and carpenter, was threatened in England by workmates when he hung doors too quickly. Tom would talk of his father's depression and – in the face of major international hostility to electric shock treatment – was adamant that, having seen it properly administered when working in a mental hospital in the North, and seen the results it delivered for his father, this approach should not be written off for those suffering intractable depression.

Tom maintained that, for good or ill, families were the foundational experience that equipped us or disqualified us for adult life, and used the concept of family frequently on courses. I knew this because I would, whenever I had a cancellation, sit in on assessments he was delivering. Trying, if I am to be honest, to pick up and copy what it was that made course attendants laugh and learn from him even though he rarely told jokes, and what it was that made them quote him and apply what he said to aspects of their lives other than media interviews or sermons. Initially, when he paused a playback and began to talk, I would get impatient and want him to get to the bloody point. Then, suddenly, the entire group would be leaning forward in recognition that he was bringing together more than one point and casting a frame around them that made shimmering sense. I would never be able to capture what it was he had done, although it was impossible not to register his instinctive teasing out and occasional scotching of certainties. He never saw a certainty that he liked at first encounter. One afternoon, when a course participant told another to 'just be yourself', Savage shook his head and pointed out that each of us has a panoply of 'selves'. The self we bring to work. The self we bring home. The self our best friend encounters. The self freed by alcohol. The issue, he proposed, was not as simple as selecting an essential self, but constant seeking of authenticity.

Then he got launched on how personality emerges in ways of which we may not be conscious. He talked of the seminarians in Maynooth who went outdoors in the evenings to have a smoke, because smoking indoors was forbidden. On nights without a moon, the darkness on the campus would be complete, and the long black cassocks worn by the men provided no contrast, so that only the tiny light-dot of the cigarettes told anything about their owners. But it told such a lot, he said, mimicking the gestures as he described each smoker. The anxious man who was always fidgeting and whose cigarette jigged in the air, scattering sparks everywhere. The talker who made great sweeping gestures to explain his point, the light-dot arcing in the air as he did so. The one who concealed his cigarette inside his hand, so light appeared only when he took a long suck on it. The one, like Savage, whose cigarette was at the end of a loose-swinging arm, a tiny round light at knee level.

The lesson was the same as the lesson from good theatrical directors: Watch. Listen. Be a silent witness, a student of others. Watch not to condemn, but to boost. To find the talent, the instinct, the capability a person doesn't know they have and push them to develop it to its fullest. He would quote Goethe to the effect that if you treat a man as he is, that's all he'll ever be, but if you treat a man as if he is what he could become, you free him to become it.

Bunny would often joke that, when he and Tom divided a group of fourteen clerics into two groups of seven, Tom invariably got the better group, based on the laughter and energy coming from the room he was in. Tom would never comment when this was said, but just regard Bunny from under his eyebrows. Of course he got the better group, because, although Bunny was insightful, witty and lovable, and although other lecturers in the centre, like Barry, were experienced and smart, Tom discovered the essence of participants, cut them away from the self-protective accretions of the years, forced them to see their own potential, and gave them individual guidance on how to release it. Every encounter with another human gave you the opportunity to build or damage a relationship, he told other trainers. If someone has come to you to learn how to improve the one essential skill, then you cannot afford to be selfish (by admiring your own performance) or contemptuous (by genericising trainees with tips and tricks anybody could offer).

Other tutors, particularly the more academic among them, tended to query the proposition that communication was the one essential skill. Tom would quote the emperor who wanted to find out what tongue children might naturally speak, if unimpeded by the language of their parents. The emperor collected a group of orphaned babies and put them in the care of women who were told to feed, clothe and clean them, but not talk to them or play with them. Within months, the babies were all dead. 'Oh', someone said, 'that's apocryphal.' 'True, Tom said, 'but it's more memorable than the studies I could quote you establishing that depressed mothers who do not talk to their babies, because they simply can't, end up with toddlers who are way behind

in developmental terms. Communication is central to every relationship, work or home. As a marriage counsellor, I couldn't tell you the
number of times I have listened to good men saying impatiently, "I
can't be doing that crap of telling her I love her, she knows that by
now" while their wives sit grey-faced with need.'

I wrote down what he said. That day, and any day, I could listen
to him, understanding that this man was the force who might help
counter the almost magnetic pull of the trivial in me. Course participants loved me because I could produce a 'shiny' – a clever, interesting
example of whatever point was being made – but I would never have
the intellectual capacity to create the great soaring arches of ideas Tom
could bring together to reframe trainees' – and tutors' – thinking. For
example, when seeking to dissuade trainees from anxious urgency, he
stated that experts always have *time*. He would mimic the way professional tennis players calmly bring back the racquet before connecting
with the ball, and make groups laugh as he then imitated the anxious
celerity of the new tennis player, rushing to connect with it. He
took his car keys out of his pocket and threw them over his head,
leisurely catching them, unsighted, behind his own back, making the
point that extra time contributes to and is a consequence of effective
communication.

None of the other priests was from the North, and they were
curious about the Troubles and how close Tom was to groups like
the Officials and the Provisionals. He said frankly that he had time
for the Officials because they were socialists rooted in poverty. When
another priest expressed his shock that he had any affinity with killers,
Savage narrowed those dark eyes and told him that if you were a
Papist living in a Papist area when 'triumphalist black Protestants led
by that bastard Paisley' descended on your streets, protected by the
RUC, carrying flaming brands and the determination to burn you out
of house and home, then knowing that a few Officials on those streets
had guns in the attic and knew how to use them made for affiliations
not based on shared ideology but the simpler need for protection. Just
as the atmosphere would turn cold with the chill emanating from

the disapproving ignorant, Tom would segue into a story from the North, like what had happened on his previous visit to Ara Coeli. He had been driving on a country road in the dark when he saw flashing torch lights up ahead. 'In that area, first thing you do is slow down to work out if they're RUC, army or paramilitaries but also to assess can you accelerate and go around them. No way around that night, so I stopped and this guy in a balaclava comes up and tells me they're commandeering my car. I ask who they are and he tells me local IRA. So I pull the Roman collar out of the glove compartment, slip it on, and look at him. "Tell you what", I say, "why don't you contact Pádraig and check how he'd feel about you taking Father Tom Savage's car?"' Because this was long before mobile phones, the man in the balaclava had no way to contact his commanding officer. Instead, he went to the back of the car, consulted with two of his mates, then walked back to the driver's window and told Tom to get moving.

Tom talked of going 'down' to Belfast. Of eating winkles as a child. Of getting his younger sister to help girls who had lived out their childhood in an orphanage to develop skills the nuns regarded as irrelevant, like putting rollers in your hair or riding a bicycle.

He told of being telephoned by the reverend mother of an enclosed order who was worried about one of her sisters, the intensity of whose religious experience, she suspected, was veering into mental illness. Savage, from his training in Purdysburn Mental Hospital, recognised the fervour of the sister's conversation as fuelled by delusions, and agreed with the reverend mother that the psychiatrist from a nearby Protestant mental hospital be called and told that this was an emergency. The psychiatrist duly arrived, took a briefing and went to interview the nun. When he emerged an hour later, he effusively thanked the reverend mother for allowing him to witness the spirit of God in action. He set off down the stairs and was at his car when Tom caught up with him, to tell him that – whatever about his identification with the religious experience being expressed upstairs – the reality was that this was, as he put it, 'a florid psychotic episode' and that if the psychiatrist did not treat it as such and section the nun

immediately, he, Tom, would ensure he was struck off. The psychiatrist went back upstairs, emerging from the nun's room much later,
accompanied by the sister, who was now singing, and brought her to
the psychiatric hospital, where he took wonderful care of her.

The point of the story was a lesson against projecting tutor needs
onto trainees or other people who are seeking our help. 'We do training,
not therapy,' Tom would say. 'It's flattering when someone portrays
you as the solution to their long-standing problems, but you must
never accede to their "felt needs". The moment you suspect a mental
health issue may be in play, or that someone needs therapy, refer them.
We have trusted psychiatrists.' 'Like your guy in the North?' someone
suggested, only to meet with a dismissive, 'Yes. A fine psychiatrist who
made one error.'

Between freelance journalism, broadcasting, photography and training
in the Catholic Communications Centre, I was making a living,
working, for the most part, with people I loved and learned from.
I was often the 'only woman in the room', a point of privilege of which
I had no appreciation. I had a family who loved me – even if Hilary had
sensibly moved to the deep southside to bring up her growing family
away from our mother's exigent expectations. I had lots of friends, and
because the silos of my life tended not to overlap, I was able to get
away with not attending parties, which I hated.

For a while, I had believed socialising was a moral duty, like cleaning
your teeth and not stealing. So I held back long hair while girls threw
up into toilets. I listened to the surprising miseries of the apparently
successful. I made myself up as if I could transform myself into something glamorous. I laughed at bad jokes and convinced boring men
that they weren't, which isn't that hard. The compartmentalised life I
was living let me off a lot of that and allowed me to spend time with
Fionnuala Kenny, host dinner parties at which people like Bunny and
Joan, Charles McCarthy and his brilliantly witty wife Muriel (librarian
of Marsh's Library) glossed over the over-elaboration of my talentless
cookery, and retreat to the books that made sense of my life. Father

Tom Savage's occasional visits to my home for cups of tea were odd, in that context, because in our house people didn't just turn up on the doorstep demanding refreshment. My mother made an exception for Savage's visits, just as she made an exception for the fact that he held his knife like a pen, which would have given her the shudders except that he was so covered in degrees, she gave him a free pass.

I learned from Tom, quoted him and valued his insight. Then came the heart-lurch when his name was mentioned, the unpreventable smile when I spotted him, grim-faced, prowling towards me, the joyful anticipation of a meeting even minutes long over coffee or tea in the Communications Centre. I knew what this was and I knew the wistfulness it gave me when I saw couples walking in front of me alongside the fencing of St Stephen's Green, holding hands, swinging arms. When Peter Lemass one day described Savage as the finest priest he knew, it was a glad blow: that he was known by the best *as* the best, and that this meant a sooner or later sundering.

That same week, he visited and I told him I loved him and he continued drinking his over-sugared tea in silence. Then he said, 'Tess, you must know I've loved you since I met you. Now, I think we should get married.' We sat in the sitting room, ten feet away from each other, this man I loved and who loved me but had never kissed me, never held me, never caressed me. He carefully put his cup and saucer down at the edge of the hearth. 'Do you think you might come over and sit beside me?' I sat on the arm of the armchair and he kissed me, announcing 'Wow!' like a little boy. Then he did his thing of conducting an imaginary orchestra and softly adapted Leigh Hunt's poem:

Say I'm weary, say I'm sad,
Say that health and wealth have miss'd me,
Say I'm growing old, but add,
Terry kiss'd me.

13

DEATH THREATS

*T*he death threats were the least of our worries. Within weeks of our telling our families and those closest to us, two kinds of letters began to arrive. The majority were from priests who knew Tom and wanted to steer him right. One I remember told him that women had two places: on their knees or on their back, and he didn't need to be making such an exception of himself when he could have sex and then do a good confession. The death threats didn't bother Tom because he knew the need to vent experienced by the troubled, and they didn't bother me because any journalist in the early nineteen seventies got their fair share of what were called 'green ink' letters.

It was the reaction of family that creased us. The frosted glass of reconciliation, forgiveness and renewed relationships renders discussion of the details redundant, but loss of contact with his parents, for several years, ate a hole in Tom. His family believed I was a Jezebel who had seduced their son/brother away from his calling. My father demanded a meeting with Tom, at which they debated theology, reaching no agreement. At the end of the encounter, Dad told Tom, 'You want to live in a pigsty, that's okay with me.' I continued to live untidily at home for three years so as not to 'give scandal', and on one of the Christmases, found beside my breakfast place a wrapped copy of *The Imitation of Christ* by Thomas à Kempis, inscribed, in my father's beautiful handwriting, 'To my former daughter'.

The hierarchy told Bunny to fire Tom. Bunny refused, on the basis that Tom was just as competent to train people in communications as a layman as he had been as a priest: witness the divorced Protestant Barry Baker. The bishops went over Bunny's head to Joe Dunn, Bunny's boss, to get him to do it. This Joe Dunn dutifully did, before he and Tom went off on a planned holiday to Malta, during which Tom threw a fully dressed Joe Dunn into the Mediterranean, to their mutual satisfaction. Tom was offered no gardening leave or severance pay and was ordered to leave Pranstown House, the Church-owned residence on Booterstown Avenue, within the month. Peter Lemass, a gentle, good man, sat him down to explain to Tom the wrong he was doing and followed it up with this letter:

> It would be easy for me to say there will be no happiness for you in this. That may not be true. What I feel is that there may not be lasting happiness for you both, but that isn't the crucial problem. You are a man called. You have the confirmation of the Church on your vocation. You are a good priest. I can't vouch for your spiritual life, but I do know that you have helped people, consoled, encouraged, and been effective. If you marry, your potential to do that sort of good, at least in the Ireland of today, is minimised. It was to do that good that you were called. A vocation is a calling to serve, to work – without you there will be a vacuum. More than that, a lot of people will be affected by your leaving – the staff in the Centre, the people you have lectured to, mentioning the importance of prayer, as I heard you do, the importance of communicating the Christian message. Your credibility as a person is in question. Some people must say 'so this guy was a phony after all.' You have been a very public priest. Other priests who may be teetering will be affected. This is a considerable responsibility. It may be that by leaving the

priesthood now, you will undermine much of the good you have done in the past as a priest.

If things were different – as in 10 years time they may well be different – if you lived in the Greek church or even in a more impersonal society than Ireland it might be different. As it is the fact of getting married means the abandonment of your priest-hood (rightly or wrongly) and that is a tragedy.

It is not too late. If you change your mind on this it will certainly hurt Terry. It might ultimately be a lesser hurt than could come her way if you marry. She is a lovely girl, she has buckets of personality, looks (hell, I don't have to tell you that). She will find someone.

Most of us lead mediocre, humdrum, lukewarm lives, we are seldom asked to make any great sacrifices, cruel decisions we never rise above the gutter. You are asked. It is an invitation, almost a second vocation. If you answer it with courage, the sky's the limit.

I was hoping to say this, rather than write it. It looks so bloody cold and clinical in print. I feel like Francis de Sales with indigestion.

To change your mind, at this stage, would not be a sign of weakness, but rather the humility to accept that you have decided wrongly.

Tom said he was saddened, not to receive the letter, but that Peter had written it. 'In time', he told me, 'Peter will realise it diminishes him and speaks to a Christianity, a Catholicism, he himself has never evangelised for. I told him, "I have set my seal on her and she on me," and he did not, would not and will not hear me.' Small pause. 'Or perhaps could not and cannot.'

Tom would not advise me against replying, if I wished to, but based on his experience, it would not, he predicted, be the most productive correspondence. With the firm pomposity of a twenty-one-year-old who knew Father Lemass less well than Tom did, I rejected his advice, determined to set down a marker:

If Tom were to decide to stay in the ministry, I wouldn't 'find' someone … I could manage. I'm not going to blather the 'I couldn't live without him' cod. But I couldn't love again, and I would be shrivelled. All of which sounds very novelettish, but is the simple truth. I love Tom in a way I'm arrogant enough to believe is rare. I love him in no sense as a dependant, a clinger. I'm prepared to face whatever is going to happen to us, to go abroad if necessary, but better still to stay here and face things with him. I love him with admiration, and a great softness I didn't know I had and a fierce steeliness I also didn't know I had. Nobody is going to nibble at the edges of this love and make it sordid, or an abandonment of something better, or a giving in to passions. Nobody is as important to me as he is, and I never expect nor want it to be easy – I have already lost the two people who were closest to me apart from him, and believe you me, it's very lonely living in a house where you are conscious of a deep loathing and contempt.

Peter did not reply, and his path never crossed ours again, although Tom always spoke of him with warmth. The other, cruder interventions by priests he knew he simply forgot about. Whenever I mentioned them in subsequent years, he would be surprised; accepting that I was telling the truth, but surprised. Tom had merciful amnesia for anything that upset him and a determination never to hold a grudge.

The first few weeks, as people came to know about us as a couple, were chaotic and sometimes cruel. We spent a lot of time in his big old red Fiat, stinking of the spilled milk he drank to assuage his ulcer, engine running to keep us warm, windscreen wipers slapping when it rained. When it didn't rain, we drove to Broadmeadows, a gorgeous empty estuary north of Portrane and sat drinking tea out of a flask, talking. Mainly Tom talking about the clergy being 'plant-minded, school-minded, memory-minded rather than people-minded'. Explaining to me that the people who thought us evil *had* to think us evil, because their beliefs were part of their identity and if they didn't state their beliefs and stand by them, they would feel weak and rudderless. Nor should we try to argue them out of their beliefs, he said, because it was pointless. Getting stuff off your chest never achieved anything, never changed anybody's convictions. He also observed that most of the people who were saying bad things about us were much less happy than we were. He would discuss what, if anything, we were learning from the high-minded exclusion of former friends, quoting Shaw's comment, 'Experience is what you get when you don't get what you want.'

Thrown on the backbone of our love, wrapped in anoraks, swooped on by seagulls hoping for food, inhaling the smell of his cigarettes, looking at the marsh flowers growing down in the mudflats, with sometimes the soul shudder of a wood pigeon, we laughed in the quiet stillness. Although he had moments of extreme sadness for his parents and for losing them, he was for the most part happier, he said, than he had ever been. As was I. Neither of us had doubts. Doubts about continuing to live in an Ireland dominated by the Catholic Church certainly, especially since Bunny's defiance of the instruction to fire Tom had been followed, not just by the bishops bypassing Bunny and getting Joe Dunn to do it, but by the hierarchy halving Bunny's budget, which wrote a long slow *finis* to the Catholic Communications Centre, although neither of us knew of this when it happened. The two of us being well-known might, Tom thought, provoke the institution to want us out of the country. Our survival would be a reproach to them. Either we needed to have nervous breakdowns (even one would do, he said fair-mindedly) or emigrate. The tolerance of the Church for the continued presence of a renegade priest might be limited. Watch out, he said, for the fifth columnists not letting on who sent them, but arriving on a mission to slither into our heads the idea that Australia was a great place to make a new start. Neither of us ever contemplated leaving the country. In one of Tom's early discussions with my mother, she told him nobody would ever employ him, and he acknowledged that nobody would employ him to do what he'd been doing for the previous decade. 'But I can dig ditches and hammer in fence posts,' he told her, which made her cry in desperation that a ditch digger was proposing to marry her daughter.

My mother's distress was not lessened in any way by learning that her Auntie Nora, who was an enclosed nun in Ronkonkoma, New York, had sent a letter to my maternal grandmother in which she condemned me and Tom at some length, held my mother partly responsible and told Nana she had put our names on the Cycle of Mercy, which apparently obviated the need to pray for us, because we were so far beyond human intervention.

Meanwhile, the paperwork began.

His Eminence William Cardinal Conway
Ara Ceoli
Armagh
24th November 1971

Your Eminence,

Since I spoke to you personally, I have given long and prayerful consideration to my decision. I now wish to make formal written application for an 'Indult of reduction to the lay state.'

I want to take this opportunity of thanking you for your kindness and consideration to me during my service as a priest of your diocese. You will continue to have my prayers and good wishes for the onerous responsibilities of your office.

I remain,
Yours obediently, Thomas J. Savage

The only person I could talk to about Tom and me was Fionnuala Kenny, who had at around the same time fallen in love with a brilliant

Polish designer named Voytek, divorced and a lot older than she was, so she encountered her own family opposition. Before she left to live in London, Fionnuala and I would meet in St Stephen's Green and swap the details of our loves. Voytek's charming 'I think maybe perhaps.' Tom buttering Marietta biscuits, slapping them together and squeezing them so buttery worms coiled out from the holes. But then Fionnuala was in London and we couldn't afford long, expensive phone calls to share our changing realities. I learned to incorporate everything into short stories, although I had yet to submit any.

I quickly lost my stringer contract with the English Catholic newspaper, as was inevitable. I lost my position as professor of homiletics in a Catholic seminary, to which I'd been recruited only months earlier. Those two losses alone dropped my income by two-thirds. The Religious Affairs section of RTÉ TV decided it could not face the controversy implicit in giving me a second series of the *In Vision* interviews, thus ushering in more than a decade of absence from television for me. How we would survive, let alone pay off the almost ten thousand quid Tom owed the bank, we could not imagine, and it drove me crazy that Tom refused to worry about this, maintaining, as he always did, that 'money is purely functional', and telling the story of Cardinal Conway handing him an envelope of banknotes to pay the first year's tutorial fees when the Church sent him to study sociology in Queen's University. On the morning he was due to visit the university to pay the fee, a woman came to the parochial house, distraught over a financial problem. Tom handed her the envelope and she departed. He then decided to go for a walk on the basis that it might give him a way to explain the issue to Plus William.

He was wandering along, puffing on his cigarette, when he heard a voice calling, 'Father Savage! Father Savage!' A horse race-obsessed parishioner was running down the hill after him, hauling a roll of banknotes out of his pocket. 'Fucken great meet yesterday,' he said. 'Fucken great.' He stuffed the bankroll into Tom's hands and got into an idling car driven by a friend. Tom walked to Queen's where he found he had almost exactly the right amount. This had either given him or confirmed in him an attitude to money where sunny optimism met reckless generosity. Throughout his life, he never found himself with money he didn't immediately look for someone to give it to. He never bought anything for himself other than cigarettes, never evinced a want for any physical object. Clothes didn't matter to him. While he was obsessive about polishing his shoes, those shoes might be ten years old and patched. He took enormous pride in having been the one sibling in the Savage house quite happy to wear darned trousers and 'turned' jackets. As long as his hair and hands were spotless and his shoes shining, he was all set. The debt to the bank had grown over the ten years of his priesthood because he couldn't ever turn down a parishioner's request for money. That often left him without the cash he actually needed.

Since one of his principles was that marriage was not a licence on either side to try to change the other, I decided that when it came to division of labour between us, I would have to take charge of money management and worry. That I could barely count and had yet to come to terms with compound interest hardly qualified me, but one of us had to do it.

I went in and out of RTÉ, smiling and giving 'Everything's fine' answers to questions, particularly from the churchman on the *Liam Nolan Hour* team, Father Pat McInerney, whom I feared would be supercilious. As a result, he ended up writing to me:

My Dear Terry,

Sorry you had to run yestereve, and did not have time for a word or two.

If there is one thing I dislike it is hearing tales about friends, without being in a direct position to reply, for or against, due to a lack of communication with same friends. In your case, tales – relating to single individuals and twains – have been coming my way now for some weeks, if not months; all received with my 'stiff upper lip' face.

May I say just one thing: I do wish you all the happiness in the world. Don't let any old wives interfere in any way. I mean <u>any</u> way, and that includes the subconscious effect of possible reaction which you might judge even friends <u>to be about</u> to experience, <u>if</u> they knew. The rot of pre-judging people is the worst effect a whispering society can have on good people.

If there is anything I can do to help, in any way, at any time, please do not hesitate to shout. Just remember, the distinction between <u>office</u> and <u>state</u> is the key to a healthy understanding of it all — whatever the positive law may say, there is no essential or necessary link between office and states, in this instance. The law can be an utter ass!

Be happy, be well, be blessed. Pat Mc

This — to me — startling letter I left out at home so my mother could accidentally read it, and she found it a catalyst, allowing her to take a deep breath and start to face down people who sympathised with her. Whereas her own mother's vast acceptance of a peculiar world allowed her to shake her head about her sister's letter, my mother wasn't having any and even let rip in a letter about the Circle of Mercy to Marty Geraghty, son of Auntie Nora's brother, my grand-uncle Martin. Marty, a priest in Brooklyn, responded quickly.

Dear Moira,

I cannot tell you how shocked I was at the report of Aunt Nora's letter. I regret it. As you probably can tell by now, that part of your letter was the only bad news for me. After reading that Aunt Bridgie wrote such a good letter, I was wishing I was near her to give her a big hug. She was always so kind and gentle.

An announcement that a priest is going to marry is still met with some surprise and I suppose when it happens close to one, the surprise can be overshadowed by dismay and even some fear ... I, for one, do hope that the day is coming when we Catholics will be beyond stigmatizing those who have left and 'punishing' them for the years of dedicated service that they did complete. Even more to the point, I hope that we will be able to move on to the idea of a married priesthood (and not a peculiarly male-dominated priesthood either).

The nearest equivalent, for Tom, came from his Aunt Enna, his mother's younger sister, herself the mother to two sons with Down's Syndrome, who Tom adored.

November '72

My Dearest Tom,

I can recall two occasions when letters from you helped me over sorrow in the past and now must try in small measure to return that kindness …

Tom, love, if these good people who hurt you because of their attitude to your action are right in God's eyes, then I haven't a hope of salvation. For the life of me I cannot see any wrong in what you are doing. I have nothing but the greatest admiration for your courage. It would have been so much easier in that world to drift along and pretend everything was grand, because you had so much to gain having made your imprint and your future seemed bright. I'm afraid I'd never have been so brave.

Don't worry about her [Tom's mother], dear, already she is much better and this is where her great love for you will show itself.

Help came from unexpected sources. Bob Cashman, then heading up the St Vincent de Paul Society, with which Tom had worked for years, commissioned him to produce a booklet. Liam McGowan, features editor of the *Irish Press*, commissioned him to write an anonymous three-part series about priests leaving the priesthood. Never did any man slave as much or ask as many questions as Tom as he dictated that series to me to type.

'That man really can write,' Liam McGowan told me when he'd read them. He would run them on Monday, Tuesday and Wednesday of the following week, with a big promotion in the paper on the previous Saturday. In that promotion, McGowan described the three features as 'searching'. A few days later, McGowan shunted another series Tom's way, about the sudden proliferation of religious cults setting up in Ireland, and this time Tom researched it and hand-wrote it before giving it to me to type. Within weeks, more work came along for him, who was by then two-finger typing at speed directly onto my computer.

Then Liam Ó Lonargáin, one of the *Liam Nolan Hour* producers, asked me casually where Tom was going to live, nodding as my eyes filled up with tears and I stood silently in front of him. He scribbled his home phone number on a sheet of paper and told me to get Tom to ring him. When Tom did, Liam set up a meeting in Broc House on Nutley Lane. To all appearances, Broc House was a good hotel, close to the university in its new surroundings at Belfield and to the main roads into the city. But Broc House had a dual personality. Once the summer was over, and the tourists had packed their bags and gone home, it changed completely, opening its doors to students taking courses at UCD. The man who supervised the annual changeover, and who overlooked the Broc House activities for the year, was a civvies-dressed priest, Tony Stanley of the Franciscan Fathers. Tony, a fully qualified and experienced hotel manager, having taken the necessary college courses to equip himself for the work, gained practical experience of hotel work in many parts of the country. The Past Pupils' Union of Gormanston College had decided, some years earlier, that a students' hostel near the as yet unopened university at Belfield would be a worthwhile provision, since many students coming to Dublin for the first time from other parts of the country tended to end up in unsuitable overpriced digs away from their friends where they paid little attention to their food, subsisting on baked beans and buns. The

Past Pupils' Union decided that they would look into the possibility of building such a hostel. And so Broc House was born.

Up to then, Tony Stanley had been a teacher of music and other subjects, but he embarked on his new career as a student of the hotel business with some enthusiasm. During the winter he was 'Father Tony' to the young men living in Broc House. During the summer, he was simply the manager of the hotel, many of his guests never realising that he was a priest. He and Liam Ó Lonargáin were old friends, and the meeting was to offer Tom a room in Broc House for the winter, or as long as he needed it. Within days, Tom's sparse possessions were shifted out of Pranstown House and he had his own room in Broc House. He and Tony would have late-night cups of tea and discussions about issues of the day. Liam Ó Lonargáin wouldn't listen, then or afterwards, to how grateful we were for his intervention, smothering gratitude with jokes and hugs.

Next into the rescue squad was Séan Egan, a dark-haired broadcaster and print journalist heading up the journalism course in Rathmines – the only such course approved by the National Union of Journalists. He decided he needed sociology to be among the subjects covered by his students, and hired Tom to deliver it.

'I'm sure many of you coming into journalism for the first time will wonder why many of the subjects on the curriculum should in fact be on it,' Tom told the fewer than a dozen students facing him on his first day. 'I'm sure this is one of the first times many of you will have studied sociology. Sociology is one of the social sciences which deals with human behaviour. With people, particularly with people as they behave in groups. And essentially, as journalists, that is what you are really about. When you look at sociology as a discipline, you will find that it does provide a background for you against which to assemble information. I believe that if you have a very basic training in some of the methods of sociology, methods of how to get information, methods of how to put information together, how would you go about finding out more information about particular subjects – that if you have this, it will certainly improve your end product as a journalist.'

One piece of good news, that year, was the announcement that Muiris Mac Conghail, former head of Government Information Services, genius current affairs TV producer/director and lifelong Labour Party member, was going to head up the RTÉ Current Affairs department. I looked forward to him ending the head-patting patronage from producers, of which I was good and sick.

A couple of weeks into his tenure, I got a message that Muiris would like to see me when I came out of studio after *The Liam Nolan Hour*. I was thrilled and an hour later knocked on the door of the office. When I was not invited to sit, I told myself that guys like Muiris like to get right to it. And get right to it he surely did, firing me on the spot. Like the five other women earning what we'll laughingly call a living from Features and Current Affairs, I was on a short-term contract, which, right now, was finishing, because women had, according to Muiris, no place in current affairs.

'Why not?'

'I can't sent a woman down the Falls Road.'

'Oh, men are more bullet-proof?'

'Get out.'

I would love to claim that I stalked out, but, in truth, what I did was slink out. Did I think about the other five or six women in the department on similar contracts to mine, and, as the daughter of a passionate trade unionist, find them out and weld them into a bludgeon, striking for women's rights? I'm ashamed to admit that this thought never crossed my mind, any more than the problems facing those other women crossed my mind. Panic can render you pretty selfish, even if you're not selfish to start with, which I was. I gathered my belongings and walked out, certain that since the hero of the working class, Muiris, had found me unworthy of employment and deployment on the Falls Road, well, you know yourself, I must have been severely lacking.

Tom's big square red Fiat would be coming back for me about an hour later, picking me up at the TV block, to which I now trudged with my black plastic bag of miscellaneous items like a released prisoner.

The lobby of the TV block was much more spacious, less cluttered and more inviting to sit in than it is now, so I planted myself against the wall on a Scandinavian sofa and worked at not crying. Tom had no job and a considerable debt. I lived at home with a father who didn't speak to me and regarded me as his former daughter and a mother under stress as a result, and now I had no job either. The thing about not crying is that it's a continuous, rather than a once-off, task when you've just been fired, so I was still labouring at swallowing back the oversized throat lump and telling myself in my head to get a fucking grip, when a man I had seen around the Radio Centre came over and asked if I was Terry Prone. I admitted to it without enthusiasm.

'My name is Billy Wall,' he said, going down on his hunkers in front of me. 'I'm the producer of a new programme, a new daily programme – *The Gay Byrne Hour.* And I was wondering if you'd consider being our scriptwriter?'

Honesty and greed fought as I considered telling him that I was unworthy of his consideration since I'd just been fired over beyond. Greed won. I patted the couch beside me in invitation and the negotiations started right there. Long before the red Fiat pulled up outside the floor-to-ceiling glass of the lobby, Billy Wall had hired me at twice what I'd been making as a reporter on *The Liam Nolan Hour,* and I was clear on exactly what would be required of me each day. I would need to start coming up with ideas straight away, he told me, because the programme would be hitting the airwaves ten days later. I would also need to talk to reporters in Cork and Galway and maybe locate a few in other parts of the country to contribute to a weekly item called 'The Shopping Basket', which would investigate the costs of shopping in different supermarkets, which, at the time, included Dunnes Stores, H. Williams, Quinnsworth, Superquinn and a couple of others. Billy Wall took my address and phone number and promised to have a three-month contract with me within days. At which point the red Fiat pulled up and Wall and I shook hands and parted.

'Who's your man?' Tom asked as he tidied me into the car (Tom always got out and opened the door for any female passenger).

'Billy Wall,' I said as he climbed in the other side, reached through the steering wheel, shook loose a cigarette, lit it and started the engine.

It was at that point I burst into tears, which caused Tom to slow the car as he considered doing a U-turn in order to go back and sort Billy Wall out.

'Billy Wall is a good guy,' I sobbed.

Gradually, the story emerged and Tom summed it up.

'You got fired by a bollix and hired by a good guy in the same organisation on the same morning.'

I nodded.

'Sounds good to me,' he said and – as always – he was right. It was the best thing that ever happened to me. The firing *and* the hiring. One wouldn't have happened without the other. Ridiculously, I would probably have felt a loyalty to *The Liam Nolan Hour*, despite the week-to-week contracts and the ridiculous interview topics, and refused Wall, had he approached me on any day other than the one on which I got turfed. The other five women Muiris fired all quietly went home or found something to do that didn't put them in front of a microphone. It was the most successful misogynistic coup orchestrated by someone who should have known better, and probably did. It was done in the small window before the EU brought in equality laws that would have prevented such discriminatory action. It must also be admitted that it was successful partly because none of the women who were victimised talked to one another or protested in any way. Each of us felt helpless as individuals and it didn't seem to strike us that collective action might work – despite the fact that this was when feminism, then called women's liberation, was beginning to rattle the old patriarchy.

The preparations for *The Gay Byrne Hour* intensified. At one meeting, Billy indicated that the programme needed letters from listeners to get topics going. Gay Byrne looked at him in silence and Billy dithered. Gay indicated that he liked the concept. The problem was a practical one. How would the programme manage during the first couple of weeks before listeners copped on that this was part of its agenda? Someone suggested that maybe Terry could rough up a couple that would give listeners the idea. Nobody around that table raised a moral cheep about writing phoney letters, and I duly went home and crafted a few on personal, highly emotive topics, drawn from listening to Tom talking about marriage problems (he was a marriage counsellor) and addiction issues (he worked for one of the consultants in St Patrick's). I did what any dramatist would do: cast a story around it and put characters into it. At the next meeting, Gay read them without comment; just nodded and put them into his folder.

For 'The Shopping Basket', I recruited my mother as unpaid help, because I knew I lacked the concentration on detail to do it correctly. We would need a dozen items each week. Those items, wherever possible, would be branded, so that a direct comparison between a particular size of Bird's custard could be made across the six chains researched. At least half the items had to be made in Ireland. The researchers, including my mother, were never to announce themselves, wear anything that would identify them as working for RTÉ, or accept any kind of freebie.

The first week, in February, should have been wobbly, but it wasn't. Gay Byrne didn't do wobbly. He arrived on the air as if he had been presenting the programme for years, moving easily from item to item. So easily that no radio critic of the time noticed that this was an unprecedented radio offering. Never before had a magazine programme failed to rely on music between items. Music allowed the mood of a show to change, so that when the presenter finished with a difficult and emotional issue, the producer could cue in a song or, more likely, a piece of orchestral semi-classical music to provide recovery time. Not so with *The Gay Byrne Hour*. Gay could and did move between fact and fun, tragedy and comedy, and, although music was always cued up to cover an emergency, he regarded an emergency as a personal challenge rather than as a setback.

On the second day, without explanation, he instructed his listeners, 'Listen to this. Just listen to it. I am not going to give you the name.' And off he went, reading one of my scripts. Reading it with such concentration, such pacing, that the misery being recounted was like a blow to the heart. When he finished, he made one of those inchoate noises he specialised in and instructed listeners to respond. *Instructed* them, that was the thing. He didn't warble around suggesting that maybe listeners would have some insight to offer. He defined the job of the active listener and went on to something else.

Next morning, when I arrived to hand over that day's scripts, I found Billy and other team members selecting from hundreds of letters that had arrived overnight. That first human interest letter generated a week and a half of passionate response. But it did more. It allowed women at home to listen to the thinking of other women in the same position. It created the possibility that the deepest secrets of a marriage or of motherhood could be safely shared on air in a way that provoked others to respond with their matching or sometimes contrasting experiences. It diminished the loneliness of a generation of women and empowered them to think outside what Pete Seeger had called the 'little boxes' in which they lived. History will rightly register the importance of women's liberation and the feminists who came through the women's pages and helped tear down the constraints hammered around women's lives, but it was Billy Wall and Gay Byrne who opened up a new world to women.

It also turned women into assertive consumers. The weekly shopping basket item quickly became so powerful that it undoubtedly speeded the demise of the least cost-effective of the supermarket chains. On one expedition, I had to go to a manager and ask about a particular Swiss roll. He looked up, recognised me, made an instant association with the programme and in naked terror said, 'To you, twenty pence.' I had to explain that if he gave me a special price I would be fired and that the price on the air had to be the same in each of their branches. For the most part, we priced staples but now and then included something unusual, like passion fruit. This caused Gay, when he reached that particular item in his script, to comment that he had never eaten a passion fruit, which in turn prompted Fergal Quinn to send him a crate of them. The producer of the programme, Adavin

O'Driscoll (named after the atom bomb the US dropped on the day she was born), halted the courier, grabbed a compliment slip, scribbled a note to Fergal saying thanks very much but Gay Byrne can actually afford his own passion fruit, and sent the lot back to Superquinn.

Emblematic of the reach of *The Gay Byrne Hour* was that when I mentioned in one script that the potatoes from a particular supermarket had a lot of green under their skins, therefore representing less value, an obstetrician who had been listening on his car radio rang the programme once he reached his hospital to tell the programme assistant that pregnant women should not under any circumstances eat such potatoes. Billy Wall, listening to the call, leaned over and asked him if he'd be prepared to explain it to Gay and before he had time to think twice about it, he was on the air. Billy, turning to me in the dark control room, snapped his fingers. 'We need a weekly doctor,' he said. 'Like him? I asked. 'No, not an obstetrician. A generalist who is a great talker. I'm sure you know someone.'

I smiled in the all-knowing way of the clever clueless and asked Tom. 'I know who you need,' he told me. 'Austin Darragh. Great show-jumping commentator, so he has acres of experience.' Austin became the weekly doctor and from the first programme was a resounding success. That was the thing about Tom. He was a connector. Not in the backslapping political way. But he loved people, found them interesting, remembered them. Years later, the two of us were in Publix, a supermarket in Florida, looking at a display of fruit and vegetables, when a man behind us said something in Irish. Without turning around, Tom answered what was said – in his Northern Irish – and also called out the name of the man who had said it. They had not talked in thirty years.

Séan Egan recommended that Tom be one of the presenters of *It Says in the Papers*, and that was the start of a run of fifteen years doing the broadcast. It became apparent that we would not starve, although that first year Tom earned only about £3,500. I remember this because I was the one who gave our receipts and payslips to an accountant. The accountant dealt with it all until he suddenly died.

We found another, transferred the paperwork, and thought no more about it until he rang to arrange a meeting, at which he told us that the previous accountant, having noted the pathetic amounts the two of us had earned in our first year, simply returned the same amounts for the second and third years, during which we had done markedly better, with the result that we owed the Revenue Commissioners a terrifying amount of money, about which they didn't yet know. Tom asked the man what we should do, and he said that one of us had to go into the Revenue and confess all. He further recommended that the one to speak for both of us should be me, on the basis that I was so genuinely innumerate that they wouldn't believe I could have dreamed up this scam. I was shaking so hard when I met the Revenue people that they made me tea and couldn't have been kinder. Tom and I owed the money. We would have to pay it back. But they would not set a deadline that might hamper our future solvency.

The two of us were freelance, but some regular commissions, like *It Says in the Papers*, to which I also contributed, made it possible to plan. The problem was that we had no idea when Tom would be 'reduced to the lay state'. We kept expecting to hear good news; it kept not coming. We stayed positive about it, although we were still, if not quite wearing a scarlet letter, at least cordially disapproved of by some. Because we didn't want to push our luck with Father Tony's hospitality in Broc House, we still spent a lot of time in Tom's car. One day as we rounded the corner in Baldoyle, we spotted workmen hammering up a For Sale notice outside the middle of three little houses facing the sea.

'Feckit, let's ask them if they'll let us look,' I said. The guys were amused and welcoming. We wandered throughout the dark little house and fell in love with it. Tom gave the guys something for a drink and we were off to Sutton for a cup of tea with Bunny and Joan. We told them about this tiny house we would buy if we had actual jobs that would satisfy a bank if we asked for a mortgage. Bunny went out into the little room where the phone lived and made a call. We could hear him say 'Tosh, these people *have* no money and no real jobs either.

But they *will* make money, you can trust me on that.' 'That's one of Bun's oldest friends,' Joan told us. 'Hugh McGowan. They were baby bankers together and did shows as Tish and Tosh. Hugh is the manager of the Bank of Ireland in Fairview.'

Mid-morning, we were possessors of a mortgage that Hugh, these days, would never have been allowed to authorise, to buy 2 Strand Road, Baldoyle. That allowed Tom to borrow a truck and bring his remaining possessions from the North. They consisted of an iron double bed of which he was inordinately proud and twelve tea chests holding ten pairs of winkle-picker shoes, several years' worth of *New Society* magazine and perhaps a hundred books. Some of the books were hardback Church histories and tomes of dogmatic theology. Scattered among them were paperbacks, one of them Robert Bolt's *A Man for All Seasons*, which, as a movie starring Paul Scofield and Robert Shaw, I had seen at least a dozen times and almost knew by heart. Opening the yellowing pages of the paperback, I found pencil underlinings beneath speeches I had loved for many years.

14

THE LATE LATE AND MICHAEL CLEARY

*B*unny and Joan were our first guests in the new house. We had four enamel mugs and four plates. Milk had to stay in the carton because we didn't have a jug. We also had only two chairs, orange padded plastic, donated by Tony Stanley. Bunny and I got to sit in them while Tom sat on the floor and Joan used her wheelchair. That was before we did the tour of the house, which required Bunny and Tom to carry Joan upstairs, while I came behind them with the wheelchair. What bothered me, as we progressed up the stairs, was Joan's buoyant faith that neither man would slip on what were pretty steep steps. Bunny had given up sailing, which he adored, because, when he took Joan out in their boat, post-polio, he became terrified by the responsibility for her safety, his terror only exacerbated by her boundless confidence in him.

After that bout of hospitality, it was back to working as hard as we could, to get right with the Revenue, pay the mortgage and keep up the hire purchase payments to the ESB for the fridge. Our eleven pseudonyms enabled us to write for competing publications, but also allowed me to write substantial stories about, for example, environmental issues, under a male name, it being received wisdom that only a man would be credible on such a complicated topic. I figured I could lose a principled feminist fight with a features editor, or send him what he wanted from a 'male' contributor and get paid money for being a man.

When Vincent Doyle, later editor of the *Irish Independent*, succeeded Brian Quinn as editor of the *Evening Herald*, he made it clear at our first meeting that unless I was prepared to do a Marj Proops and attack public figures twice a week, my shelf-life would be short. I told him to stick his two columns a week. Rash. On the other hand, because I had invested in technology way beyond what I had previously needed, I had options. I went home, changed the font, wrote two columns and submitted them to Vinnie from my sister's address. He paid me more for *not* being me than he had paid me for being me.

Because so many envelopes arrived at the house now occupied by Tom, addressed to a vast number of people, male and female, the postman one day asked our next-door neighbour, a pensioner, Mr O'Neill, if a commune lived in number 2. Mr O'Neill took this amiss and gave out yards to the poor postman, which left the issue of who all these people were somewhat up in the air. I did make sure our rescue accountant knew about them and declared everything to the Revenue, but I got so used to operating more than a dozen identities that on one occasion, at a meeting in the Fairview Bank of Ireland, manager Hugh McGowan told me that if I was going to do multiple forgeries on documents for him, maybe I wouldn't do it while seated directly in front of him.

Tom and I grabbed any kind of work offered us. To my mother's relief, this didn't include ditch-digging on Tom's part, but it did include some surprising possibilities. Like when Joe Foyle got in touch with Tom, much to his surprise, because Foyle would have been regarded as an extreme right-wing Catholic activist; the last man, you might think, to want to work with a controversial former priest. But that, apparently, was what he was considering. He wanted to meet Tom to look at the possibility of Tom working with him as a speed-reading tutor. Around this time Mr Foyle had, in a newspaper interview with

Ginnie Kenneally, said that 'University definitely reduces a bright girl's marriage prospects, because men do like their wives to be less intelligent than they are themselves. I don't mean they want to marry bird-brains. Most of us welcome advice and even criticism from our wives in private, but no one likes to be publicly outsmarted, least of all by his wife. A girl who does well in university finds it hard to conceal her own excellence, so she is bound to frighten away all but the most intelligent and self-confident men – and those are in short supply.' He went on to express the belief that a secretarial, domestic science or artistic training was more likely to lead girls to a happy and fulfilling life. He even got into the fertility business, recycling the suggestion 'that the tension and tiredness caused by working while setting up a home may prevent conception'.

Tom, when I raised this with him, said that meeting a man for a cup of tea didn't commit him to that man's views. When he came home, he was enthusiastic, explaining that Joe Foyle had timed Tom's natural reading speed, and then given him a lesson in how to read faster. Post-training, Tom was reading at twice his original speed. He sat me down, laid out his test papers and subjected me to the same test, which caused him to lose interest in the whole thing because, without any training, I read faster than he did after he'd been improved, while meeting all the data-recollection tests. I did point out to him that if you live in books and have an impatient nature, you may develop a fast reading pace. He disengaged regretfully from Joe Foyle.

Meanwhile, the hierarchy had retreated from what had promised to be a golden era of straight-talking priests, nuns and brothers, best exemplified by the 'Black and White' *Late Late* shows handed over completely to the religious. Tom Savage deciding to become a layman was coincident, rather than causative, of the hierarchical abandonment of Joe Dunn's vision, but that abandonment, in retrospect, is stark. Whereas high intellects like Fergal O'Connor had been media darlings a short half-decade earlier, the airwaves were largely ceded, at this time, to 'men of the people' like Eamonn Casey and Michael Cleary. The bishops halved Bunny's budget in a move that was part of a pattern of disengagement that soon saw the Radharc team being spoken of in historic terms, and Father Pat Ahern down in Kerry creating *Siamsa*.

Bunny, who had taken a pay cut in order to take on the role of director, resigned. As did Barry Baker, Kay Daly (Bunny's secretary), Aidan Meade and Dominic McNamara. The Redemptorists let Bunny have a wing of their Marianella headquarters in Orwell Road for a peppercorn rent and Carr Communications was set up to provide communications training and consultancy for businesspeople, rather than clerics.

We were too busy surviving to care much about what we had left behind, and, in the case of Tom and me, too happy to waste time longing for it. When you are madly in love, you tend to notice other people in a similar condition. You see them everywhere and you relate to them. Hand-holders. Forehead-leaners. Kissers. One dark evening, on the old Airport Road, I hadn't been paying attention to the affections of anybody outside of the Fiat in which me and the man in my life were travelling, when Tom interrupted our conversation.

'See that car up ahead?'

I had half-registered that the male driver had his arm around the smaller female passenger, and that she was more than halfway across the front seat space, her head on his shoulder.

'Now you watch the driver,' Tom instructed, suddenly crashing down a gear and accelerating like a Formula One driver. We roared out to come level with the other car, then slowed so I could see the driver scrambling to get his arm away from the girl's shoulder and push her back across the front bench seat. Inevitably, because of the almost attacking speed of our car, the driver couldn't fail to turn to his right, to see why any vehicle was overtaking in such a marked manner. I got him in startled full face: Father Michael Cleary.

'Bastard!' Tom said.

Nobody ever gave the word 'bastard' more explosive condemnatory relish than Tom Savage gave it. Tom continued to speed until the lights of Cleary's car disappeared, then took his foot off the accelerator, muttering a definition of Cleary as the ultimate hypocrite. Father Michael Cleary, the popular radio priest, was never behind the door in promulgating traditional Catholic values and condemning those who didn't live by those values. Top of his list of hate figures were the men leaving the priesthood in growing numbers, many because they couldn't cope with loneliness and celibacy. Cleary didn't have to cope with either loneliness or celibacy, having – as emerged much later — fathered a family with Phyllis Hamilton, his housekeeper. He didn't cope well with fidelity to her either, having sex with dozens of other women, one of whom – a single mother he had previously counselled – Phyllis Hamilton discovered in bed with him. This was no secret at the time, yet nobody nailed Cleary for it. He was untouchable. A real Dub. One of our own. No side to him. A man who told it like it was. A man who never saw a camera or a microphone he didn't love. A man gifted with unique freedom, the 'singing priest'. It's difficult, now, to explain the impregnability delivered at the time by his high profile. The abuse horror of other 'singing priests' was later told in the courts, but the contemporary consensus was that the Church was lucky to have such authentic, unpompous men of the people.

Between the sustained hostility of the establishment and of the Caseys and Clearys, many of the men who left the priesthood suffered greatly. Some found themselves impoverished, able to do no job other than, say, teach Latin and Greek, for which there was not much demand outside Catholic schools – which would never employ them. So it was that when, some months later, my husband-to-be was invited to join two others on *The Late Late Show* to discuss the reality facing the men who decided to leave the priesthood, he decided to do it, even though it would reverse him into what he had been, rather than keep him in what he had become. 'Someone has to face them,' he said, showing me the list of topics he had written down as the researcher talked on the phone. Estranged families. Lost jobs. Lack of references. Anonymous threats.

I went with him to RTÉ, a silent journey because when Tom was focused on a challenge, you did not interrupt his thinking. He would whistle now and then – something he invariably did when he was tense, which wasn't often. He went off to make-up and I didn't see him again until he appeared on screen during Gay Byrne's introduction: 'And our third panellist. Tom Savage. Journalist. Was Father Tom Savage. Didn't drink. Didn't smoke. Never had a problem with women –'

Tom interrupted, causing me, in the green room, a private heart attack. What was he about to confess?

'Sorry, Gay, I need to correct one thing,' he told the presenter. 'I did smoke. I always smoked. Since I was sixteen.'

For the only time in the item, laughter eddied around the studio. Then Gay got down to business. The other two men deferred to Tom, partly out of fear, partly out of a belief that since he was a TV professional – to the extent that he frequently presented the late-night God slot on RTÉ and UTV – he could best handle the tough questions. Tom became the de facto spokesman for a generation of Irish men leaving the most admired role in Irish society. At the end, the three men came off the set during the commercial break to applause and claps on the back. Tom cut across all the congratulations and propelled me in front of him into the green room, where he stood watching the big screen. Father Michael Cleary was the next guest. This was back in the day when nobody knew in advance who was going to appear on any section of the *Late Late*.

'If you want to watch him, why don't you sit down?' I suggested.

'I'm not going to sit down because if that bastard makes one negative reference to men leaving, I'm going right back out on the studio floor and taking him on,' he responded, rocking on his heels, ready to run if speed was required. In the event, it wasn't. Cleary was all smarmy positivity. The audience loved him. It wasn't until after his death that he was exposed for his sexual exploitation, and it wasn't until years after his death that it was revealed (by the *Irish Independent*) that he had herded single mothers-to-be into an adoption society where the standards matched his own and where one mother was given a baby she now – half a century later – has proved through DNA testing was not her own.

Michael Cleary had little in the way of overt power, but as much covert power as he wanted. The Church shrugged and let him do the sort of crappy broadcasting he'd never have managed to do as a layman. But the rest of Ireland let him off the hook, too. Those who believed themselves to be his intellectual superiors – and there were many, with some justification – shrugged in collective dismissal, never thinking that their shared contempt, while making them feel good, nonetheless left huge power in his hands.

What most puzzled Tom, as the third year of seeking laicisation rolled around, with him living in Baldoyle and me in Clontarf, was that friends like Bertie Watson, who had applied around the same time, had received their laicisation months, if not years, earlier. Bertie and Kay were now married, and he was teaching in Oughterard. The two of us were laughing over one of Bertie's witty letters when Tom suddenly decided something must be done. He found the Italian tele-phone number of a fellow Maynooth graduate, and telephoned him. Would he do a great favour? Tom's request for laicisation had gone to the cardinal on such and such a date. Since then, he had heard nothing. Would his friend perhaps do a little investigation to see where Tom's progress towards reduction to the lay state was at? Sure. No problem. Neither of us expected him to come back for days, but less than an hour later, the phone rang.

'Tom. You asked me to find out where you are in the system. I'm sorry to tell you, you're not *in* the system. At all.'

'Sorry?'

'The Vatican has no record of your name or your request. None.'

'How the hell …?'

'You want my best guess?'

'Of course.'

'Big Bill Conway decided to sit on your application. Never forwarded it.'

'Holy shit.'

'That would just about sum it up, the way I see it.'

Tom thanked him, gave me the briefest summary of the conversation, took his car keys and walked out of the door. He drove directly to Armagh, where, at Ara Coeli, he marched straight past the receptionist and the priest who sat at a desk outside the cardinal's office and, ignoring their protests, opened the door and banged it closed behind him. Conway, at his desk, looked surprised but undisturbed. Tom sat down and accused him of not sending on the request for laicisation. This evoked a tranquil nod. Why? Tom asked. Because, Conway told him, he had hoped Tom would be his successor and that, given time, he might change his mind.

If he thought this would flatter Tom, he was wrong. Tom told him that he had no goddamn right to play with the lives of human beings. Furthermore, he had no right under canon law. And if Tom didn't find out within 48 hours that Conway had lodged the request within the Vatican, he would go public about this outrageous, inhuman and unchristian act.

The following week, Tom's friend in Rome rang, laughing, to tell him the application had appeared. About four weeks later, the laicisation came through. We had spent more than three years waiting for something we should have received after a month, during which time we had lived separately in order to support the values of a Church that had actively prevented us from undertaking the sacrament of matrimony.

Once the laicisation came through, nearly everything else fell into place. Gerry Reynolds, the Redemptorist, had asked at the outset to officiate at our wedding, and Brian D'Arcy was happy to support him. Broc House was the inevitable venue for the reception. My sister, Hilary, and my friend from school, Anne Sheehy, were to be my maid of honour and bridesmaid. Bunny was Tom's best man. Tom's brothers and sisters all agreed to be guests. And, a few weeks before the wedding date, my father came to me and said he had been wrong and, if we were willing, he would give me away.

The day would have been perfect, if it hadn't been for Hilary falling down the stairs before leaving her house, this fall complicated by her having her youngest son, baby James, in her arms when the descent started. He departed her embrace and described a parabola in the air from the top of the stairs which ended when his little head connected forcefully with the hall floor. James's head had to be medically checked out. Hilary rang to tell me that she might be a little late. Nobody had a mobile home or a free human to contact Bunny and Tom in St Gabriel's church – local, but not close – to explain the absence of the bride. Gerry Reynolds later said he envied Tom because Bunny filled the time, like any good broadcaster, by telling Tom outrageously funny stories. Eventually, little James was cleared and Hilary and her husband, Jimmy, set off for Clontarf. Because Hilary was maid of honour, she had a lot to do throughout the day, whereas my poor brother-in-law Jimmy, marooned in a sea of people, most of whom he had never met, could do nothing but worry about his son. When they arrived home at the end of the wedding day, going into James's room, Jimmy was felled when the baby opened his eyes and smiled at him.

The wedding itself had its moments. Tom's brand-new shoes had the price on big labels on the soles, which were what the congregation mainly saw of him. Gerry Reynolds, when it came to the sermon, was fairly nervous about delivering it in front of the man who had trained him. This was complicated by someone opening a door in the wings of the altar, creating a sudden draught, which lifted his script off the podium and blew it away from him permanently. Poor Gerry, stricken, began to ad lib. Tom, beside me, his face in his hands, began to whisper. 'Gerry, wind it up before you get to the effing blessing of the effing sheep.' I was sure the two of us would be hit by a thunderbolt.

Once the deed was done, it was over to Broc House, where Tom was so focused on making his speech that he couldn't eat his meal, which was just as well because, having lived on boiled eggs for three months in order not to look like Mount Everest after a heavy snowfall, I was so hungry I ate his as well as mine. The great thing about our wedding reception was that nobody was at it who did not like the two of us and wasn't loved by us. Then it was off to the Killiney Castle Hotel for the first few nights of married life. In the *Sunday Press* that week, June Levine reported why: 'Terry Prone was married to journalist Tom Savage in Dublin last Thursday. And, yes, it was she reading *It Says in the Papers* on Thursday morning and Friday, the morning after the wedding. She had to be at work at 5 a.m. to prepare the radio headlines from the national newspapers and the telex machines.'

At the weekend, we headed off to the Canary Islands for our honeymoon. The air hostess was convulsed by me sugaring Tom's tea and instantly worked out we were honeymooners. Sad that such simple mutual gestures would be definitive only of the newly married. We talked, as the plane veered out over the Atlantic, of how we would live our lives, Tom expressing dismay at the family tradition in Clontarf of 'coolnesses' where one of my parents mightn't speak directly to another for several months at a time. 'Let's not do that, Tess. And if we have a row, don't tell your mother. Because we'll make it up, but the memory of it will stay with your mother and taint her view of our relationship.'

He believed arguing to be the most pointless destructive habit in marriage, next to 'Getting something off your chest in the belief that it is good for you. In reality it is likely to make you even more angry. If you want your partner to change, or if he or she has said something to embarrass you, humiliate you or offend you, don't blow up at them. Go away, come back and indicate in an unemotional way what it was about their behaviour that upset you.' I happily agreed, confident that we would never have a row, and claiming to be less vigorous than Hilary in disagreement. Tom murmured that Hilary might kill you in a blind rage but she'd never wish you dead.

We walked down the steps of the plane in Tenerife into such sunshine, Tom began to tan almost immediately. I had been looking forward to this honeymoon with mixed feelings, because, about a week before the wedding, when I noticed Tom not smoking and asked about it, he announced that since he was marrying a woman with a weak chest, he had given up the fags. This seemed badly timed, and I expected him to be of doubtful disposition during the honeymoon. In fact, he was as equable and funny as normal. The hotel had a television where Tom could watch sport, albeit not the sport he wanted, and we had brought lots of books. We swam in the sea and the pool. Tom had a rushed, splashy crawl. But for the most part we talked. Mostly, *he* talked and I studied him as I would study him for forty years, fascinated by his characteristics and his contradictions. Latin phrases and references to Ancient Greek mythology were threaded throughout a conversation that was lightly spattered with rural humour and profanity. He talked about poverty around where he had grown up; poverty so deep that in one family the mother ate her lunch with the plate in the drawer of the kitchen table, so that if an unexpected visitor arrived, she could just shove the drawer closed and not be shamed by her incapacity to feed the visitor, too. He talked of another family where it wasn't until the social services arrived with the Guards that the young son with the profound intellectual disability was released from a kennel out the back of the main building. He talked about being Irish. 'Very few organisations express the essence of Irishness,' he told me one day when I queried his regard for the GAA. 'It catches people when they're young – builds on their sense of family, of place, builds on their sense of belonging and creates a unique pride – like my pride in having an all-Ireland medal and a Sigerson Cup medal. The other organisation embodying the essence of Irishness is the amateur drama movement.'

Tom was buoyant about our future. He said he would be successful in the next phase of his life because I saw possibilities in him that he would never have identified. He knew just how good he was at sport, at lecturing, at preaching, at assessment. But he had learned to become a print journalist because I told him he would be good at it. He loved the version of himself reflected back from me, loved that the first time I saw him in a short-sleeved shirt, outside the then Regency Hotel where he was picking me up to give me a lift, my breath stopped, because of the big muscular arms on him and the broad thick wrists. He enjoyed that I was always picking out shirts and sweaters and suits for him, although he never bought any clothes for himself.

Even though he was, at that stage, estranged from his parents, he never stopped talking lovingly of them. His father was a quiet, skilled workman who drove all his kids nuts with his perfectionism and who had suffered grievously from the isolation and loneliness when forced by bad post-war years to work for long stretches in England. His mother, Mag, worked for 53 years with J. P. Kearney & Son, Willville, Carlingford, She delivered and breastfed five babies long before maternity leave and then educated those children way beyond what could have been expected. That required the children to be trained in their responsibilities from toddlerhood. Mag wasn't going to be there to make beds, so it was their responsibility to make their own beds and clean the house before setting off to school. Because of that, Tom had no notion that women were different from or lesser than men. Apart from occasional comments about the rear ends of women golfers, he was as egalitarian, on all issues, as his mother had been, and from the start assumed I would be leading anything we did. He loved the company of clever women, including Mary O'Mahony of the Mental Health Association, Justice Minister Máire Geoghegan-Quinn and, later, Garda Commissioner Nóirín O'Sullivan.

We were competitive in different ways. Tom always wanted to win, whereas I never wanted to lose, no matter what it cost me. He was at first amused one day in Tenerife when I asked him to show me how disabling it was to have your arm pulled up behind you. I couldn't see it would be that painful, until he did it, but fought the urge to scream until, horrified, he let go and turned me around to face him. 'Jesus, Tess. You'd let me break your arm rather than give in.'

There was the truth of it. He knew he was brave. I was afraid I was a coward. He talked of boarding school teaching him, from ten years of age, ways of coping with all the loneliness, isolation and being in a difficult environment. 'Therefore, almost whatever eventuality occurred in life, I always felt that I would adjust and that the outside world would never know whether it had had an impact on me or not.'

Some attitudes, where I had expected clerical overhang, went the other way. He recounted a nun ringing him in panic to say that two of the sixth-year girls were in love with each other and his response to her was: 'Love comes in such rare instances that maybe we shouldn't rush to question the form it takes.'

Just as he stopped smoking and never expressed a longing for cigarettes thereafter, so nothing in his life as a priest seemed to call him
back, despite how well the priesthood had suited him. 'It gave you
total freedom to be uninvolved – or to be involved only on your own
terms. It was actually the perfect place to be. And you learn early on to
hedge your personal involvements. You build fences, you keep them
up and you decide that's the way life is.'

His black Labradors had all been named Laddie, and he would
mention the relief of living alone in a parochial house where, having
spent the day ministering to people, he could come in, close the door
and stand with his back to it in the silence, relishing the few hours of
solitary reading or listening to music that lay ahead, the dog at his feet.
His musical tastes were catholic with a small c. Popular classics like the
Chorus of the Hebrew Slaves from *Nabucco* jostled with Gregorian
chant. His own party piece was a song called 'Little Green Valley'. But
his ultimate favourites were country music: three chords and the truth.
He was a genuine connoisseur of country music, right back to the first
recordings, and believed it to be the poetry of blue collar workers.

He would write to me, even if it meant bringing the letter with
him to hand over. In one of the many I kept, he described me as 'the
complete focus of my life. Anything that I do, or say, or see, anything
that happens to me or two others that I experience – all these and
more I want to share with you first.' Many of the hand-written notes
he discarded I would keep, just for the pleasure of looking at his
elegant handwriting, distinctive in that the letters never sat on the line
but floated a fraction above it, which gave a joyous cast to whatever
he wrote. In 1997, *Woman's Way* asked us and two other couples if
we'd allow a graphologist to do a blind assessment of us based on our
handwriting. They would give us a piece of text, we would write
it out in our normal handwriting, the graphologist would look at it,
knowing only which one of us was male, which female. The piece
of text had nothing to do with our lives or careers. We did it with
maximum scepticism and forgot about it. Until the report came back

from the graphologist. 'This is a quietly spoken man who enjoys his own company,' he wrote of Tom, having never met him. 'He is a very spiritual person and has a great understanding of people. He has a natural reserve with people. His mind works quickly and is always ahead of his actions. I think this man is not a great socialiser as he prefers to be in the background rather than taking the limelight. I think this is a really nice man.'

Twenty-three years after our marriage, in my second novel, *Racing the Moon*, Darcy, one of the twins at the centre of the story, writes with wistful hopelessness about her ideal man. Her ideal is a faithful portrait of Tom:

I want a man who is independent of me and linked inextricably with me. Who will fight for me, who will wait for me, who will toil in the wilderness for love of me, like Jacob did for Rachel … Jacob worked seven years to win Rachel '… and it seemed as but a day because of the greatness of his love'.

I want a man generous in plan, in thought, in possessions and in time, not simply generous in reflexes or reaction. A man gritty with his sureness of himself and where he stands, bulwarked against my inundating inevitable attempts to modify, improve and change him. A man of ideas and silences, of speculations, reflections and earned, unstated certainties.

A man not needy of audience or approval. A man whisper-hoarse in spoken voice, that roughness lost in the singing of his songs. A man of steel and silk strengths, of clean soap smells and spice-sweated sleepfulness.

I want a man who walks and stands in the unselfconscious ease of the athlete, whose hands have the control and disci-pline of sport, a man gentle in the control of mechanical things. Who does not weep to prove sensitivity, and who scrapes, sandpaper-raw, to remove adherent sentimentality. Who can be part of a team. Arms-linked, minds at one with other equals, then walk away into his own individuality. A man so self-defined as to be without need to change others.

I want a man of quiet developing beliefs, not all of them shared with me. Of trusts and unequivocal relish. A man of wisdom, of reading. A steadfast man. Steadfast. A man whose temperament is like the great movements of the deep ocean, not the shoreline fussiness of the shallow sea; no tetchy volatility.

I want a man who never bores me, is never predictable, except in his casual presence in my life. A man who has only to look at me, head glecked a-tilt, to send the breathing ragged in me and the curling weakness between my legs, who puts his hands on me in demand that meets demand and is unfazed by the vivid recklessness of the response he gets, a man who will take me like a train thundering unstoppable and nestle me afterwards like a cat with kittens.

I want a man who is superb at whatever he does, be it carpentry or high art, of whom I can be proud, who is proud of me, of what I do.

I imagine him to be a big broad bludgeon of a man with an unhandsome face of angles chiselled and textures punished, eyes dark and filled with secrets, no ready sunshine smile but a slow-shared humour pulling the edges of the mouth.

That is him. That is my man.

That was him. That was my man.

15

Being Bombed

In the seventies, Tom ran a peace organisation called PeacePoint. It suited his deep knowledge of the North. He had been the priest sent by Cardinal Conway to welcome the British troops into Northern Ireland when they were regarded as likely protectors of Catholics.

As we were driving in the North before dawn one morning, I asked him if he could tell whether a tiny hamlet we were passing through was Protestant or Catholic. 'Protestant,' he said without hesitation. 'See the first-floor windowsills? See the thing in the middle sticking up? For putting the Union Jack in on the Twelfth.'

On that occasion, we met a printer who was producing some Peace-Point leaflets outside the restaurant where we were to have lunch. I was startled when a shot rang out and both men dropped to the pavement on either side of me. As did a couple of other people. A man who stayed standing laughed and – as the fallers stood up again – explained to me that it wasn't a shot, it was a car backfiring. I didn't know what he was talking about because I had never heard a car backfire, but apparently it sounds like a gun.

Inside, over lunch, the topic of random shootings came up and Tom said it was a misnomer. No such thing as a random shooting, he said.

The shooters mightn't know the identities, but they always knew the religion of the people they shot. Catching my puzzled look, he said an IRA man would know a Protestant on sight and vice versa. I scoffed at this. Tom took out his pad and pulled off a page. Then, on that page and the next, he quickly sketched the number of tables in the restaurant and numbered them, handing the pad to the (Protestant) printer and nodding in a general way at the diners.

'You put the religion of each table beside that table, and I'll do the same,' he said. The printer nodded and the two of them got to work. Within minutes, they had completed pages – and the pages matched at every point.

'Tess, you're looking at two communities deliberately not intermarrying for more than four centuries,' Tom said. 'Of course they're going to have differences in physiognomy.'

'Also differences in grooming and wardrobe,' the printer added. 'There's a particular blonde hair dye that doesn't sell at all in Catholic areas.'

On 7 March 1973, Tom had a PeacePoint meeting in London. I tagged along and found something to research for *The Gay Byrne Hour* while I was there. The following day, we were heading for the airport through a grey, drizzly London when, mid-morning, the IRA bombed the Old Bailey. Our taxi was directly outside, so the windows were blown into the car and all over us. The blast, the noise and the resultant screams caused the driver to halt the cab. It didn't stay halted. Tom leaned forward and jammed his index and second fingers into the driver's neck. 'Drive,' Tom ordered. 'Just drive.' The driver drove, never looking at us through the rear view mirror. He undoubtedly believed Tom was pushing a weapon against his neck. 'Keep driving,' Tom told him and sat back, giving me a look that severely disincentivised me from opening my mouth. At Heathrow airport, I tipped the man all the English money I had – roughly three times as much as the fare – and whispered, 'I'm sorry.' He got back into that black cab in eyes-down silence and drove away while I turned to Tom and demanded to know what the hell he thought he was doing. He looked at me in a slightly puzzled way. 'Tess, did you want to spend several hours – two people with Irish accents – being interrogated by the London constabulary?'

I turned him so he could see his own reflection in the window beside us. 'You think the airport cops are not going to have reservations about letting two people covered in blood onto a Dublin flight?'

Tom was used to bombs in the North, but it came as a shock to everyone when, on 17 May 1974, co-ordinated bombings killed more than thirty people in Dublin and Monaghan. Tom and I had driven into town in his car and I had dropped him off in Talbot Street. I was heading to Nassau Street to buy books in Hanna's and we were going to meet up again in the Shelbourne Hotel. I parked and was waiting for the chance to brave the traffic to get to the shop when the end of the street exploded. I wasn't sure whether the explosion was due to a gas leak or a bomb, but I started to run in the direction from which the crowds were moving. Just before the point where the road turns left into Lincoln Place was a circle of death and destruction; burned clothing, torn-off limbs, unconscious children and undoubtedly dead adults. The screams of ambulances competed with the screams of the wounded and the horrified, and gardaí were already moving people away to let the paramedics in. I remembered I was driving a Northern-registered car, so I left the scene and ran back to the big old red Fiat. Then the journalist in me clicked in and I drove to Independent Newspapers and got to the newsroom, which was already chaotic with shouting, telephone-ringing and keyboard-thumping. I found the duty editor and told him what I had seen. Before I had got two sentences out, he pushed me ahead of him to a long desk with lines of big typewriters, made sure a sheet of blank paper was rolled into one of them and sat me down in front of it. I started to type, and as soon as I had three paragraphs done, a copy boy tore it off and ran with it to where a Linotype compositor typed it again, this time to make the metal words that would, embedded in ink, put my words on newsprint. It was only when I typed 'Ends' at the conclusion of what I had written that I tuned into the bellowing around me to discover that several bombs had gone off in the evening rush hour. One of them in Talbot

Street. My skin crawled with terror for Tom, but all anybody could tell me was that maybe a dozen people were dead, hundreds injured and nobody had any names yet.

I headed for the Shelbourne. It took me nearly an hour, through diversions that sent me in circles. Several people I knew were there and some had come from Talbot Street. Had they seen Tom? Sorry, no. But the word was that it was bad. Someone had a hotel radio on and did the flapping shut-up gesture, so everybody in the coffee lounge heard that more bombs had gone off in Monaghan town. Knotted with helpless fear, I thought about trying to get closer to Nassau Street, but I could hear Tom's voice in my head telling me to stick to the plan and not confuse the situation any more than it already was. Then followed the longest three-quarters of an hour of my life. Finally, covered in sweat and dust, he came up the Shelbourne steps and I stepped into his hold, smelling the sweet cleanness of him and the sweat with it. People I'd talked to earlier grabbed him and sat him down, demanding to know what he had seen.

'Tea,' he said and I asked a waiter to deliver it with more sugar than he would normally bring. The waiter looked at me sympathetically as if he knew I was trying to cope with shock, when in fact all I was trying to do was meet Tom's constant sugar need. Because he had been in bombings before, he said, he was able to help, getting doors that had been blown off in the blast to serve as stretchers. Someone asked who on earth would have done this, and Tom looked at them from under raised eyebrows: come on, who the hell other than the most triumphalist loyalists would have any interest in doing such damage?

As soon as he had had several cups of tea, we headed out and he apologised for not asking me where I had been. 'You can read it in tomorrow's *Indo*,' I said. He looked across at me with admiration. 'That's the difference between you and me, Tess,' he said. 'Yeah,' I said. 'I know. You go and help. I go and type.' He nodded, as if this was a correct division of responsibilities, adding that this was what Peter Lemass didn't understand. Once a priest, always a priest. Not in the sense of delivering sacraments, but in the sense of giving help. Then came the practical *non sequitur.* 'Have to get rid of this Northern-registered car first thing Monday,' he said.

Much later, Tom was to work with some of the men behind those bombings. President Mary McAleese, having campaigned for election, first time around, as a bridge-builder, set about delivering on the claim by actively building bridges north of the border. She contacted the barrister Noel Whelan and Tom Savage, asking them if they would have any problem working together on a project. They each laughed. Working together when Noel was on the staff of Fianna Fáil and Tom was Albert Reynolds' communications adviser, they had developed a warm and strong relationship. The president said this was good news. Would they come to the Áras for a quiet dinner, without partners? They agreed, asked no questions, and pitched up on the night, formally dressed, two tall dark men meeting each other's eyes in puzzlement in the elegant reception rooms of Áras an Uachtaráin. Whatever this was about must be related to Northern Ireland, to judge by the accents of the other men – and only men – present. Sitting down to dinner, Tom beside a man in a pink-frilled shirt he knew to be a multiple killer, Noel in a similar position, did a mutual non-shrug: we'll hear in her own good time.

In due course, President McAleese stood to address the assembled paramilitaries. Or perhaps 'recovering paramilitaries' might be a more accurate description, since they had, not long before, signed up to relinquish violence as a *modus operandi.* She told them the reason she had invited them was that abandoning violence wasn't enough. Now they needed to know how to work democracy. To move from the bullet to the ballot box in an informed way. Noel and Tom were asked to stand up, and were introduced by the president. She explained that Noel Whelan was a legal expert deeply rooted in party politics who knew every aspect of planning for and managing elections, while Tom Savage knew all about political communication. The two men, she said, had agreed to provide whatever help those present needed as soon as they needed it. Which slightly exceeded what they had agreed to, but spoke to her understanding of the two of them. They'd be up for it and she knew it without going into the details.

A few weeks later, they were told to be in the car park of a hotel north of the border at a particular time on a particular day, and to expect to be away from home for several days. Seated, talking, in a southern-registered car, they watched the arrival of a van with blacked-out windows. Signals were exchanged and the two of them, carrying their small suitcases, climbed into the back of the van to go they knew not where. For three days they worked in a secret location with about twenty men to fit them for the democratic process, and tough work it was, particularly for Noel Whelan, who was introducing them to a system of which they had no experience. Noel's expertise in the system south of the border was relevant – but also irrelevant. He had to constantly adjust to deal with the realities of electoral processes north of the border. By day two, he and Tom decided not to deal with separate groups but to amalgamate them and work jointly with them, because Tom had been educated north of the border and, having worked in social care in Armagh, was able to produce specific examples of Noel's concepts which locked them into the mindset of the course participants. Then they were returned to the hotel car park. No reports went to the president. Or to the Department of Foreign Affairs. No subsequent meetings happened. The two undertook an important task and then shut up about it.

In the early years of our marriage, finance demanded that the two of us work two and three jobs simultaneously. Tom lectured in sociology, broadcast *It Says in the Papers* and worked the overnight duty roster in the RTÉ newsroom. I edited *Nikki*, a teenage magazine, for the Creation Group and briefly served as the first women's editor on the then new *Sunday World*, while at the same time writing somewhere between fifteen and twenty-five scripts a week for Gay Byrne. Even though some of the other jobs paid better, *The Gay Byrne Hour*, with the opportunity to watch the maestro in action, was the favourite.

Gay Byrne was a native speaker of broadcasting. He understood the grammar of it, the peculiar inflections of it, the dangers of it, the way to make it heard and attended to, and he understood all that to a unique depth. He had the courage of a lion and needed it. And an abiding realism: he regarded himself as highly professional but much less relevant than he actually was, seeing himself as a coincidence of history, rather than a catalyst for change. The way he saw it, the previously impermeable walls of Irish society were becoming chalky and porous around that time; and he and Adrian Cronin began to shape *The Late Late Show* into an outlet for dissent and challenge in a way unintended when the programme began. One way or the other, Gay, who produced as well as presented *The Late Late*, had an instinct for where the public mind was headed, plus the courage and skill to help it along.

He used an autocue so naturally that audiences had no clue that such technology was even in play. He listened like a hawk, identifying among the detritus of ordinary conversation the gem to be pulled out and focused on. Programmes like Graham Norton's have an endless supply of A list celebrities who can be relied on but who can still be edited, post factum and before transmission. Gay had nothing but the people in front of him, lengthy preparation, a phenomenal memory, an entertainer's instinct and an unerring capacity to work out what the viewer wanted at any given moment. He could cope with the exigencies of live TV like the night in 1997 when he rang to tell a viewer named Rita Hanley that she had won a car in the previous week's competition. Rita told Gay that her daughter Linda had in fact entered the competition on Rita's behalf, and that Linda had died the previous day. 'She got knocked down,' she told him. 'She was in a car crash last night.'

Gay ignored the horrific irony of the situation, quietly asking her if she wanted to continue the call. When she said she did, he began to ask her about her daughter and invited poet Brendan Kennelly, who was on the panel that night, to contribute. Kennelly delivered lines from one of his own poems and the bereaved mother cried. Nobody other than Byrne could have rescued the situation so gracefully, so sure-footedly.

The pace, the purpose, the ad breaks were all set by him. And that was when things were going right. It was when things were going wrong that he ascended to another level of art – because what he did was art, not craft. If every camera but one went down, Gaybo would manage and how he did it would become a war story among the techies, who adored him. They adored him because he was the quintessential pro. Always on time. Script to hand. Research done. Pronunciations checked. And pronunciation mattered enormously to him. He was one of the few broadcasters in Radio Éireann who loved the pronunciation unit run by Brigid Kilfeather and Una Sheehy. Long years of elocution classes left him with an acute ear for oral error. He knew where the emphasis fell in a foreign word, he knew how to handle a silent aitch, and the south Dublin soft 't' drove him crazy.

The various histories of Irish broadcasting come back, again and again, to him being excoriated in the Houses of the Oireachtas or in the media, with demands that he be silenced or fired. The Church threatened his livelihood many times, and yet – despite being the most devout of Catholics – he stood up to them again and again, making programming, including the one about what life was like as a gay Irish person, that blew the doors off the silent coercion which had characterised those lives for so long.

Yet Gay was a devout coward on some things. Medical topics gave him the screaming heebie-jeebies. He had to steel himself to do them, but nobody watching him interview a woman whose entire face, post-cancer surgery, had to be completely reconstructed, would have known the discipline he mustered to conduct the interrogation. At the end, he reached out and gently touched her cheek with his palm.

It was always about the audience, never about him. The night he trounced psychiatrist R.D. Laing for coming on the show three sheets to the wind, the issue wasn't his personal affront but rather a clinical laying down of the law. To look at the footage all these decades later is fascinating. When a man in the audience shouts at Gay in defence of Laing, you can almost see, as Gay turns to hear him out, the cogs in the broadcaster's brain welcoming this unexpected and ostensibly unfriendly input. It was all grist to his mill. That's what they all were. Bands. Politicians. Comedians. Writers. Harmonica players. All fuel for his fire. He could spot the charismatic shining hungry ones a mile off. What he wanted was performers who were interesting, different, lively. If they were funny, that was jam on the egg. Nobody ever 'gave' to comedians or played the straight man more generously than Gay Byrne.

Even when he and the topic were inconsonant, he was able to conceal his own views. In the early seventies, for example, something called the 'voice phenomena' of Raudive and Jürgenson fed into the Colin Wilson-fuelled hunger of the day to believe in something more modern than Christianity, and outside rational experience. The theory behind these phenomena was that the voices of the dead somehow turned up on audio recording tape. I believed this was a higher-tech version of listening to a big seashell and said so on the show. Gay believed that this was a profitable manifestation of mass hysteria with a scientific overlay. But it was great television and proved that believers will always find something in which to believe, for a time.

The technical guys loved Gay Byrne because he did what he said he would do, at precisely the moment he said he would do it. He would pick up the microphone and loop its cable around his hand (to minimise movement noise) as he was finishing an item, giving everybody plenty of notice that he was about to turn to the audience. He moved like a dancer, suffused with adrenalin, the neat averageness of him suddenly outsize in its authority and confidence, yet concentrated all the time on managing the infinitely delicate balance between the emotions of the people in the tiered seats in front of him and the people stuffed into their couches at home.

He understood change without understanding what he understood. He had no theories or philosophies about it. He was simply in tune with the waves breaking on the shore of old Ireland. When he did the first special in which members of the gay community talked openly of their lives in a world that criminalised the expression of their love, they knew he would be courteous and fair to them, not because he agreed with them, but because he wanted to explore ideas whose time had come. Gay had a deep understanding of TV that precluded ding-dong contention. While he never sought the thesis/antithesis/synthesis argument to a conclusion, he never bought the idea that mutual battery, using non-sequitur statements of disagreement or hatred, amounted to a discussion.

Gay Byrne was not modest, but he never told stories about himself and his triumphs. At a dinner party, he was either the perfect host or the perfect guest, cueing others to tell their stories, keeping the conversation going, but rarely, if ever, talking about himself. That was partly because he didn't remember what others saw as breakthrough moments in radio and TV, such as the time a famous controversialist was due on the programme on some hot topic but didn't turn up, sending a lengthy statement instead. Gay told the audience that the guest had sent this material and then he contemptuously tore it up and tossed the whole lot in the air. Reminded of it, decades later, he shrugged: no recollection of it whatever. Just as important, there was no need for a recollection, because his life wasn't a competition between himself and others. Not for him the sad traditional sequelae of the old man: a series of yarns in which he stars as the victor. Gaybo was just there to do TV. Novelist Brian Cleeve wrote a thinly disguised fictional version of him, a character brought to life by the studio brightness, the circling cameras, the red lights. Brought to a larger life than was his by nature; and when each show ended, the character shrank into a grey emptiness. That was not a fair portrait of Gay. He was not empty. But he was not an extrovert. He liked his own company – significantly, he preferred solitary activities like cycling, motorcycling, walking and reading. When he came to our house, he would wander along the bookshelves, select three books, ask permission to borrow them, and return them within a month, without fail.

A few weeks after I got home from hospital, in a wheelchair, after a major car crash, he and Kathleen arrived on their bikes to our home in Baldoyle. Tom brought tea and biscuits in time to hear Gay ask me, for the third time, how I was coping apparently so easily with the catastrophe.

'You're not asking that for her', my husband said, handing him a mug, 'you're asking for *you.*'

'You're absolutely right, Tom,' Gay said. 'To this day, I'm not over what Russell Murphy did to me. Do you know, for the first year, my very signature was unreadable? I was destroyed. Just destroyed. So close a friend ...'

Having bamboozled Gay into giving him power of attorney, Russell Murphy stole and squandered Gay's life savings. To a man of a generation that saved and took care of its family responsibilities that would always have been a blow, although Gay was young enough – just about – to earn his way back to comfort. But that someone he loved would do such damage to him, so gratuitously, so carelessly, wounded him so deeply that he had to work hard to trust anybody thereafter. If this could happen at the hands of a dear and trusted friend – godfather to one of his children – what else might? It rocked him to the core and collapsed many of the certainties by which he lived.

The exceptional certainty that could not be collapsed – ever – was his wife, Kathleen Watkins. He always talked of Kathleen as infinitely powerful and decisive in their family life, particularly in the last year of his life. When she said that he shouldn't even think of going back to presenting his Sunday afternoon programme on Lyric FM, no matter how much he loved it, he simply accepted that she knew what was best for him and went along with it.

Towards the end of his life, he worried that he had not been kind enough to those who worked with him, although most of us who spent time on his teams relished his rare crisp reproofs nearly as much as we lived for his brisk words of praise. He loved talent and attended upon it like a sacrament, building Joe Duffy and countless others into major figures in broadcasting and journalism. He never offered advice unless it was asked for. He was appreciative and kind and wouldn't permit anybody to tell him that Ireland wouldn't be the country it is today without him. If you started any of that stuff, he would reach for the cap and the stick and announce he was for home.

What John Boland described as the 'regular and sometimes quite unpleasant spats' on social and political issues between Ulick O'Connor and Dennis Franks, the former a combative writer and journalist and the latter a posh-voiced earnest actor of Polish-Jewish descent, who died in 1967, pushed ratings from the outset. O'Connor continued as a panellist after Franks' death, paired with whoever looked like they could survive his venom. Which, on one Saturday night, was me.

This wasn't a case of a lamb to the slaughter. This was a case of a pig-ignorant lamb to the slaughter. Because we had no TV, I had never seen the frequent quarrels between Franks and O'Connor. Which is not to say that I didn't know about them. Because of the scarcity of channels, back then, the few channels there were had a grip on viewers' imagination which is impossible to imagine now. In addition, TV was where the ideas of the day played out, so the arguments that began on a Saturday night ran through the following week, whether on the bus or at the pulpit or in the Dáil. Just as you can get lung cancer from second-hand smoke, you could get a second-hand but acute understanding of what happened on TV even if you hadn't seen the particular programme. I assumed that, since TV was an extension of show business, it was all acting and it was your job to go on and be slightly larger than life in your adherence to a particular viewpoint. You could have a grand battle for ten minutes and then go and have soft drinks (in my case) or hard liquor (in their case) with the person who had ostensibly been your enemy up to that point. And so it was that, when I was invited on to the panel of *The Late Late* along with Ulick O'Connor, I figured it would be fun, because, although I'd never met him, I'd read his book on Behan and knew he wrote like an angel.

A key reason for my ignorance was that nobody told the truth about O'Connor at the time. Just as nobody told the truth about Dennis Franks' sexuality. This was the era where everybody knew but nobody admitted knowing. Where people who suffered at the hands of misogynistic bullies kept their mouths shut, lest it be assumed that they couldn't take the heat. The fault, in other words, lay in their weakness, rather than in the crude nastiness of the attacker. So it was only in 2019, after Ulick O'Connor died, that my former boss Mary Kenny, confessing to be reluctant to break the old Irish rule about saying nothing but good of the dead, wrote a column for the *Irish Independent* wherein she touched on how nasty he could be:

> Combative I don't mind. But I usually felt humiliated after a bout with Ulick: he did not play by Oxford Union rules, where it's supposed to be about the debate, not the person. On one occasion, I appeared next to Ulick on a panel at a public media discussion in Dublin, and perhaps I annoyed him by delving into my handbag for notes. 'Mary Kenny – would you stop rummaging in your bag for your Tampax!' Ulick announced loudly, nostrils flaring sneeringly. Now, I have no sense of prudery about the issue of menstruation – it's a fascinating aspect of women's history – but the note of misogyny in Ulick's voice was unmistakable. Real misogyny in men is quite rare, in my experience: most men like women. But that's the way Ulick was.

I had no warning of this as I sat down beside him just before the countdown, filled with excitement and goodwill at the prospect of the televised arguments ahead of us. I asked him something about his most recent book, genuinely curious to know if what I quoted had been said in innocence by his subject or was carefully planned. He went berserk. No messing; straight-up berserk. It wasn't just his nostrils that flared. His *ears* flared. He foamed. All of it more terrifying because it had the one-to-one intimacy of an unseen garrotting. There was no shouting. There was plenty of swearing. Swearing in a hissing whisper, delivering the volume and spitting steam of a talking pressure-cooker. The force was interrupted by floor managers calling for each of us to count to ten – he did it so calmly I thought I must have imagined the earlier abuse. But the whispered tirade resumed as the signature tune boomed its way into the studio.

It has to have been one of the weirder *Late Late Shows*. I was there to create laughter, disagreement and interest. O'Connor, when he contributed out loud, was his usual contemptuous self, personalising his disputes with me. This was not done to create a *frisson* of faux tension. He meant every word of it. But what was most challenging was that every time his microphone was off, during ad breaks for example, he would go back to his hissing abuse of me, my stupidity, vested interests, impertinence and incompetence.

The programme ended and the audience milled around on the studio floor, the lights dying in sequence, taking the sparkly magic with them and reducing each of us to who we were, although I wasn't that sure of precisely who I was at that point. Suddenly, Tom, who had been sitting way up at the back of the audience, out of the view of any wandering camera, was in front of me.

'Tess, what's wrong?'

I fought not to cry and told him what had happened. The minute he understood, across the studio with him to where O'Connor was talking to a group of worshipping audience members. Tom spun him around and grasped him by the lapels of his jacket with such force that the jacket split down its back seam. It crossed my mind that Tom might get himself killed, given that Ulick O'Connor had won awards for boxing, but O'Connor didn't fight back, understandably, since he had no idea who Tom was or what was eating him.

'Gay! Gay!' O'Connor called out and Gay immediately responded. Tom released the lapels as Gay came level with the two of them in a suddenly hushed studio.

'What's wrong, Tom?' Gay asked, which flummoxed O'Connor, who was, after all, the one being assaulted. Tom gave Gay a short, quiet account. Ulick started to square up to Tom. Gay called the floor manager and the director and ordered that O'Connor be brought to one dressing room and Tom and me to another, those dressing rooms separated by a length of corridor. Gay encouraged the audience to head down to the green room, patted Tom on the back and said he'd be with us shortly. He then went to the other dressing room, along with the producer, and interviewed O'Connor, who claimed nothing at all had happened and that I had made it all up to get attention. The two RTÉ men then came to us and I went through what had happened. Off they went again. Then Gay reappeared, on his own this time, and told us it was all taken care of. The producer arrived, nodding and explaining that Gay had told Ulick that he believed my account of what had taken place. Gay indicated that this was purely data-driven: why would I make it up? Appearing on *The Late Late* was more attention than anyone could otherwise hope for, so why would I invent a story that gained me the attention of only about ten people?

Tom walked out onto the corridor to talk with Gay while the producer double-checked that I was okay and got me into my coat. We walked to Tom's car and, as always, he opened the passenger door first and got me in.

'Well, that's the last time Ulick O'Connor will appear on *The Late Late Show*,' he said. And it was. However, it wasn't the last time our paths crossed. Many years later, following a car crash that nearly killed me, coverage appeared in newspapers of the inevitable legal actions, and I received a letter from Ulick O'Connor, wishing me the bad outcome he said was inevitable because I would be revealed in court for the liar I was. It was the first time I had encountered such long-term venom on the part of someone who remembered a damaging encounter in a way that made no sense but that was satisfactory in getting him off a hook he had perhaps baited once too often.

O'Connor's disappearance from TV, unsought by but undoubtedly caused by me, was an object lesson in – to use Gay Byrne's pet phrase – 'how quickly they forget'. Nobody noticed his absence because he had appeared sporadically rather than every week, but also because *The Late Late Show* was changing, as were viewing habits. The awful cruelty of television fame is that, within a shockingly short time, you can go from household name to 'Wasn't he the guy who …?' I never talked about what had happened. Neither did O'Connor. Nor did he seem to learn from his removal from RTÉ's biggest programme. In 2001, when publicising his newly published diaries, he told journalists that Gay Byrne was a man who was 'hard to like', who read very little and who had 'failed to fulfil his potential'. This infuriated one of the stars Gay had nurtured. Joe Duffy, in *Ireland on Sunday*, wrote that at 67:

> [Gay is] flying up and down the country on a Harley-Davidson, living life to the full, while Ulick (only five years older) is using his breath to badmouth decent people. As for Gay not being well read – that's a joke. I can personally testify that he read every single book covered on his radio and television shows over 35 years. He is without doubt one of the most well-read people I have ever met. Mention any subject and Gay has read a book on it – including every major new novel. Gay told me he has read five books in the last week alone. For the record, they are Seán Moncrieff's new novel, entitled *Dublin* (and in Gay's words, it's 'bloody good'), a new thriller by Terry Prone, Pat Liddy's book on Dublin, a novel by Eibhlín Ní Dhuibhir and cancer-beating cyclist Lance Armstrong's autobiography. And he'll no doubt read Ulick's new book, if he gets an hour to spare next week.

Even when Ulick O'Connor managed to get bits of radio work, he screwed that up, too. Vincent Browne wrote of how, when O'Connor was a participant on a radio programme Browne was presenting, 'He had a go at a journalist and when I attempted to stop him he railed on and on. He had complained that there was a policy in RTÉ to keep him off the airwaves. I said that, sadly, there wasn't, but if I had anything to do with it there would be.'

16

ANTON IS A LOVELY NAME

*I*t took me by surprise, because I didn't think the baby was due for another two weeks. But the signs were inescapable. I showered, dressed and went into the box room we used as an office to input the two columns due that week, somewhat distracted by Tom, who was bothered by the sight of me typing away but every five minutes or so going into a contraction-crouch. Columns complete, we got into the car and headed for Mount Carmel. As Anton arrived into our lives, I thought it was a hallucination that I could hear my own voice, but it turned out that the labour ward radio was playing the Andy O'Mahony programme on which Tom and I appeared each week.

Once the baby was handed to me, the relief was total. For more than six months, I had lived in dread of this moment, because, around about the tenth week of pregnancy, I had an asthma attack that put me into Jervis Street Hospital in the middle of the night, where an exhausted radiologist X-rayed me without protection. The consequent terror washed away when I held this perfect, strong baby who looked at me in the most straightforward 'Okay, who are you, then?' way. When I let Tom have a hold of him, the baby's fingers began to explore the velvet jacket Tom was wearing. The paediatrician who came to examine him said he was a good two weeks overcooked. So I had my dates wrong by a month.

His name had been easily picked months before, when I wandered into the room where Tom was watching a football match and heard Mícheál Ó Muircheartaigh bellowing something about Anton O'Toole going down the sideline. 'Anton is a lovely name,' I said. Tom, whose total concentration was on the game, glanced up, nodded, said 'Grand' and that was it. As the nurses got us settled into a room, I realised that, because of having his ETA wrong, I now had a problem. On the following day, Monday, I was due to meet Vincent Hanley, a broadcaster then breaking into international work with MTV. When I mentioned this, the nurses shrugged. This was, they pointed out, a hospital, so if I wanted to go off and interview 'Fab Vinny', I should do just that. Anton would be in good hands.

So first thing the following morning, I took a taxi to the hotel where we were due to meet. As I was setting up my cassette recorder, I thought Vincent didn't seem his usual chatty self and said so. 'You told me you were pregnant,' he said defensively. 'Oh, sorry. The baby was born yesterday,' I told him. The thought of that totally put him off, but once the tiny red light went on, he delivered a gorgeous interview. That captured, I was back to Mount Carmel to feed Anton and discuss the world with him, because he seemed so eager to come to terms with it. Sometime that day, before Tom arrived to visit, I fell in love with this baby in a way I had never anticipated. I had not been that pushed about having a baby. Neither had Tom. If it hadn't happened, we'd have been fine. Tom had a particular loathing of what he saw as a particularly Irish thing of parents living vicariously through their children, and wanted no part of it. So, for the first twenty-four hours, Anton was like a pleasant if conversationally inept guest. A baby, in short. A perfectly acceptable baby with all the right bits and big black eyes. But that was it. Then, suddenly, he was much more than a random baby. He was the only baby who had ever existed, and I would have died for him.

Later, when Tom arrived from one of his three-a-day jobs, I virtu-
ously held Anton out to him with a sense of relinquishing my life. As
he took his son, he handed me a tiny box. I unwrapped it and found
a diamond eternity ring I knew we couldn't afford. My thanks were
drowned by a yell from Anton, speedily quelled as his father began
to walk around the little room, telling his son about the day he'd had.
Very soon, this would morph, every evening, into Tom putting Anton
on his thighs and gently stroking the baby's forehead towards his
eyes, causing him to close them, briefly and resentfully, while telling
Anton all that Anton had experienced that day. Each evening, when
Tom came home from work, Anton would be taking the house apart
because of 'five o'clock colic' and Tom would walk him up and down
the landing, singing and talking to him until the agony died down and
the screams with it.

Watching Tom, that first full day of his son's life, it was as if he had
never said he wasn't pushed about fatherhood. He was transformed, a
quiet ecstasy taking hold of him that never let go. He believed every
sigh or squawk Anton produced was the best sigh or squawk in the
history of childhood, and that it was his job to explain to the world
how exceptional this baby was. The Mount Carmel nurses, watching
Tom, told me I was lucky. Funny thing, that. You marry a man because
you've spotted he's generous, witty, diligent, sweet-natured, clever,
kind and insightful – and spend the rest of your life having other
people pointing, in a marked manner, to those qualities and assuming
you haven't spotted them.

On that Tuesday morning, I couldn't find the eternity ring. At first
it was a minor irritation, but it turned into a major crisis. Almost
everybody working in Mount Carmel came to help search one small
room. It was not found. So when Tom arrived to collect new son and
wife, he found the latter strangling so hard on sobs and apologies that
it took him a while to work out the reason. When he apprehended it,
he sat down on the bed beside me, put one arm around me and held
my hand with the other. 'Tess. I had the pleasure of giving you the ring.

You had the pleasure of receiving it. Now, let's take Anton home and introduce him to Baldoyle.'

That's what we did. I took Anton everywhere with me, including when I was doing the *Gay Byrne Hour* shopping basket item. His early months were heavy on travel and changing locations, even if they were a bit light on luxury. We didn't have a cot and so he spent the first half year in a drawer. I had sworn to Tom, haunted by Cyril Connolly, that we would never have a pram in the hall, but Deirdre Purcell handed on two items her two boys had used, the first one of those light buggies that looks like a small cluster of folded walking sticks, the second a baby seat you could put on a table, which enthralled Anton because he could bounce it. Anything that allowed movement, he liked. Unfortunately, his love of action caused him to roll over several months before the baby books said he would. He did it on our bed and fell off, striking his head off the floor and screaming with pain. I bundled him into the car and took him to Sutton Cross, where our GP David Chapman lived. David opened the door and took the baby while I shouted the details over Anton's screaming. 'That's some impressive volume you have there, Anton,' David whispered as he probed the baby's head. 'And I'd say that was some impressive bang you took, was it? Painful, I imagine?' Anton lowered the volume of his cries in order to hear David, and in no time was doing that convulsive after-shock gulp that follows extensive upset. I began to apologise to the two of them for inadequate and inattentive motherhood. Anton broke my heart by reaching for me and David laughed. 'Great thing about babies is a secret nobody tells young parents. Babies don't know what's coming, so they fall like drunks, all relaxed, and rarely do themselves major harm. Right, Anton?' he said.

It was so consoling, that statement. Right up there along with the one from Professor Geoffrey McKechnie of Trinity College. Geoffrey, who was married to Mary Finan, the PR genius, once observed that babies had no precedent to go on. They had no idea what was normal or to what they were entitled, so as long as you fed and watered them and hugged them a lot, they were grand. This proved true of Anton, who, three months in, got over five o'clock colic so decidedly that we nearly forgot what his crying sounded like. He was an inquisitive, agreeable and amused toddler who adored the father who had so adored him from the outset – the day after he was born, Tom had walked into his journalism course in Rathmines and announced to his students (including Tommie Gorman) that he was a father. As soon as Anton could walk, Tom brought him to almost all the meetings he could, and – perhaps because he was Tom, or perhaps because he was a man – this was interpreted as adorable. Mary McAleese was amused to be introduced to Anton as if the toddler was a visiting dignitary.

Tom decided to test out his Aunt Enna's prediction that his first-born would heal the estrangement between him and his mother. He put Anton in the car and set off for Cooley. When Mag opened the door, Anton was handed to her without introduction, and she took him with the big practised mother hands of her and wept into his soft golden hair. Tom's father made tea and several years of misery ended, right there, as Enna had said they would.

I did the feminist thing, early on, of giving Anton dolls and putting trucks and guns to one side. In fairness, he was never into weaponry, so the absence of guns was not a problem. What he was into was anything with wheels. If it was capable of forward motion, he loved it on sight. Trucks, diggers, wheelbarrows, tanks – you name it, he loved it. If any of the dolls I gave him were the right size to serve as crash test dummies in his somewhat combative use of vehicular toys, well and good. He did have a beloved teddy ('Tedser' his father christened the toy, and it stuck) but Tedser was for bedtime. Daytime was for driving. From the time he was four, Tom would take him down to Bull Island in the car, put him on his lap and let him steer the slowly moving car for hours, back and forth, on the hard-packed sand. I figure the statute of limitations has run out on this crime.

Those were gloriously happy years. Tom told a newspaper that I had 'a huge capacity for unconscious, forgetful fun. Strangers coming into the house hear the noise and think we have at least two children, whereas it's usually mother and child having a pillow fight.' The fun was shot through with a terror that never left me. I was sure that my inattention would cause Anton to die in a horrific way or be maimed for life. My recurrent nightmare was of forgetting him on a bus and ringing CIÉ to find out if he'd been found, only to be impatiently told that I would have to go to the Lost and Found office. Which, in the dream, I always did, rising panic in my swollen throat. The Lost and Found office fella to whom I tremblingly confided my problem would gesture dismissively at a piece of furniture, like an umbrella stand, in a corner, which had swaddled babies neatly stuffed into each segment. The horror, in the dream, was that I couldn't distinguish Anton from any of the other forgotten babies. Then I would realise I was being shaken and hear Tom's voice: 'Tess. Tess. You're having a nightmare.' I would cling to him in gratitude and he would ask if it had been the lost Anton dream and I would say yes.

Tom rarely had nightmares. On one occasion, I woke to find him moaning in his sleep and shook him awake. 'Jesus, Tess, thanks,' he said, rolling over and preparing to go right back to sleep.

'Wait,' I said. 'What was the nightmare?'

'They weren't passing the ball through quick enough.'

Neither Tom nor I had much interest in politics. His father voted Fianna Fáil and his mother Fine Gael and they religiously cancelled each other out at every general election, whereas Tom was instinctively Labour Party. I imagined my father voted Labour but had no certainty about my mother and – although I interviewed politicians on radio – I had never encountered one in a real way until one day when the phone at home and a hoarse, quiet voice said 'Terry?' and I confirmed who I was. 'This is Dr John. Dr John O'Connell,' he said.

John O'Connell was one of my heroes, in the same way Noël Browne had been one of my parents' heroes. O'Connell was the doctor of the slums, a fighter for the poor who had distinguished himself by battling the Distillers Company over what one of their products, Thalidomide, had done to hundreds of Irish children. Thalidomide, 'magic bullet' for pregnancy, allowed expectant mothers to sleep and controlled nausea. It also grievously warped the development of the foetuses carried by those mothers, so they were born without several limbs, or born with tiny versions of proper limbs, so that a child might have a hand growing out of their shoulder. Doctors didn't spot or report these anomalies quickly enough, and even when they did, Ireland took a lamentable length of time to take the drug off the market, whereas in the US, the Food and Drug Administration refused to authorise its sale, thereby saving the limbs of hundreds of thousands of potential victims. John O'Connell fought the manufacturers for compensation and that was what I knew him for. When, on the phone, he told me who he was and said he needed my urgent help before the election, I told him I knew nothing about politics and would be useless to him.

But when John O'Connell wanted you to do something for him, that thing got done, and so the following morning I was in his office being introduced to a young American political student interning with the O'Connell campaign. Dr John's idea of a political campaign was a cross between the Twilight Zone and Haiti, mid-earthquake. The young American had wonderful ideas, new to Ireland, like telephone canvassing, and the candidate wanted him to do them all, single-handed, yesterday. When the American tried to explain to John that this was unreasonable, John would throw tantrums on a scale I had not previously witnessed, even in the theatre, where tantrums are florid and at high volume. I found myself in that fugue state that often happened when I encountered high emotion; it ceased to be real for me and became a performance where I had to work out what role to play. In this instance, I worked out that I was the director. When John accused the bright young intern of being lazy, uncommitted and incompetent, I pointed out that the *Irish Medical Times* came out on time every week because everybody on the editorial team knew precisely what they had to do and the deadline they had to meet and that the same system would improve the campaign. John looked at me as if this was Grade A wisdom, rather than the bleeding obvious, and the American nodded tentatively. We stuck A3 sheets of paper on the wall with each task written on it, and John realised that the American could not possibly begin to tackle all of them. Other people were going to be needed. Finding people of vaguely left-wing persuasion who hadn't fallen out with John was one problem. Finding *anybody* who could start work right then was another. But it was done. As was an autobiography based on interviews with him, written in a fortnight and published three weeks later. Getting Dr John in front of as many electors as possible was a priority, because once you met him, it was easy to believe in him.

That this man had become a doctor was astonishing, coming as he did from dire poverty. His father had been in the British Army in the First World War in France, coming home blind in one eye, to chronic unemployment, with a pension worth less than forty euro a month today. John's mother was illiterate. His father taught himself to read, although John maintained that, to the day of his death, 'the full stop and he were strangers to each other. He could write a ten-page letter with no full stop to halt the run of it from start to finish.'

John was the youngest of six, the oldest of whom died of rheumatic fever, the next of tuberculosis. Three of O'Connell's siblings died in their teens of TB, or 'galloping consumption' as it was then known.

And yet John wanted to be a doctor. When he approached the local GP for guidance he was met with derisive laughter. Medicine was not for young fellas coming from the tenements, he was told. He silently and politely set out to prove that wrong. Intellectually brilliant and incredibly hard-working, he passed the exams to get himself into medical school working as a bookie's tout to pay the fees. No matter how hard he worked, the only footwear he could afford was plastic sandals that squeaked with every step he took, provoking smirks from his fellow students. He promised himself that once he qualified as a doctor, his prime objective would be to get rich. He met that goal, first coming up with *MIMS*, the first drug reference book for doctors, a huge seller which he later flogged, along with the *Irish Medical Times*, to a UK company owned by former Conservative minister Michael Heseltine. But he was only at the beginning of his journey to extreme wealth when a Jewish doctor friend of his who had studied with him came to see him and said, 'Why don't you go out with me one night to see some unusual patients?' He took him to the oldest tenements until they reached one with the hall door open and led him up several long staircases to a tiny room at the top of the building, where he knocked on the door. No answer. John's friend knocked again and eventually pushed open the door to reveal a big room, unfurnished and empty but for a bundled figure on a bare bed at the far wall. John was about to step into the room when his friend put out restraining hand. 'Look at the floor, John,' he whispered. 'Look at the floor.' The floor was a moving grey carpet and John had no idea what to make of it. His friend said, 'That's a mass of lice. He's dead. They leave the body the minute somebody dies.' Sickened, John staggered out onto the landing and asked why he'd been made to witness what he had just seen. 'Because this is where you should be. This is where we need you' came the answer, quietly relentless in its insistence.

O'Connell, always searching for a cause, found it in serving the Dublin slums while at the same time establishing the *Irish Medical Times* and turning it into a money-maker nobody could match. Even the consortium that spent millions buying it from him couldn't make it as successful as he had, and he ended up buying it back for much less than he had sold it for. He also decided that to fight for the people he took care of required him to enter politics, so he joined the Labour Party and became a TD. He then fought with effectively everybody in that party, developed a particular hatred for leader Brendan Corish, and ended up fighting elections as an independent. Eventually he made the big leap into Charlie Haughey's Fianna Fáil and it was when Haughey was his hero – that didn't last, either – that he dragged me out to Kinsealy and got C.J. to retain us to media train the Soldiers of Destiny, despite their leader despising me and Tom since the 1977 general election.

That was when Jack Lynch made a last-minute call to Bunny. Did he have anyone who could advise Lynch on party political broadcasts? Tom Savage, said Bunny. Lynch asked for Tom to go immediately to RTÉ. So Tom went and was told by RTÉ staff he knew that it was all very simple: the politicians just had to sit at a desk in studio two and read their script off autocue. When Tom asked why this should be the way of things, the RTÉ guys told him it was the way it was always done. Tom nodded thoughtfully and invited them to agree that amateurs reading bad scripts off autocue tended not to generate good television. Then one of them pointed out that each party had X number of hours, Y number of cameramen, Z amount of studio time and about an hour in the editing suite allocated to them. They could play around with these as the fancy took them. Plus the camera operators, bored filming bad autocue readers, could film outdoors if Tom wanted them to. Tom went outside and talked to Jack Lynch, whom he had never previously met, in the Taoiseach's car. Between them, they chopped the script into chunks that Lynch could say to camera while leaning out of the window of the Merc. The cameraman set up his shot, and Lynch, once he understood that fealty to the original script was not called for, delivered a confident and comfortable performance in one take, patting the warm paintwork of the car door at the end of his final piece to indicate to the driver to get moving. What was captured was an unexpected sense of excitement and movement.

The next speaker was to be Charles Haughey. Except that because Haughey wasn't speaking to Jack Lynch, he would not deal with Tom or countenance the suggestion that he be filmed outdoors and talking to camera without an autocue. Tom and the RTÉ guys shrugged. They would edit Haughey into the package, but it was going to look odd. Nothing they could do about it. The result was a vivid, new-style party political broadcast, except in the middle where Haughey, like a dead man, talked to camera in studio. As the embattled always do, C.J. learned the wrong lesson from it. Instead of figuring that this Tom Savage person had managed to make Jack Lynch look energetic and persuasive, C.J. decided that Tom belonged in the enemy camp. Once we had worked with Jack Lynch we were anathema.

Gossip about Haughey's hatred of us reached us. While we knew that C.J., as Machiavelli noted of Louis XII of France, esteemed no one unless that person was armed or had something to give, low esteem didn't seem to cover his loathing for us.

As time went on, we did more political work, although it has always been a tiny portion of our turnover, and we moved from one party to another because we were selling not affinity but skills-building. In consequence, down through the following decades, we worked, at different times, for Fianna Fáil, Fine Gael, Labour, the Green Party and the Progressive Democrats, and developed a few deep friendships with people in each of those parties. But that's for another book.

17

LITTLE RED RIDING HOOD

*S*tupid is bad at the best of times, but unfixable stupid in the middle of agony is worse. I was surrounded by stupid people in uniforms who let on to be doing important things but who were really only avoiding having to listen to me. I had two important issues I wanted sorted. One was the pain in my arse. The other was doing the live broadcast on Rodney Rice's programme on Monday.

The uniforms deferred to other uniforms and behaved as if I was a lunatic who didn't even need to be humoured. I could just talk to the surgeon about that. When he came in. No, they couldn't tell when he would be in. Or I could talk to the neurologist. When *he* came in, I explained, as calmly as I could, that I couldn't fail to turn up for a live broadcast and they could put me together just long enough for me to get to RTÉ and then get on with whatever stuff they thought was so important. I would promise to come back.

Sometimes, when I was going through this, my mother was there, crying. Sometimes, my sister was there, not crying but looking as if she was going to bust someone straight in the mouth for not doing something they should have done. At dusk, Tom was there. Always. Just there. Not crying. Not looking sympathetic. Not arguing. Just there. Sometimes I would know he was holding my hand and sometimes he would be quietly asking them questions. That was when the serried ranks of a surgeon with juniors to right and left stood at the bottom of the bed and surveyed me. I told them about the Rodney Rice programme and the surgeon patted one of my legs through the coverlet. I must remember, I thought, to go after that bastard and crush him on the wall like a bluebottle after I'd done the Rodney Rice show.

'Tess.'

Yes, I thought.

'Tess.'

'Yes', I said, annoyed Tom hadn't heard my thought.

'Tess, listen to me. The Rodney Rice programme is over. No, no, wait. It's over. Stop trying to go to it. They wouldn't understand you if you got there. Your teeth are missing.'

I lay there, running my tongue over the ruin of my mouth.

'Not all of them,' I said.

He watched me for a long time and I shouted it at him. He did a quieting down gesture.

'You still have some, yes, you do. But you're difficult to understand.'

I went to sleep. That happened a lot. It was like I was watching a show on a television with dodgy reception. When I woke up, Tom was still there, but with a nurse who looked like Little Red Riding Hood because she had a small round basket over her right arm.

'Tess. This is Nurse Joan Dennehy.'

The nurse took off her coat and put it over a chair.

'She is an agency nurse.'

I had no idea what that meant. He turned to Little Red Riding Hood and said he assumed it would be better if he went outside for a while. She nodded and then sat down beside me.

'Tom says you have a pain nobody is reaching.'

Oh, God, I said. Yes. In my arse. I kept telling all the nurses about it but all they did was talk of referred pain and do nothing except make me generally furious and then unconscious. She watched me while I talked with a fierce quiet attention, and a couple of seconds after I finished, she nodded. I tried to explain that for some reason my arms weren't working and so I couldn't point her to the precise place.

'You don't have to show me,' she said. 'I know.'

Yeah, right, I thought as she worked around the tubes coming out of me and moved her hands under me and suddenly the pain of days was gone. I cried and tried to thank her and she just went and got Tom and I tried to explain what she had done and he wiped my face and told me she would be with me every night. Every night, he repeated comfortingly. Every night until he got me home. That phrase was so comforting, I cried more and he smiled at me. Be grand, he promised me. Be grand.

And it *was* grand for me. I didn't understand the cracks the staff night nurses made about Little Red Riding Hood silently arriving each night with her roundy basket. They resented her, seeing her as a reflection on how well they had been performing, but used her presence as a way to avoid having anything to do with me. They were horrible to her, my sister told me later. Nurse Dennehy seemed used to that. She arrived at twilight as silently as dusk and every night gave the same silent kindness. I would sometimes hear Tom and herself talking in whispery monosyllables. Even when she left in the morning, it wasn't as bad as it had been. I explained this to Tom, using a Shakespearean reference.

'Nurse is like sleep – knits up the ravelled sleeve of care,' I told him. Except that I couldn't find the word 'sleeve' and it took him a while to work out 'ravelled'. He got it eventually, though. He always did. Other than him and Joan, it was like I was in a foreign country where even shouting at the natives didn't make them shape up and understand bloody well plain English. Sentences would form in my head and I would say them out loud. But the stupid people around me didn't understand what I was saying. Lovely sentences, filled with meaning, wasted on them. Their fault. How could it be otherwise? Nobody told me that my face was swollen to twice its size, cheeks backloaded into my mouth fighting for space with a bitten tongue, missing teeth creating shapeless uncontrolled space through which fumbled words fell as dead as wet cement. The two people who mattered – Tom and Joan Dennehy – seemed to have no problem understanding me. Tom because he could read me like a book. Joan because she didn't interrogate me, just watched me, worked it out and then did things silently.

I was still in the hospital when I realised that Tom was repeatedly playing a guessing game with me. I would ask him for something in the room and he would lift up a towel. This? I would growl a negative. This? Jesus, what was wrong with him? This? Eventually, he would light on the right item and I would be grateful in a strictly measured way, relative to how long it had taken him. Pull over those things, I would think. Pull over the book, I would say. Tom would lift a book off the bedside locker. No, for Chrissakes, how could a book solve the problem of the bloody light in my eyes? Then he would go all around the bed suggesting different possibilities until he hit on the curtain. I was never grateful for his infinite dedication to my needs. I was nothing but discomfort, interruptions, needs, each replacing the last in a daisy chain of misery, precluding anything but demand. The opposite of command and control. Demand and hope.

I knew, for example, in the second week after my arrival in the hospital, that the bit of my right leg near the ankle was hurting under the plaster, but I might as well have announced I was Napoleon for all the attention I got when I told the nurses about it. Tom arrived at dawn, before going to work at *Morning Ireland* (he was the first producer of the programme), so I told him about it and he told them again. Blanchardstown Hospital, back then, was built like an old-fashioned railway carriage: single rooms opening out onto a corridor. I could hear him telling them and them convincing him they were paying attention, because this was a nice husband and, apart from inflicting the night nurse on them, didn't do much that was objectionable. Tom went off, produced *Morning Ireland*, went to our company office and did a day's work there (my parents were in charge of Anton), then came in to see me before going on to edit the *Medical News*. He knew by the sight of me that nothing had been done.

'I spotted Brian Hurson on the corridor,' he murmured. 'He'll be here shortly.'

He arrived, did Hurson the orthopaedic surgeon, all big handsome bumptious good humour, surrounded by lesser beings. He did his performance and then Tom said quietly that he might want to take a look at the right leg at the ankle, because – raising his voice over the interruption about it being protected by the plaster – because it had moved in thirty-six hours from severe to acute pain. The surgeon looked him and put his hand on the plaster over the pain-filled bit then muttered something to one of the people beside him. Within seconds, an instrument was slapped into his hand and an electric buzz came from down around my ankle as he cut a small square viewing window into it. A flurry of conversation ensued and Hurson swept out, stopping to have a quick word with my husband. Then Tom came over to me and kissed me.

'See you in the morning, love,' he said aloud, then whispered in my ear. 'Something's amiss and they're taking you to theatre to find out what's wrong.'

Suddenly it was porters and trolleys and barrelling along darkening corridors to double doors opening ahead and the circle of bright light overhead and the anaesthetist asking me to count backwards from ten and me losing it as I got to six. They found an inflamed seeping infection, which convinced them my husband was a genius. My husband sat beside me the following evening, holding my hand until Nurse Dennehy arrived and he told her what had happened that had caused him to cancel her the previous evening. When it was all sorted, she asked him to go back over the accident. She knew what he had told her the first night, but …?

What had happened was that we had a branch of the business in the west of Ireland near Spiddal, and Tom and Anton, who was then about six or seven, had headed off on Friday, the last day of August, to the thatched cottage we rented there, so we could have a final summer weekend before school resumed. I was to join them a couple of hours later. It being the last day of August, most of the traffic was coming the other way, holiday-returning home. As I came round a bend in the road in Leixlip I found a car on my own side of the road driving towards me. The driver had pulled out to pass a line of traffic and hadn't managed to get back in. He was doing about 50 mph, I was doing about the same, and we collided head on, my little light Mazda and his station wagon. My car was reduced to 170 quids' worth of scrap metal and when the fire brigade came they had difficulty getting me out. Apparently one of the firemen said 'Pull her out over the back of the seat; she's a goner anyway', and I said, 'Don't bank on that.'

I was taken to Blanchardstown Hospital with a broken left arm, both legs broken in several places, broken face, broken ribs, just about everything smashed except my right hand. In theory, it should have taken ages for them to identify me and then find Tom. But what happened was that, as the evening drew on, and Anton was tearing around the little cottage in Spiddal, his father sat him down.

'Anton, I'm going to need you to be quiet for the next little while. Your mother's had a car crash and I need to work out where.'

'How do you know she's had a car crash?'

'You know the big phone in her car? I can't get through to her on it. Now, if it was just not working, Tess would have pulled into a hotel and phoned me from there. But she hasn't, and she's an hour-and-a-half overdue. That means she's had a car crash, and I'm going to ring every garda station from here to Dublin to find out where it happened.'

That's what he did. The guards answering the phone knew the voice, partly because of Tom doing *It Says in the Papers*, partly because when he did overnights in RTÉ for *Morning Ireland*, they were used to him ringing to ask if anything had happened in their area. No, Tom, they said on this night. Not here. No, nothing like that. No crashes. Until he hit Lucan. Yes, we have her, came the answer. Not good, Tom, tell you the truth. She seems to have been hit by a much bigger car – station wagon, you know? He must've pulled out to pass a line of traffic, sure all the holiday-makers are on their way back up from the West, and he didn't get back in, so the two cars collided. Maybe fifty miles an hour each? Yeah. Not good. Fire Brigade had to cut her out and she's in Blanchardstown. Anything we can do for you? Oh, you're heading out of Galway? Take your time. Someone here says they said she'd be in the operating theatre for hours.

Tom rang my sister to tell her what had happened. Yes, she would take Anton, no problem. He wrapped Anton up warm, got him into the back seat, and started for Dublin. Anton could hear him quietly saying 'Poor Tess. Poor Tess,' to himself until Anton fell asleep.

Tom arrived at Blanchardstown having unloaded Anton to Hilary, around eleven, to be told that the surgeon would be coming out shortly, that the work was nearly done. An exhausted medic with a face mask dropped to chin level eventually sat down in front of him, wiping his face one-handed to stay awake. They had put metal bolts in the legs and left elbow and were now plastering both legs. It had been bad, bad …

'Will she survive?'

The surgeon looked at Tom and thought about the question.

'Is she a fighter?'

'Oh, yes.'

'Then she'll probably survive.'

It was the next day when my mother was allowed to see me, and she never got over the sight of the unrecognisable blood-clotted, swollen, bruised, stitched head. The following day, the *Sunday Press* put a forbidding sunglasses picture of me on their front page above a report: 'Journalist Terry Prone suffered serious injuries following a car crash at Maynooth, County Kildare, last Friday evening. She was taken to Blanchardstown Hospital suffering from multiple fractures. Last night the hospital said her condition was "stable".'

In the beginning, it was no visitors because of intensive care. Then it was no visitors because Tom decided they would do me no good. But he was there, every morning and every night, despite working three full-time jobs. Calm, casual. No crisis-making, no great sympathy. Just there, noting progress, policing what was done and not done for me.

When my face shrank back to something like normal, he brought Anton in for quick visits, but other than my mother, Hilary, Tom and – occasionally – Anton, nobody else was allowed to come in. The one person who broke the visitor ban was our employee, Gavin Duffy. I would hear him on the corridor, giving lip to the nurses to distract them from barring him, and then he would arrive, tell a series of outrageously funny stories about the people we worked with, and, just as the laughter headed into painful territory for me, get up and go.

Four weeks after the crash, the nurses dropped me. From a considerable height. They got me back up onto the bed and minimised what had happened. I wasn't wearing it.

'I'm going home as soon as my husband arrives,' I told them. 'Please pack up my stuff.'

Not at all, they said, I needed to relax. It had been a tough day and they understood I mightn't be in great form. *After you dropped me, you mean?* I was going home, I told them. No matter what they said or did.

I could hear them, an hour later, accosting Tom in the corridor. Mr Savage, your wife is a little confused today. She says she's going home. I could hear Tom saying that was fine. No, no, it is not fine. Your wife is in no condition to be released. Fact is, Mr Savage, your wife is a big heavy woman and everything except her right arm is broken, so she has to be lifted, washed, dressed, fed. Everything. You simply wouldn't be able to do it.

'Oh, I spent a good chunk of my earlier years lifting syphilitic oul' fellas,' Tom's voice said dryly. 'I think I can probably lift my wife.'

Syphilitic oul fellas? I let on not to have heard anything when they came in, still rabbiting on, faster and louder, for fear I'd start in on how they had dropped me – this big, heavy and heavily injured woman – and threaten to sue them. I sat silently while Tom gathered clothes and rammed them randomly into a bag.

'You might get a robe on her,' he said to one of the nurses.

Whether they liked it or not, I was going home. Warnings were issued about leaving hospital unauthorised. Tom winked at them, which confused them. Porters materialised and helped me from wheelchair into car. Tom checked he had everything and told them, with the sudden crispness of someone who suspects something has happened of which he had not been told, that he would deal with the paperwork later. Then the engine started, country music came on the radio, and I was going home, him driving more slowly than was his norm, lest he hit a pothole at hurtful speed.

'Syphilitic oul' fellas,' I prompted.

He got launched on how he had taken a qualification in psychiatric social work in Queen's University Belfast, interning at Purdysburn Mental Hospital, which at the time was effectively a dumping ground for men in the tertiary stage of syphilis. Men who, for one reason or another, had either not been identified as sufferers early enough to undergo the brutal treatments of the time, or had not been successfully treated. The last stages were known as general paralysis of the insane, which meant that the men involved could no longer walk or take care of themselves. A big athletic intern was useful in that context, and so Tom lifted, carried and cleaned those patients.

In addition, he would occasionally be asked to bring in a Mrs Black. Lovely woman, he said. Middle-aged. Neat as a pin. Charming and chatty as he drove her to the hospital. Continued to be charming and chatty when the case conference began and the lead psychiatrist started asking her general questions while the students in the tiered seats wondered why on earth this lovely little woman had been dragged in to be presented to them. She would locate herself in place and time, provide details of various hospitalisations. All the time polite and precise. Those not in the know would be looking at one another, bored and confused, when the lead consultant would lean forward.

'Maybe you could tell us a little of what your neighbours do,' he would suggest.

Her eyes would light up, her cheeks would flush and she would launch on her vivid account of how the neighbours on the left of her house would take their rifle and poke it through the letterbox of her house and shoot into her hall and the bullets would go round and round and up the stairs and between her legs and into her vagina.

Tom and the others would sit extra still, unsure how to react. The consultant would ask a few more questions and each time the same story would emerge. When the consultant moved on to other things, Mrs Black would revert to her prior condition as a sweet woman in her middle years.

'She was a classic example of paraphrenia,' Tom said, as we came close to our house in Baldoyle. 'Completely sane, north by northwest, but with this narrow streak of complete lunacy. Now, I'm going to have to go up on the footpath here, so it's going to hurt.'

He got the car as near to the front gate as he could, and, seeing that the path from gate to front door was perhaps five feet in length, getting me into the house might have looked easy. It was not. By the time I was planted in the double bed he had brought down and positioned in the dining room of the tiny terraced house, I was ready to throw up from pain, and sweat was pouring down Tom's temples from effort. He left and came back with half a glass of water and a pill. One of the nurses had slipped a bottle of pills into his pocket as he took me out of Blanchardstown, indicating that he was going to need them to keep my pain at bay.

'So one of them was human,' he said. 'Tall red-haired one.'

We observed five seconds of silence in gratitude to the tall red-haired one.

'I need to go to the toilet.'

'Could you hang on for fifteen minutes? By then the painkiller will have kicked in and it'd make the stairs easier.'

I nodded, which the broken bones in my face instructed me was a mistake. Gradually the pain eased and the relief created a wild euphoria which made me adorable in my heroism, I believed, as I made witty comments during the clumsy journey upstairs and downstairs. Tom might not have testified to my adorability, since he was doing the heavy lifting. Neither of us registered that the red-haired one had donated a bottle of powerful narcotics and that I was as high as a kite. Nor would we have cared. Anything was better than the whole-body agony prior to analgesia.

Anton wasn't there that first night. His grandparents were minding him, and were prepared to continue minding him, but his father believed that the sooner he came home, the better, and that he might even be a help in 'caring for the cripple', as Tom put it. So the following morning, Tom washed me, changed my clothes, and left me in bed with everything in reach he could think I might need, while he went first to the Irish Wheelchair Association in Clontarf, where they lent him a wheelchair for me and taught him how to use it. There's more to a wheelchair than meets the eye, as you soon find out as a passenger, when amateurs enthusiastically commit themselves to your forward motion to a degree that causes you to face-plant on the pavement. After that, he collected Anton from school and brought him home, by which time I had worked out a genuinely useful task for Anton to perform. My left arm was so severely broken that it was used by the sister in Blanchardstown as evidence to prove staying in hospital was impera- tive when she was trying to persuade Tom not to help me escape. I had only started physiotherapy on that arm, she told him, and needed to do it twice a day for six months, which is why I would have to move to Cherry Orchard Hospital for six months' rehabilitation. When Tom resisted her advice, the sister said bluntly that if I wasn't put through the physio every day, I would end up with my left arm permanently bent at right angles, which would make everyday tasks, ranging from putting on a dress to carrying a tray to driving a car, almost impossible. I resolved to do the physio twice every day at home until I was sure I could straighten my left arm in a Hitler salute. Well, okay, maybe that wasn't the objective, but in my defence I point out that I was pretty stressed at the time by virtue of being dropped on a hard floor.

When Anton arrived home with Tom and the wheelchair, his first question was could he do a wheelie in it. I shrugged, which was an error of judgement, since I was near the end of the efficacy period of the last dose of narcotics and my ribs didn't want to know about shrug- ging. Anton got into the wheelchair and quickly became so expert that he could get his feet up in the air and sustain a position, utterly still, with nothing touching the ground other than the wheels, for several minutes at a time. I explained to him that unless I did daily physio I might end up with an arm that would not unfurl. He thought about this and explained to me the range of activities, outside of those already listed by the hospital sister, from which I would be precluded. I would not be able to wire-walk. Or use a skateboard. Or reach the press where the biscuits were kept. The two of us considered these dire possibilities for a few minutes and then I told him that I couldn't do the physio on my own, because my body would chicken out of the necessary arm-straightening. I needed someone strong to force the arm. He volunteered immediately, and we set ourselves up in the correct position.

'Now, let's first see how much I can straighten it without pushing,' I said.

Anton watched in dismay and disbelief. My elbow was on the table, and so when I straightened my arm my fist should have hit the table. Instead, it stopped a good twelve inches from it. Lifted up, my arm was resolutely bent. He would have to force it further on the road to straightness ten times. Was he up for that? Of course he was, and he did it firmly and with a will. One, he counted. Two. Three. Four. Then he glanced up from the arm and saw his mother was mauve in the face, with eyes awash with tears. He stopped.

'You must keep going,' I growled at him.

Five. Six. By the time we got to ten, he was crying, too. Thoroughly and helplessly.

'Maybe I'll get your dad to help me this evening,' I said.

If I had suggested blacklegging to a striker, I would hardly have met with such ferocious rejection. This was *his* job. *He* would do it. And he did it. Twice a day he did it, for several weeks, rewarding himself for completing the ordeal each day with a good set of wheelchair wheelies. By the third week, the arm could straighten completely, and after that it was just maintenance, which I could do single-armedly. These days, whenever I do a task that requires me to fully extend my left arm,

I am always grateful to a resolute little boy who gave me that gift, albeit through much personal distress.

A week after coming home, it seemed obvious that going back to work in the daytime would be better than being stuck in the house on my own while Anton was at school and Tom at work. Having run out of narcotics, I was on to the hard stuff – aspirin – for the washes of pain that happened throughout the day, but I was getting good with the wheelchair. I had always secretly wanted to be in a wheelchair, because so many children's books when I was a kid glamourised that state so much. Katy of *What Katy Did* was in a wheelchair for a period and Clara, from *Heidi*, similarly, although each later learned to walk again. Wheelchairs seemed to make you much more popular with everybody, so I thought it would be great to be in one. Which it was, to the extent that it allowed mobility and coffee transport. That latter is important. People think getting on to crutches is a step up, literally, from being in a wheelchair, but whereas you can carry liquids around in a wheelchair, it's impossible when you are using crutches, which also give you sore elbows and calluses on your palms.

The wheelchair, on the other hand, was mainly positive, although not for our next-door neighbour, Des Kenny, who at that time was running one of the organisations for the blind, he having no sight as a result of an accident involving a toy, specifically a sword, when he was about four. The first couple of weeks after I went back to work, the phone on my desk would ring and it would be Des.

'I fell over bits of your wheelchair again,' he would say, resignedly. 'I brought them into the office with me, so if you want to send over a courier …'.

The courier company must have wondered why the National League of the Blind was regularly sending me the foot supports from a wheelchair, but they were the least of my worries. Top of the worry list was the agony centred on the broken bones of my face, which tended to become unbearable every three hours. Even though I was taking only over-the-counter painkillers, I was determined not to take them more than every four hours. Accordingly, with resolution and diligence, I drove myself and those around me crazy postponing necessary pain relief. Bunny, Tom, Dominic McNamara and I would go to Jurys café for lunch because they had a wheelchair-accessible toilet. Then, about a week after I resumed work, we arrived one morning into our offices on Taney Road to find workmen knocking down walls. Tom looked a question at Bunny, who explained that his wife, Joan, who had been in a wheelchair since a bout of polio in her twenties, had asked him the day before how I was managing in the toilet business. He explained the Jurys Inn approach and she told him off, insofar as it was possible for so gentle a woman to tell anyone off, explaining that it wasn't good for my insides to be postponing going to the loo. He promptly ordered a team to create a wheelchair loo, which greatly simplified my life. It also meant we could lunch in our local, the Goat Grill, where I was unnerved, on our first visit, when one of the waiters asked Tom what I wanted to eat.

'Ask her yourself,' Tom said. 'It's only her legs are fucked. Her mouth is working fine.'

I didn't discover the full truth of the facial damage until we went, for the last time, to spend Christmas in the little thatched cottage we rented from Údarás na Gaeltachta a couple of miles from the branch of our business in Spiddal. Anton was in bed on the night we began to decorate the Christmas tree. Singing Christmas hymns in Latin along with the radio, Tom suddenly found himself surrounded by butterflies. We never found out how this was – perhaps it had to do with eggs being laid in the thatch overhead having their maturing process hastened by the heat of our fire – but it was magical.

At one point, I glanced away from him and the butterflies and looked at the box of silver baubles he had put on my lap. Much later, I published a short story about a husband and wife, fictionalising what then happened.

Six bright silver balls sat, segregated, egg-fashion, in the box, reflecting back six fattened faces at her. Bloated by the convex mirroring, the face was nonetheless different, nose tilted at an angle, forehead dented, the dent rimmed by pale raised scarring. A squealing whimper came through her clenched teeth and the six reflections blurred. Her husband, unhearing, came back to the wheelchair, still singing, and began – deftly – to loop skinny wire hooks onto the baubles.

'Jesus,' he said, breaking off from the male voices. 'Don't dribble on the bloody things. Oh. You're crying. Why're you crying? Your face, is it?'

She nodded. He mopped her with the tea towel from off his shoulder.

'Yeah,' he said thoughtfully, taking some of the hooked baubles and beginning to position them on the tree. 'I'd forgotten you wouldn't have seen yourself since the accident.'

His tone was casually observant, as if commenting on a one-degree change in external temperature or the lateness of a newspaper. She roared at him in wordless agony, bubbles forming and bursting in the gap between top and bottom teeth. He finished hanging the baubles, came back and mopped her again.

'You have a thing called keloid scarring,' he said informatively. 'That's why the bump on your head has a kind of rim on it. If you really want to, later, you can have it sort of filed down. But probably if you just grew your fringe a bit longer. Other than that, your face is going to be a bit different. But you'll get used to it. I have.'

You are without sympathy, she thought. You are without imagination. You lack the capacity to understand the true horror of being behind a strange distorted face, of knowing that it will never present to the outside world what you are used to it presenting. You have no patience for 'talking out' of problems and your favourite phrase is 'there's the status quo, and there's worse – which do you want?' You have already got used to my battered face and you will never understand why I should have a problem doing the same. It wouldn't even occur to you to say that you see my face more than I do: you simply don't empathise enough to argue it through at all.

She held out her arms to him and he put his head down on her neck. In a desperation of trust and need, she hugged him awkwardly, hiding her hospital-pale face in the always tanned warm skin of his neck.

'Now', he said, straightening up as if everything had been settled and returning to the task. 'Butterflies and Christmas. What more could we want?'

18

LOSSES AND RUMOURS

*W*hen Anton was small, we did occasional freelance lectures for Bunny. But on Stephen's Day, when he dropped into our house in Baldoyle with presents for his 'golden godson', Bunny told us his company was at a point where he had to fold the tent or make it into a serious business. To make into a serious business, he needed the two of us. The company, right then, was staying afloat because he wasn't taking a salary and Aidan Meade and Dominic McNamara, company employees, were on starvation rates. However, he added, if we joined him, we would receive a carried interest.

'The hell is a carried interest?' Tom asked. It was a shareholding you didn't have to buy, which was just as well, because we had no money. The two of us had, for one year, worked together in the Institute of Public Administration and it was like holidaying in a foreign country where you were paid the same amount every week and if you were sick you stayed solvent. That had been the first advantage of the IPA. The second, for me, was Colette Cullen. My secretary. Imagine. At twenty-one, I had a permanent and pensionable job as editor of the civics magazine *Young Citizen* and my very own secretary, a sunny woman who ran interference on my behalf with my boss, Jim O'Don- nell. *Young Citizen* was utterly pointless and if schools hadn't been forced to buy it, it would have died sooner than it did. Even leavening it with clever features about pop music by Brian D'Arcy wasn't going to make thirteen-year-olds care about proportional representation, although I still recall with pleasure a particularly vitriolic piece D'Arcy wrote about Donny Osmond, whose every shining tooth he hated.

The most memorable morning in the IPA was the one when Colette suddenly arrived into my office, grabbed the potted plant off my desk, threw it out of the window, closed the window and turned to me with her index finger across her lips: silence. This was so untypical of her that it took me a minute to register the polite knock on my door. Jim O'Donnell, my boss, arrived in, accompanied by a man he identified as Inspector Dinny Mullins, who had become a legend as the head of the Drugs Squad, formed to combat the major problem emerging in the seventies on the streets of the capital. Dinny sat down, I asked him if I could interview him for *Young Citizen*, and I did. After a compelling hour, Jim, who had left the Inspector with me, retrieved him and I waited for Colette to reappear. When she did, she was red in the face and sheepish as she leaned out of the window to retrieve the potted plant, which had survived its eviction remarkably well. (The office was on the ground floor.) She patted it into place and returned it to my desk.

'The girls gave you that at Christmas. Because you're so innocent, they knew you wouldn't know it's a marijuana plant. It was only when I realised Jim was going to bring Dinny Mullins to meet you that it struck me.'

I kept that plant on my desk for the rest of the time I was there, which wasn't that long, because although Jim O'Donnell was a courtly, witty and pleasant man, he would wait until an edition of *Young Citizen* was printed and at that point find a typo which he would reprovingly bring to my attention. The last time he did it, I told him I was out of there and wasn't working out my notice. Fine, he said, and left me to gather my possessions, helped by Colette, to whom I donated the marijuana plant. We stood for a minute in the office, the two of us, me clutching a fattened briefcase stuffed with everything I needed to take with me. She smiled that ineffably sweet smile at me.

'Colette, I'll come back for you. Don't know when, but I will come back for you.'

A hug and then the fastest walk to the car to prevent the tears showing. Tom stayed slightly longer in the IPA, editing *Public Affairs*, before leaving to set up the *Irish Medical News* in competition with Dr John O'Connell's *Irish Medical Times*. I was freelancing under my own and other names, even having pseudonymous short stories published in *New Irish Writing* by David Marcus, whose office was a floor higher than Mary Kenny's in the *Irish Press*.

Tom and I knew we could fit what we were doing around whatever Bunny needed us to do, and so, in the first week of January, we joined him, quickly realising that to pay the rent and proper salaries, we would have to immediately start turning over about four times what had been the turnover up to then. When I presented Bunny with a business plan requiring expenditure on equipment, he laughed. 'Tess, I'm an ex-quizmaster, you're an ex-actress, Tom's an ex-priest. Would *you* lend us money?'

Then AnCO, the state training body, wanted six-month media skills courses for unemployed graduates, so we pitched for that and won it, training people like Richard Crowley, Brian Dowling, Gavin Duffy and Linda Cullen. Within months, we had bought equipment and moved into to the Old Railway Station in Dundrum.

But the finances were tight, all the time. One day, our bank manager rang looking for Bunny, who was delivering a course out of house. Tom? Ditto. Terry? The staff member he reached didn't know. Okay, Hugh said, tell Bunny I am bothered you people are pushing the envelope of your overdraft. Oh, Hugh, she responded in a lethal burst of honesty, it's much worse than you realise. We're at least two thousand quid past where we should be. Hugh turned untypically cold and said he wanted a phone call from Bunny, me or Tom within the hour.

I was the first to arrive. I couldn't reach Bunny or Tom, but asked our auditors to come in for an emergency meeting. They said I should tell the bank manager that the company was trading insolvently and was going to be wound up. I told them they were fired, rang Hugh, and asked him what I had to do to reduce his discomfort. By close of business, he told me, the deeds of my house and Bunny's house must be in his possession. I effected that, reaching Bunny and explaining the situation to him.

Within months, we had righted the finances enough to get our houses back and find it retrospectively funny. Except for Bunny no longer parking his car at the front of the building, but near the side door, which allowed him to get into his office without passing the staff member who had precipitated the crisis by her frankness with Hugh. He was afraid that if he met her one morning before he had a smoke and several cups of coffee, he might kill her, and he was not joking. Bunny had a ferocious temper, which surfaced maybe once a decade, but when it did, it was spectacular.

The project that most captured his heart in that decade, was getting the international development organisation Gorta's funding up to a million a year. It was an unimaginable target for an organisation without fundraising infrastructure, and required Bunny to travel the country to give motivational talks to persuade people to form fundraising groups. It worked phenomenally well, helped by videos showing where the money went. One of those videos took Tom to the wilds of Kenya for twenty-one days, where the memorable culinary experience was provided by local nuns who fed him lettuce washed in Milton steriliser. But the major factor in Gorta's success was Bunny doing the fundraising radio and TV ads.

Eventually Gorta's chief executive came to see Chief (as first Tom and then all of us called Bunny) to confirm that a sustainable million a year had been reached. Bunny was delighted but also relieved, because it meant that he could step back, stop the provincial touring that took him away from Joan, and quit the TV ads he did for free. However, the Gorta man wanted Bunny to continue and told him the organisation would buy him the Jag he had always wanted. He was lucky to get out of Bunny's office alive. Chief was sickened that someone who had worked with him for years would perceive him to be amenable to what he regarded as a filthy bribe. The relationship was over and we had no further dealings with Gorta. However, that was to cause Bunny major problems, because, as the public saw it, what happened was that Bunny, who had been the TV personification of Gorta, disappeared off the screen, and this coincided with him quitting afternoon television. Together, the two absences gave rise to a conspiracy theory that Bunny had abandoned his lovely 'invalid' wife, Joan, stolen all the Gorta money and fecked off to live in sin in Spain with the singer off afternoon television. The rumour would surface, now and again, in pub talk. Then our receptionist weakened, one morning, in the face of a particularly insistent caller wanting to discuss something with Bunny. Although the rule was that such callers had to give an outline of their needs to the receptionist before being put through to Bunny's office, that morning she was hassled and transferred him. I was waiting to go in to see Bunny when she said the caller must have got through his issue really quickly, because he was off the line. I knocked and simultaneously entered Chief's office, to find him, head down on his desk, his shoulders shaking with sobs. Eventually he mopped his eyes and sat up straight.

'That's the third this week, Tess.'

'Third what?'

The third caller who had rung, convinced that Bunny was either away in Spain (or in Limerick prison, where another rumour had him) and eager to prove it by finding him unavailable. Each time, the minute Bunny's distinctive voice greeted them, they banged down the phone. I went outside and rang Gay Byrne, who had heard and dismissed the rumour. 'They come with the territory,' he said. 'You obviously haven't heard about the grief Kathleen Watkins's alcoholism causes me. I'm dragging her out of the pub every night after closing time, footless. Her, I mean. Not me.'

He had Bunny on his programme the next day, the two of them exploring how such myths start, with Gay mimicking the sanctimony of sympathisers who thought better of him because of Kathleen's mythical alcohol problem, and thought better of Joan because of Bunny's mythical abandonment of her. 'I've always been one of the guys in the white hats,' Bunny said. 'I'm not good at being one of the guys in the black hats.'

For a few weeks, after coming back to the office, post-car crash, it seemed as if service as usual could resume. Until the day I was prepping Alex Spain, managing partner of SKC, for a *Prime Time* interview. I asked him some question in a properly accusatory way and, as he came to the end of his answer, experienced a mental windscreen wipe. I found myself looking at him, asking myself who he was and what he was talking about. He looked at me in wary expectation.

'How does that gel with what you said earlier?' I asked, implying it didn't, although I couldn't remember what he'd said earlier. Alex assumed I knew something he didn't and floundered to answer. I finished the interview as quickly as possible and excused myself. Tom was in our shared office. I explained what had happened and asked for help. 'C'mon,' said Tom, grabbing the handles of the wheelchair, 'we'll do it together.' Alex was delighted to get double value and as I watched the playback, it began to come back to me. But the memory wipes, combined with aphasia (word blindness) made it inescapable that, for the moment, I needed to do something other than interviews and assessments. I decided to look at the books with Bunny's personal assistant.

'You and Bunny and Tom are brilliant at what you do,' she said. 'But you're useless at running a business. This company made a loss in every one of the ten years since it was set up. No marketing. All the business is surrender or referred business, which is great, but there isn't enough of it.'

Two weeks later, I had a new marketing plan which depended entirely on cold-calling by Bunny and Tom and a series of potential businesses for them to call. The good thing was that – especially since Tom had done a TV series which had been popular – they were both known and would immediately be put through to the chief executive in any business. All they wanted was half an hour to find out about his (it always was a he) communications policies, internal and external.

'They won't have any,' Tom said.

'Doesn't matter. It'll get them talking. And neither of you are to come back and say the MD was supportive. Supportive won't pay our salaries.'

Business began to trickle in, including a two-day course with Nixdorf, the computer company, to be undertaken by Bunny, who came home after the first day and said he wouldn't be going back the next day. 'They have these computer programmes that do fantastic things like tell you what your gross profit is on a daily basis,' Bunny said. "The sales guys, who aren't bad, go out and sell this stuff. But they don't really understand it. In effect, they're selling things they don't understand to customers who don't understand what they actually need, and so, very quickly, the complaints come in and the engineers have to be sent out to patch the programme so it does what the customer thought it would do in the first place, but that's costly, so they're either making no money on what they're selling or actively *losing* money on it. I told them to send the engineers out to sell the stuff.'

This sounded like it made sense and since the company quite happily paid us for the second day Bunny hadn't done, we forgot about it until a Scot based in Belgium rang Bunny and introduced himself as Ian Dand, in charge of marketing for Nixdorf, globally. Ian told Bunny that when head office examined their end of year figures, they were depressed by the flatlining in one country after another, even though a recession was holding economies to the floor. But what puzzled them was one little peak in the figures in Ireland. When asked about it, the Irish chief executive said he'd been advised to use his engineers as salesmen. A corporate decision had been taken to install this approach right across Europe, but it would require the communications training of engineers, who, by their very nature, didn't talk, even if they *could* talk. Could Ian Dand come to Ireland to talk to our company about helping to develop those training programmes?

He flew in the following week and stayed for ten days, watching our training in action, and taking frantic notes, making lists of what to us were truisms, but which to him were key lessons to be taught to his engineers. By the time he was ready to go, he had three separate programmes fully articulated. He rang Bunny a few days later, told him to invoice the Irish HQ, which would be expecting a bill for course development, and cost the programmes his management had now agreed. Bunny put down the phone, looking stunned. It had never struck him that the company would want us to provide training all over Europe, but they did. Ian Dand had convinced them that control and standard-setting lay in having this tiny Irish company undertake the task. He – Dand – would participate in each programme to cover aspects of the marketing approach, and we would always be supported by a software expert who could resolve emerging technical problems, but the bulk of the training would be provided by Bunny and Tom. How many countries? Seventeen. How soon? Yesterday. Had they agreed our fee structure? Yes and would immediately detail how they proposed to manage the travel. If it was okay with us, Ian Dand said, they would book all flights and hotels. That was fine with us, we said.

For eighteen months, Bunny and Tom were in touchdown or take-off mode. Once, they encountered each other in Athens airport by accident. In the French training centre, which was structured like a wheel with the reception at the hub, the receptionists would tell latecomers looking for the course conducted by Mr Savage to stand still and listen. 'The room the laughter comes from is where he is.' By all metrics, the training was outstanding in its success, allowing an international shift in approach, which radically improved the finances. It unexpectedly suited Bunny, because he couldn't get distracted by trainees asking him about television programmes and he couldn't use any of his old RTÉ stories, so it hugely refreshed his line of attack as a trainer.

We had learned how to do business. We were making money. So I rang Colette Cullen and asked her to have lunch with me in a pub close to the IPA. 'It's been a while, I know, and it may not suit you, but I promised I'd come back for you and here I am. Will you consider joining us?' She smiled that breathtaking smile and shook her head. My heart plummeted. 'I don't need to consider it. The answer's yes,' she told me and we disgraced ourselves overturning soup bowls with our intemperate embraces. A month later, she was our head of administration, putting in systems to manage rooms and tutors that have been sustained to this day in The Communications Clinic. She was so charming she could persuade anybody to do anything, as happened once when an Irish language translation was required overnight. Whenever we needed something translated into beautiful idiomatic Irish, we asked Pádhraic Ó Ciardha, who eventually reached the top in TG4. On this particular occasion, Colette, having talked to Pádhraic, said in a puzzled way that he wasn't as funny and agreeable as usual, but had nonetheless promised that he would drop in the translation the following morning. Next day, I arrived, as always, at dawn, to find a figure stuffing an A4 envelope into the ankle-height letter-box of the Old Railway Station. As he turned to get into his car, I recognised him and leaped out of my own car to ask him if that was the overnight translation. He nodded. All I could do was laugh. Cully, as Bunny called her, had rung RTÉ, where Ó Ciardha was based, been misdirected without realising it to Pádraic Ó Gaora, who was understandably less than enthusiastic about doing a fast turnaround translation for a stranger, but who still did it for the charming woman on the phone. I explained and apologised and he went away somewhat relieved that he would be paid for this once-off job. And that it would be a once-off job.

The only negative attached to the overseas work was that Tom seemed more distracted than usual. Now Tom never met a brown study into which he didn't want to go. Anton, early on, described him as the dormouse in *Alice*: if you left him alone, he would drift off to sleep and have to be dipped in the teapot. But during those months, which coincided with me beginning to walk again, he was distant enough to worry me. It was from Ian Dand that I heard the story of Tom conducting a Train the Trainer course in Greece, where neither the trainer nor any of the participants spoke English, interrupting the trainer, moving to the top of the training room, and in a combination of Ancient Greek and mime, explaining the right way of doing it. Tom just nodded listlessly when I mentioned Dand's delight about this. Eventually, when he had just returned from delivering a course in Lyon, I asked him what was wrong.

'Tess, between sessions this week I was sitting by the river, thinking about how unwell I've been for months and I suddenly realised I know what it is. I have cancer. No, I'm absolutely sure of it.'

He was right. David Chapman, our GP, telephoned first thing the following Friday, after Tom had tests and X-rays, to tell him that he didn't have lung cancer, which was what he had expected after decades of smoking, but he *did* have stomach cancer. After his daily surgery, David came around and answered all our questions. It was bad. Big. Size of a grapefruit. Unclear whether it had metastasised. Surgery and then chemo or radiation or both. Tom listened in an oddly casual, relieved kind of way. The odds on successful surgery and survival? Eight to one against.

Tom showed David out, came back and put an LP on the record player. A slow tune. He danced with me. And while he danced, he talked into my hair about what a great life he had lived and how he had no regrets, other than the possibility of not seeing Anton grow up. He was tranquil. I was distraught, particularly about what this might do to Anton, who had suffered plenty as a result of his mother having a life-changing accident. 'We'll tell him the truth,' Tom said. 'That's all we can do.'

The following week, the surgery happened in the old Adelaide Hospital, a Protestant establishment where the nurses wore polka-dotted uniforms. I was in a waiting room during the operation and my mobile phone never stopped the whole time. Mary Harney of the Progressive Democrats was demanding to know what the Fianna Fáil-led government was paying my company and for what. (Pádraig Flynn, who was not loved by Mary Harney, had retained me as his adviser.) Eventually, a grubby, sweaty man in scrubs appeared and introduced himself as Bill Beesley, the surgeon who was operating on Tom. He said he had taken out some of the organs around the cancer, although he couldn't tell whether or not they had been invaded by it. One of those organs being the spleen, which would affect Tom's immune system. The surgery had gone on for four hours and the man looked exhausted. I asked him about chemo and radiation and he shook his head. He thought he had taken it all out, he told me, and that Tom wouldn't need either. But if he was wrong, neither chemo nor radiation would help. So when he was able, which would not be for a couple of weeks, I should take Tom home and take care of him. I nodded and thanked him and later was brought to Tom's room where he was coming out of the anaesthetic, looking questioningly at me.

'Sweetheart, they got it all. No chemo. No radiation. All you have to do is get better.'

He smiled and did a thumbs-up gesture and went back to sleep. Four or five times that afternoon the two of us played out the same scene, because whenever he woke up, he had no recollection of the previous conversation.

The following ten days were tough for Tom, but he did what he was asked, and he was amused, when David (our GP) and his wife, Valerie, visited, to learn that Beesley was a mathematical genius who had won the Lottery twice and who, when his wife wanted to go to Brown Thomas, would drive her, wearing a chauffeur's cap, and park directly outside, ready to murmur implacable nothings to any Guard who queried him.

Beesley had taken out three-quarters of Tom's stomach. His appetite, never formidable, disappeared and he lost three stone, a big muscular athlete becoming a slender man who needed new suits two sizes smaller. But he was alive, getting better and as engaged as ever in sport on TV, although worried that his golf swing might be affected by a missing rib. It wasn't; he was still able to play off four, although he never played in Ireland again because he could not keep warm outdoors here. Then, when we were in Florida the year Obama was elected, I noticed he wasn't playing there either and asked why not. 'I have limited appetite for playing golf with guys who call their President the N-word,' he said.

19

THE STITCH

We sell the company for millions more than we ever thought it would be worth and set up another, with Anton as MD. He has the new entity in profit in its first year. Bunny retires. Tom and I keep working.

Then, on his way to work in the vintage Merc, thinking through the sequence of the course to which he's contributing, Tom gets the stitch. The distinctive, unmistakable stitch that says pneumothorax. Collapsed lung. It's happened before. He calls the office on the way to A&E to get someone to cover for him. Neat and orderly it is, the start of Tom's three-year landslide of health disaster, recovery, relapse.

Early on, he tried to explain to the two young doctors at his bedside that the tube supposed to relieve the problem had been put in the wrong place. Trust him on this. He'd been here before. The two men nodding but doing nothing, promising that once Naveed arrived, all would be well. Naveed they spoke of reverently, like he was God. Then this Pakistani doctor arrived with a backpack on him. Tom watching him, listening to the courtly politeness of him, understanding the reverence, praying that this smart man would do something soon to alleviate the pain and the oxygen shortage. He did.

Tom's son, banished during a procedure, sitting on a kerb at the hospital car park, motorbike leathers on him, unshaven, harassed by a security man, snapping 'Jaysus, if I was going to nick one of the cars, you think I'd be reading the *Daily Telegraph?*' Me, walking behind a porter pushing Tom in a wheelchair after an emergency admission along a corridor when the lift, as we pass, disgorges a suited man who moves into step with us in a parody of our procession. Turning to snarl at him and meeting the 'Gotcha, didn't I?' laughter in our son's face. Nothing he can do and everything he can do.

Home from hospital, Tom, finger over lips – 'Don't let Tess know'– turfing the contents of a cup of soup into the ash bucket beside him in the sitting room. Talking with his brother Seamus about the hope they share: just to live long enough to be remembered by their grandchildren.

The next day, it's all over.

Anton, reached in JFK on his way to a vacation destination, turns round and comes back for his father's funeral in the little church in Grange in Cooley, County Louth. I sit, dazed, as the communion procession slowly passes the pew I'm in. Nobody turns to look at me. Except one tall grey-haired man whose gaze insists I look at him. Pádraig Flynn. Present and correct.

Then the cardinal, the man Tom played football with five decades before, sits in an armchair placed for him on the altar and Anton steps to the microphone and looks at the tiers of Tom's relatives and friends to the right and left of him and the rows in front of him.

'I stand today,' he begins, 'on the altar where my father said his first Mass.'

A heartbeat pause. Then: 'Not many men can say that,' he adds, and a sob of soft laughter whispers around the old church.

BIBLIOGRAPHY

Southside Provisional: From Freedom Fighter to the Four Courts
Kieran Conway
Orpen Press, 2014

Beyond the Fringe
British comedy stage revue written and performed by Alan Bennett, Peter Cook, Jonathan Miller, and Dudley Moore from its debut at the 1960 Edinburgh Festival. It also played in London's West End and then Broadway.

A Man for All Seasons
Robert Bolt, 1960

Dr John – Crusading Doctor and Politician
Dr John O'Connell
Poolbeg, 1989

Here's the Story
Mary McAleese
Penguin Ireland, 2020

Carry on Talking
Peter Bander
Colin Smythe, 1972

Memoirs of a Radical Lawyer
Michael Mansfield
Bloomsbury, 2009

Index